BOOKS BY LARRY WOLFF

*Postcards from the End of the World*
*The Boys and Their Baby*
*The Vatican and Poland in the Age of the Partitions*

POSTCARDS FROM THE END OF THE WORLD

LARRY WOLFF

# POSTCARDS FROM THE END OF THE WORLD

*Child Abuse in Freud's Vienna*

ATHENEUM · NEW YORK

1988

Excerpts from *The Interpretation of Dreams*, by Sigmund Freud.
Translated from the German and edited by James Strachey. Published in the United States by Basic Books, Inc. by arrangement
with George Allen and Unwin, Ltd. and the Hogarth Press, Ltd.
Reprinted by permission.

Excerpts from *The World of Yesterday*, an autobiography by
Stefan Zweig, translated by Helmut Ripperger and B. W.
Heubsch. Translation copyright 1943, renewed © 1970 by the
Viking Press, Inc. Reprinted by permission of Viking Penguin,
Inc.

Excerpts from *Die Welt von Gestern* by Stefan Zweig reprinted by kind permission of Williams Verlag AG, ZUG.

Excerpts from *The Complete Letters of Sigmund Freud to
Wilhelm Fliess*, edited and translated by Jeffrey Moussaieff Masson, reprinted by permission of Harvard University Press. Copyright © 1985 by Sigmund Freud Copyrights Limited and J. M.
Masson.

Copyright © 1988 by Lawrence Wolff

Atheneum
Macmillan Publishing Company
866 Third Avenue, New York, N.Y. 10022
Collier Macmillan Canada, Inc.

Designed by Jerry Kelly

Library of Congress Cataloging-in-Publication Data
Wolff, Larry.
  Postcards from the end of the world.
  1. Child abuse—Austria—History—19th century.
  2. Filicide—Austria—History—19th century.    I. Title.
HV6626.5.W584  1988      362.7'044      87-33484
ISBN 0-689-11883-X

10 9 8 7 6 5 4 3 2 1

Printed in the United States of America

*For Dorrit Cohn*

"Die aber wie der Meister sind, die gehen,
Und Schönheit wird und Sinn, wohin sie sehen."

—Hugo von Hofmannsthal
*Der Tod des Tizian*

# Acknowledgments

As a graduate student I had the great good fortune to study Austrian history with Wayne Vucinich, Gordon Craig, and William Slottman—three marvelous teachers who offered three different treasuries of insight into the history of the Habsburg empire. Earlier, in college, I received the most fortunate of all possible introductions to the richness and complexity of Austrian culture, in tutorial with Dorrit Cohn; it was she who helped me begin to appreciate Hofmannsthal, Schnitzler, and Musil.

This book could never have happened without the confidence and enthusiasm of my agent, Molly Friedrich, or without the excellent intellectual guidance of my editor, Tom Stewart. From the beginning of the project, I have benefited from the suggestions and encouragement of friends and colleagues, especially Mitch Katz, Amy Cohen, Maria Tatar, Michael Wilson, Mort Klass, and Sheila Solomon Klass. I have also received essential institutional support from Boston College and Harvard University.

My parents, Robert and Renee Wolff, have offered me great encouragement—in this as in so many other things—while my son, Benjamin Orlando Klass, has been supremely inspirational—in this as in so many other things. Perri Klass has been involved in every detail of this project, and has given me once again an intellectual and literary standard without which my work would possess little coherence and no grace at all.

# Contents

# Introction

~§§§~

The Family by Egon Schiele
(Reproduced by courtesy of Dr. Rainer Handl
and the Österreichische Galerie)

I N November 1899, the leading newspaper of Vienna published
on the front page a short article under the heading "Postcards
from the End of the World." Some entrepreneurial spirit had
undertaken to print postcards in anticipation of the imminent apocalypse, for the year 1900 was about to begin, and popular superstition presumed that there would be some sort of portentous manifestation for the turn of the century. The story was reported with a
certain irony: "If the world really does come to an end in the
coming days—and there are plenty of fearful people who believe
that it will—all will certainly have need to notify their friends and
acquaintances with postcards, as to whether or not they witnessed
the great crash." So two kinds of cards were being printed, one of
misfortune in case of apocalypse, and the other of congratulation in
case of "the averting of the generally feared danger." One could be
prepared for either eventuality. Actually, chronologically rigorous
people insisted that the twentieth century would not begin for
another year, not until 1901, but such disputation did not stop the
postcards from quickly selling out their printing. The card for catas-
trophe included a notice of emergency safety regulations, and was
decorated with a picture that represented "fear and anxiety."

The very next day after the appearance of the article "Postcards
from the End of the World," there began in Vienna a courtroom
trial, which marked the beginning of an unprecedented sensation,
something so shocking that people could remember nothing like it
ever coming before the public. It was the trial of a mother and
father, Joseph and Juliane Hummel, who had tortured to death
their five-year-old daughter. This case was followed two weeks
later by another trial, even more tremendously publicized, of a
father and stepmother, Rudolf and Marie Kutschera, who had tortured and mutilated seven of their children and finally killed one of
them. To our eyes, these two cases are immediately recognizable as
a part of the tragically widespread phenomenon of child abuse. The

3

world of 1899, however, barely recognized the concept of child abuse, and a powerful Victorian sentimental ideal of the loving family made it hard to believe that parents brutalized their children. For the Viennese of 1899 these two trials were compellingly inter-esting—but they were also unfathomable, uncategorizable, unas-similable, for there were no references or precedents to help make any sense out of such horror. These cases of abuse were radically different from the great sensation of the previous month, the far more familiar scenario of an unmarried mother, Hedwig Keplinger, who despairingly shot herself and her illegitimate daughter in the woods outside Vienna. What was new and different about the Hummel and Kutschera trials, however, was at the same time so agonizingly unacceptable for the public of 1899, that the issue of child abuse, after a month of stupendous publicity, was allowed to disappear altogether. The cases failed to make a lasting sociological impression, failed to establish the prevalence and urgency of child abuse as a social problem, and so, in time, they were forgotten, repressed, consigned to historical oblivion.

Historians know very little about the history of childhood, of relations between parents and children. They know still less about the cruel and painful side of that history, the history of the abuse that children have suffered. Past centuries have left us little evi-dence to construct that history, for the brutalization of children was always a strictly private family matter, unrecognized as a public social evil. In the late nineteenth century, in America and in En-gland, societies were founded to prevent cruelty to children, but it was not until very recently that child abuse as we know it—the abuse of children by their parents in their homes—made its mark on the public mind, and was widely recognized as a not uncommon medical and sociological syndrome. The breakthrough in public awareness came in 1962, with the publication of the article "The Battered-Child Syndrome" in the *Journal of the American Medical Association*. Since then, child abuse has become a subject of contin-ued concern and interest; before 1962 the phenomenon was still largely unrecognizable and unbelievable. It is therefore historically interesting that child abuse was brought to light in Vienna in 1899, brought to light and then once again submerged in darkness to await rediscovery. The Viennese cases provide us with an extraor-dinary picture of how child abuse was perceived and interpreted in an age that had not yet accepted the fundamental concept of child abuse. Furthermore, the responses and reactions of 1899 help us to appreciate why it was then so impossible and unthinkable for the discovery of child abuse to make a lasting sociological mark, why it had to be obliterated and forgotten.

These cases offer insights into the cultural conception of parents and children one hundred years ago. The general attitudes under examination are those of the Western world at the turn of the century, at the end of the Victorian era; those attitudes constitute our own cultural heritage. These cases of child abuse, however, were also more specifically formulated and interpreted according to the cultural values of fin-de-siècle Vienna—and that provides a special significance. Vienna in the 1880s was still the waltzing city of Johann Strauss and "The Beautiful Blue Danube," but in the 1890s there emerged men and movements of such importance that fin-de-siècle Vienna is now generally recognized as a formative cultural crucible for the elements that shaped the twentieth-century world. Mahler and Schönberg in music, Klimt and Kokoschka in art, Hofmannsthal and Schnitzler in literature, Kraus and Wittgenstein in the philosophical critique of language—these were some of the figures who constituted fin-de-siècle Vienna, and acted so influentially upon our own century. As the capital of the doomed Habsburg empire, turn-of-the-century Vienna also offered a political education to the young Adolf Hitler, who fully appreciated the potency of such Viennese forces as enraged German nationalism and popular anti-Semitism. For Hermann Broch, Vienna was the city of "the gay apocalypse." For Karl Kraus, it was "an experimental laboratory for the end of the world." In 1899 the Viennese bought postcards and waited for the crash. This was the crucible in which the entirely new and mysterious element of child abuse suddenly appeared, and it was in the mingling with the other heated elements that the sensation acquired its distinctive Viennese characteristics. Just as Viennese cultural forces determined the reception and interpretation of child abuse in 1899, so the study of these child abuse cases casts new and intriguing lights on the whole cultural complex of the city.

There is one individual genius, of course, whose spirit more than any other predominates in our historical appreciation of fin-de-siècle Vienna. These cases unfolded in the Vienna of Sigmund Freud, and it is Freud's presence in the city that makes them particularly fascinating as episodes in cultural history. No one has contributed more than Freud to the shaping of our own ideas about parents and children, and in November 1899, at the same time that everyone was reading in the newspapers about the Hummel and Kutschera trials, there appeared in Vienna, barely noticed, a book, *The Interpretation of Dreams,* containing Freud's first public elaboration of the Oedipus complex. In the decades that followed, those positions were reversed: Freud, *The Interpretation of Dreams,* and the Oedipus complex rose to the pinnacle of fame and intellectual influence, while child abuse was disregarded and submerged. In November 1899, at the very same time that Freud was exposing the antago- nisms between parents and children in a revolutionary way, the Hummel and Kutschera trials drew attention to different but not unrelated—and no less shocking—family antagonisms. Today there is heated controversy over the development of Freud's ideas about parents and children in the 1890s, but it has not been appreciated that Freud's Vienna was the scene of a great child abuse sensation, decades and decades before the formulation of the battered-child syndrome.

The historical study of the Viennese child abuse cases of 1899 takes on some of the characteristics of both archaeology and psycho- analysis. The cases have lain buried and forgotten for almost a century now, bizarre labyrinthine structures, awaiting excavation and rediscovery. They must be carefully uncovered and recon- structed, so that we can understand the significance of the different elements and artifacts, as they were understood in 1899. In this archaeological work, however, one must bear in mind that the child abuse cases were not buried only by time. They were forgotten, perhaps purposefully forgotten, repressed; their graphic details and alarming implications were precisely what made it impossible to preserve the memory and draw the indicated sociological conclu- sions. It is important not only to bring to light what has been buried, like the archaeologist, but also, like the psychoanalyst, to understand how and why it was buried, forgotten, and repressed. There will be moments when the uncovered structure seems utterly alien to us, and there will be other moments when it feels uncannily like the world we live in today. For child abuse remains one of the most terrifying tragedies of our own times. We can recognize it perhaps more easily than could the world of 1899, but it remains painfully difficult to face, and excruciatingly resistant to prevention or intervention. The rediscovery of these child abuse cases delivers to us postcards from the end of the world, and if those cards show us pictures that represent fear and anxiety, it may be because there is something in those old pictures that we find disturbingly familiar.

# CHAPTER ONE

## The Story of Hedwig Keplinger: Murder and Suicide in Fin-de-Siècle Vienna

*Franz Josef I with his children*

## THE BODIES IN THE WOODS

ON the Friday afternoon of October 13, 1899, a Viennese shoemaker's assistant took his ten-year-old daughter for a walk in the woods outside the city to hunt for mushrooms. It was the child who wandered a little from the path through the woods, and suddenly came upon the dead body of an elegantly dressed young woman whose face was covered with blood. Two steps away was a second corpse, a much smaller one, the also elegantly dressed dead body of a little girl, maybe six years old. Whether her face too was bloody was not immediately evident, for it was covered with a little hat of white lace. The daughter of the shoemaker's assistant, who had found in the woods not mushrooms but corpses, cried out for her father, and they hurried out of the woods to inform the police. The police, when they appeared upon the scene, determined that this was a case of murder and suicide.

Then the details of the scene were scrupulously noted, and the Viennese, when they opened their newspapers the next morning, were presented with a remarkably complete description of the bodies in the woods. The young woman, a bullet wound in her right temple, was of medium height with brown hair. She was wearing a dove-gray suit with white trim, a black jacket, black stockings, and yellow shoes. On the ground beside the body was a yellow hat with a dark blue ribbon and a veil—also a revolver, a six-shooter, two shots fired. The dead child, a bullet wound in the left temple under the white lace hat, wore a red dress with brown stockings and, like the dead woman, yellow shoes. In her little ears the child wore gold earrings with blue stones arranged in a floral design as forget-me-nots. Beside the body was a dark blue jacket and a blood-spotted handkerchief.

An examination of the dead woman's pockets turned up a gold watch on a chain, a key, and a black leather purse. In her mouth were traces of a yellow foam which seemed to suggest that she had taken poison, a phosphorus solution, before the shooting. Nearby on

9

the ground was a blue silk reticule whose contents were carefully itemized: yellow deerskin gloves, also a pair of child's gloves, a bit of sugar, a ham sandwich, a box of bullets, a photograph of a man. On the back of the photograph was written, "I have loved you till my unhappy end." This writing was dated October 11, 1899, two days before the bodies were found.

It was soon known that the woman was Hedwig Keplinger, age twenty-three, and the little girl was her illegitimate daughter Olga, age six. They had disappeared three days before, supposedly going on a picnic. On the same day that the bodies were found, a messenger brought a letter to Hedwig Keplinger's sister; he had been instructed to wait three days before delivering it. In the letter Hedwig Keplinger declared that she had given up all hope, that she had received a visit from the man she hoped to marry, that he would not marry her after all. Therefore, she wrote, she was determined to kill her daughter and then herself.

From the very first appearance of Hedwig Keplinger and her daughter in the Viennese press, it was evident that this was a story of special fascination. Certainly theirs was not the only fatal tragedy of that day in Vienna. In a cement factory one worker jokingly aimed and fired a supposedly unloaded gun at his fellow worker and friend—and the gun was loaded. In this case the wounded man survived, but, at the same time, in a sheet metal factory another worker was caught in a rolling machine and immediately decapitated; he had a wife and four children. These two local items appeared in the *Neue Freie Presse,* the most important newspaper in Vienna, under the headings "An Unfortunate Shot" and "Misfortune with a Rolling Machine." Neither of these incidents received anything like the attention that was devoted to the elegantly dressed bodies of Hedwig Keplinger and her daughter. The story of the corpses in the woods appeared under the far stronger heading of "Murder and Suicide"—in German, *"Mord und Selbstmord."*

During the next few days their story became a minor sensation, reflecting Viennese attitudes toward parents and children, as well as murder and suicide, at the turn of the century. It was immediately called to mind a month later at the time of the child abuse sensation in November. The story of Hedwig Keplinger would then serve to define by contrast what was so exceptionally, unspeakably dreadful about those later cases. Then there would be no neat bullet wounds at the temple. Then it would no longer be possible to dress up the horror of the tale with items of elegant clothing. For us, as for the Viennese of 1899, the story of Hedwig Keplinger and her daughter is the all-important prologue.

## THE LEGENDARY EMPEROR

In 1899 Vienna was the capital of the Austro-Hungarian Empire, and the Emperor Franz Joseph who resided there had just the year before marked the fiftieth anniversary of his coronation. He was sixty-nine, ten years younger than Queen Victoria, but like her he had come to the throne at the age of eighteen, and like her he had achieved a certain mythic status by virtue of the remarkable length of his reign. From the year of his accession, when he oversaw the suppression of the liberal revolution of 1848, Franz Joseph was a figure of conservatism. His was the competent but unimaginative conservative rule of a man who supposedly never read a book in his whole long life except the army register. Unlike Queen Victoria, Franz Joseph was always a monarch who really ruled, absolutely until the Austro-Hungarian compromise of 1867, constitutionally thereafter but still with great power. He lived and ruled until 1916.

Robert Musil's enormous novel *The Man Without Qualities* is the most profound literary recreation of Habsburg Austria in its last years, the empire of "Kakania." To Musil the old Emperor appeared as already "legendary" in his own lifetime, so much so that his subjects "were sometimes overtaken by doubt whether he existed at all."

> The number of portraits one saw of him was almost as great as the number of inhabitants of his realms; on his birthday there was as much eating and drinking as on that of the Saviour; on the mountains the bonfires blazed, and the voices of millions of people were heard vowing that they loved him like a father . . . But this popularity and publicity was so over-convincing that it might easily have been the case that believing in his existence was rather like still seeing certain stars although they ceased to exist thousands of years ago.

The tense and tenuous existence of the doomed empire seemed spiritually to depend on this devotion to a star which, if not already long dead, was certainly too old to live much longer. Adolf Hitler, as a young man in Vienna, was also struck by the complete identification between the ruler and his empire. In *Mein Kampf* he recalled that Austria-Hungary was "so bound up with the person of Franz Joseph that the death of this old embodiment of the empire was felt by the broad masses to be tantamount to the death of the empire itself." In fact the empire disintegrated just two years after his death.

For Hermann Broch, the brilliant Viennese writer who analyzed the city's "gay apocalypse," the essence of the legend of the old Emperor was his "absolute seclusion." In this respect his family legend resembled Victoria's: she lost Albert to typhoid in 1861, becoming forever after the widow of Windsor; in 1898 Franz Joseph became a widower under far more dramatic circumstances. The Empress Elisabeth had been one of the most famously beautiful women in Europe; she was also perhaps a little mad, and she could hardly bear to live in Vienna with her husband the Emperor. On September 10, 1898, on the edge of Lake Geneva, she was fatally stabbed by an Italian anarchist. In the Emperor's letters to his mistress in October 1899, there was no trace of the newly discovered bodies in the woods, but rather the anniversary memory of the body that fell by Lake Geneva the year before. The Empress had virtually arranged the long-standing romance between her husband and the actress Katharina Schratt, and after the assassination, the Emperor could comfortably reminisce, writing to his mistress about his dead wife.

> I went before two o'clock to the painter Benzur to see the portrait of our dear transfigured one which he had painted . . . It is very successful and, moreover, the best portrait that has been painted of the Empress. It is an exceedingly beautiful picture, the bearing excellent and her face as it was at a more youthful age, and with a very pleasant expression.

This was written on October 23, ten days after Hedwig Keplinger and her daughter were discovered dead. If the Emperor knew the story, there was certainly no reason for him to think it worth mentioning in a letter to his mistress. And yet one of the reasons the story was so fascinating to the Viennese public was because, strangely, it was thematically related to the story of the Emperor and the imperial family. The words "Murder and Suicide" inevitably raised the memory of the century's most important and most sensational case of murder and suicide.

Ten years before, two other bodies had been found in the Vienna Woods, fifteen miles outside the city. They were not found in the open air under the trees, like Hedwig Keplinger and her daughter, but rather in the bedroom of a hunting lodge in the woods at Mayerling. These two were the Crown Prince Rudolf, thirty years old, the only son of the Emperor and Empress, and with him the seventeen-year-old Baroness Mary Vetsera, his lover. Rudolf, frustrated at his exclusion from the affairs of state, irrevocably married to a princess he did not love, had fallen in love with a beautiful girl and proposed to her a suicide pact. On the night of January 29, 1889, during the Viennese carnival season, the pact was carried out in the hunting lodge at Mayerling. Over the objections of the Emperor, the doctors who examined the bodies remained regretfully certain that it was the Crown Prince who had pulled the trigger both times, first to shoot the girl, then to shoot himself. The suicide pact, in execution, was really murder and suicide. Stefan Zweig, when he wrote his Viennese memoirs, still vividly remembered Mayerling, though he had been only seven at the time.

> From the very earliest days of my youth I can recall another day when Crown Prince Rudolf, the Emperor's only son, had been found shot dead in Mayerling. Then the whole city was in a tumult of despair and excitement, tremendous crowds thronged to witness his lying in state, the expression of shock and sympathy for the Emperor was over-whelming.

Zweig was writing fifty years after the event, and soon after that, in 1942 in Brazil, he and his wife committed suicide together. His childhood memory of Mayerling was indelible, and in 1899 the story would have come easily to everyone's mind.

There were in Viennese society and the society news always two figures who served as living reminders: the Dowager Crown Princess Stephanie, Rudolf's widow, and her daughter the little Archduchess Elisabeth. In fact, Princess Stephanie and her daughter could even be seen as the grand imperial counterparts of Hedwig Keplinger and Olga: two abandoned women, two fatherless girls. What might have made this analogy perceptible to the Viennese public of 1899 was the coincidence that, only a week after the two bodies were discovered in the woods, it was publicly announced that Princess Stephanie was to remarry. Rudolf had not loved her, and now she was ready to give up the grandeur of imperial widowhood to marry a Hungarian count, becoming thereafter simply the Countess Lonyay, no longer the Dowager Crown Princess. Her parents, the King and Queen of Belgium, disapproved of the remarriage and threatened to cut her off completely. Franz Joseph, her father-in-law, was not much more understanding, and, four days after writing about the portrait of the late Empress, he wrote to Katharina Schratt about Princess Stephanie's coming remarriage. "Let us hope," he concluded, "she will be less difficult to manage."

In October the Emperor had his mind on family matters, and he made no imaginative connections; the Emperor, after all, was not an imaginative man. And yet the members of the imperial family could be curiously entangled in the inner lives and fantasies of their subjects. Sigmund Freud, perhaps the most brilliant and imaginative of all the subjects of Franz Joseph, found the members of the imperial family in the dreams of his Viennese patients. "The Emperor and

Empress (or the King and Queen) as a rule really represent the dreamer's parents," wrote Freud, "and a Prince or Princess represents the dreamer himself or herself." For the Viennese public, the news of Princess Stephanie's remarriage followed so immediately upon the sensation of Hedwig Keplinger, that both women, with their daughters, were in the public eye at virtually the same moment. The link to Mayerling was there from the very beginning, when the two bodies were found in the woods, and publicized under the heading "Murder and Suicide." And then it was announced that the Dowager Crown Princess was to marry a Hungarian count, a stepfather for the little archduchess, just a week after Hedwig Keplinger had given up all hope of marrying and taken her daughter for a picnic in the woods.

### "A CERTAIN HATRED OF THE CHILD"

The morning after the discovery of the bodies, the newspaper had all the most precise details about clothing and accessories, but still only a vague idea of Hedwig Keplinger's personal history. By evening, however, that too had been thoroughly gone into, and the *Neue Freie Presse,* in its evening edition, put the story on the front page, bottom center. The heading was no longer "Murder and Suicide," but rather "A Big-City Novel"—in German, *"Ein Grossstadtroman."* The heroine of the novel was now identified as "the pretty Fräulein Keplinger."

What had been discovered during the course of the day was something about the identity of the man in the photograph inside the blue silk reticule, the photograph that Hedwig Keplinger had inscribed on the back: "I have loved you till my unhappy end." He was not the father of her child, and neither was he the man whom she had recently set her hopes on marrying. Rather the love of her life turned out to be a third figure from the years in between those other two. Her story was thus unexpectedly complicated; it was, in short, a novel.

Hedwig Keplinger had come to Vienna six years before, at the age of seventeen, from Styria, from the provinces. She came to the capital to go into domestic service. Soon after her arrival she was seduced and abandoned, left with a child. She sent the child away to be cared for outside the city, so that she could go on working. Then a rich man became interested in her, a certain Robert W., the man in the photograph, and for a period Hedwig Keplinger was kept in luxury. Eventually Robert W. grew tired of the affair, and she was on her own again. Before he dropped her, however, he was thoughtful enough to introduce her to an engineer who seemed like a possible candidate for marriage. The engineer was just about to go off to Bulgaria, where he had been given a very well paying job, but he wrote letters to Hedwig Keplinger from Bulgaria, and from their correspondence came an informal engagement. Only the week before, the engineer had come to Vienna on a visit, and there he learned for the first time that Hedwig Keplinger had a six-year-old illegitimate child. Upon learning that, he told her that he could never marry her.

This was indeed almost the outline for a novel, the novel of a girl from the provinces who comes to the big city. There were a million and a half people living in Vienna in 1899. The novel was not to be a simple morality tale—death as the wages of sin for a fallen woman—but rather a socially concerned work about the harshness of contemporary urban life. It could even have been a novel about social class relations, for the single most important item of information in the evening edition account was the fact that Hedwig Keplinger came to Vienna to work as a domestic servant. Those who had read the morning papers, and fed their imaginations on the dove-gray suit, the yellow deerskin gloves, and the blue silk reticule, could now revise their conception of Hedwig Keplinger. Lest there be any doubts on this matter, the newspapers further revealed that her father in the provinces worked in an iron foundry.

There was only one moment in the article when the *Neue Freie Presse* went beyond plot summary to consider the case psychologically. This was, interestingly, also the only moment when it was recalled that there were *two* bodies in the woods, that Hedwig Keplinger was not the only character in the story, that she had murdered her daughter.

> The engineer explained to the girl that he couldn't marry her, since he didn't want to acquire an illegitimate child in marriage. With that the girl now saw her last hope shattered and regarded the child, whom anyway she always dragged around with her as a heavy burden, as the cause of this collapse. It could be that from this a certain hatred of the child was established in the heart of the mother, and drove her to her dreadful resolution.

The speculative phrasing of that last sentence was rather unjournalistic, and suggested that perhaps the newspaper really was ready to plunge into fiction. On the one hand, there was here a recognition that the child was murdered by her mother, and an attempt to account for that. On the other hand, there was just a hint that the newspaper, which certainly sympathized with Hedwig Keplinger as she passed from seducer to seducer, also managed to find some sympathy for her attitude toward her "heavy burden."

This was Freud's Vienna, and the readiness to psychologize, especially the frank suggestion of "a certain hatred of the child," was almost Freudian in its implications. Freud was right there in Vienna in October 1899, waiting for the appearance of his masterpiece, *The Interpretation of Dreams*. And in that book, for the first time, he publicly presented the Oedipus complex, which would establish in modern psychology the crucial significance of both sexual attraction and deadly hatred between parents and children. In September Freud was still on vacation in Berchtesgaden in the Bavarian Alps (it would later be Hitler's favorite mountain retreat), and from there he sent the final pages of his book manuscript to the publishers. "I dread Vienna," he wrote to Wilhelm Fliess in Berlin, his closest friend; Freud always claimed to hate Vienna, but could not bring himself to give it up until 1938, after Austria became a part of Nazi Germany. Returning to Vienna from his vacation at the end of September 1899, Freud dreaded the city even more intensely than usual, because he awaited its response to *The Interpretation of Dreams*. He did not expect the book to be favorably received.

In the book itself Freud anticipated his readers' indignation at the Oedipus complex in the section on "Dreams of the Death of Persons of Whom the Dreamer Is Fond." Fathers or mothers, brothers or sisters, sons or daughters:

> The meaning of such dreams, as their content indicates, is a wish that the person in question may die. And since I must expect that the feelings of all my readers, and any others who have experienced similar dreams, will rebel against my assertion, I must try to base my evidence for it on the broadest possible foundation.

It was no small thing, Freud recognized, to insist that family members could wish each other dead.

> Before this idea is rejected as a monstrous one, it is as well, in this case too, to consider the real relations obtaining—this time between parents and children. We must distinguish between what the cultural standards of filial piety demand of this relation and what everyday observation shows it in fact to be. More than one occasion for hostility lies concealed in the relation between parents and children.

Freud pleaded for an open-minded hearing, pleaded that he was no monster, but he expected to come up against a wall of sanctimonious, hypocritically sentimental Victorian reverence for the ideal of the loving family. He appealed to everyday observation, but he could hardly have anticipated that just as the book was about to appear, Hedwig Keplinger would murder her daughter. Still less could he have imagined that the leading newspaper of Vienna, on the front page, would stray so far from "cultural standards of filial piety" as to admit to the possibility of "a certain hatred" between mother and daughter.

What more convincing evidence could one have required, to prove that parents and children might indeed wish each other dead, than a parent who actually carried out that wish? And the child abuse cases in November, when the book was already out, would provide even more devastating evidence of hatred. Freud, however, was right to fear complete rejection, and the newspaper's suggestion of "a certain hatred" was soon dropped, virtually retracted, when the case of Hedwig Keplinger was given its final summation in the Viennese press. Freud himself did not seize upon Hedwig Keplinger in self-justification. In fact, he never commented on the case, and there was no trace of it in the short letter he wrote to Fliess only days after the bodies were discovered.

October 17, 1899<br>IX., Berggasse 19

Dear Wilhelm,

   What would you say if masturbation were to reduce itself to homo-sexuality, and the latter, that is, male homosexuality (in both sexes) were the primitive form of sexual longing? (The first sexual aim, analo-gous to the infantile one—a wish that does not extend beyond the inner world.) If, moreover, libido and anxiety both were male?

   Cordially,
   Your
   Sigm.

Both Sigmund Freud and the Emperor Franz Joseph, in their private correspondences, showed themselves otherwise preoccupied. To each his own, of course: for the Emperor a beautiful portrait with a pleasant expression, for Freud masturbation, homosexuality, libido, and anxiety. Freud never wrote a word about the murder and suicide at Mayerling in 1889, and likewise he made no contribution at all to the "big-city novel" of Hedwig Keplinger a decade later.

## "A FEELING FOR FORM, AN APPRECIATION OF BEAUTY"

What was the other news of the day? What else was Vienna reading about on that same front page of the evening edition of the *Neue Freie Presse,* October 14, 1899? The leading political news concerned the new Austrian ministry of Count Manfred Clary-Aldringen. This was in fact a critical moment in the history of the impossible Austrian nationalities question, which was already ravaging Austrian political life and would ultimately destroy the empire during World War I. Even after the Austro-Hungarian compromise of 1867, by which the Emperor's Hungarian lands received virtual political independence in their internal affairs, the Austrian half of the empire remained bitterly nationally fragmented among Germans and Czechs, Slovenes and Italians, Poles and Ukrainians, Serbs and Croatians. The center stage of the struggle in the late nineties was the province of Bohemia, where Czech and German antagonism was so intense that Adolf Hitler would still be able to play upon it forty years later when he demanded the Sudetenland from Czechoslovakia. In 1897 the Austrian minister president Count Casimir Badeni had decided, as a great concession to the Czechs of Bohemia, to insist upon the bilingual administration of the province. The Germans of Bohemia demonstrated, then rioted against the Badeni language laws. German representatives in the Reichsrat, the parliament in Vienna, furiously obstructed all parliamentary activity. Finally, in October 1899 the Emperor called upon a new minister president, Count Clary-Aldringen, to repeal the Badeni laws. That October was long remembered as a black month by the Czechs of the empire. During the following months it became their turn to riot in the streets and obstruct parliamentary government, and the empire was on the verge of a long period of ministerial absolute rule under the emergency powers of the Emperor.

The foreign news of the day on October 14, and for a long time thereafter, was the English involvement in South Africa in the Boer War, which had just begun. This together with the news of the Clary ministry, dominated the upper half of the front page. The lower half, under the title "Little Chronicle," gave three columns of lesser news. The Emperor was awarding special honors (the Cross of the Order of Leopold and the Cross of the Order of the Iron Crown) to diplomatic officials of the Austrian embassy in Constantinople. Although Edmond Rostand was visiting Vienna, the Burgtheater, on account of repertory complications, would be unable to present a performance of Cyrano de Bergerac in his honor. The great Viennese actor Joseph Kainz (a famous interpreter of Cyrano) was being scheduled to play King Ahasuerus in Franz Grillparzer's Esther. Gustav Mahler, director of the Vienna Opera, had appointed a new conductor from Frankfurt to conduct Don

*Giovanni.* In the city of Graz in Styria, contributions were being solicited for a Goethe monument. In Vienna's famous Danube park, the Prater, an international horse show was about to open. And the girl who always brought supper to the guards at a particular Viennese guard station was accidentally shot in the neck when a watchman was handling his service revolver. It was among these notices, in the center column of the three, by far the largest item of the "Little Chronicle," placed between the Goethe monument and the international horse show, that one found "The Big-City Novel" of Hedwig Keplinger. By the next day, her position in the paper would be more prominent still.

That the story of Hedwig Keplinger was set amidst such items in the "Little Chronicle" pointed to what was most characteristically Viennese about its reception. For the case was an item of theatrical gossip, a show, and above all—billed explicitly as a novel—a literary event. Only the question of genre remained uncertain. When the story had first appeared in the *Neue Freie Presse,* it was introduced with a curious frame: A shoemaker's assistant and his daughter were hunting for mushrooms in the woods, and the little girl strayed from the path. This was a German fairy tale; the tone was unmistakable.

And then the catalog of clothing began, the garments of the dead woman and child, all included and described without any apparent standard of selection; no detail was omitted as irrelevant, since the purpose was to present a sort of textual painting. Colors and fabrics were essential, the elements of the whole visual representation. The two pairs of yellow shoes picked up the gold of the child's earrings, the gold of the mother's watch, the yellow of her hat and her deerskin gloves, and even the foam of the poisonous phosphorus solution. The child's dark blue jacket was matched by the ribbon on the mother's hat, the blue forget-me-not stones set in the child's gold earrings, and of course the blue silk reticule. The child's red dress was the color of the blood that spotted her handkerchief, the color of the blood that flowed from the bullet wounds. The description of the clothing of the dead suggested an odd, but distinctly artistic editorial sensibility.

Stefan Zweig was a young poet in Vienna at the turn of the century. He eventually discovered his intellectual vocation as an international pacifist during World War I, and as a highly successful biographer who ranged from Erasmus to Marie Antoinette. Zweig, a Jew, left Europe in the 1930s, and before he and his wife committed suicide together in Brazil in 1942, he wrote a vivid memoir of the Vienna of his youth, *The World of Yesterday*. The literary renderings of Hedwig Keplinger's story fit perfectly with Zweig's recollection of a city ruled by "an artistic monomania, overvaluation of the aesthetic carried to the point of absurdity." And this, Zweig suggested, was possibly a problem of compensation.

> There is hardly a city in Europe where the drive towards cultural ideals was as passionate as it was in Vienna. Precisely because the monarchy, because Austria itself, for centuries had been neither politically ambitious nor particularly successful in its military actions, the native pride had turned more strongly toward a desire for artistic supremacy.

At Princeton in the 1960s and 1970s, the historian Carl Schorske did more than anyone else to bring about the rediscovery of the lost world of Zweig's recollections, the world of fin-de-siècle Vienna. Schorske in his historical essays, like Zweig in his memoirs, emphasized the idea of compensation through art and the creation of a Viennese "aesthetic culture." Aestheticism, art for art's sake, was by no means uniquely Viennese, but in Vienna it was not only more "passionate" (as Zweig remembers), but far more influential in society at large. Art, according to Schorske, became for the Viennese bourgeoisie "an escape, a refuge from the unpleasant world of increasingly threatening political reality." The political situation of October 1899 was certainly ominous: riots and demonstrations over the Badeni language laws, the collapse of parliamentary government, the imminence of emergency absolutism.

In the 1890s Vienna became one of the cultural capitals of Europe. The literary circle of Young Vienna included two of the geniuses of modern literature, Hugo von Hofmannsthal in poetry and drama, and Arthur Schnitzler in drama and fiction. Hofmannsthal, as a teenager in the early nineties, was writing some of the most beautiful lyric poetry in the German language, and, as a dramatist, he would eventually join with Richard Strauss in such stunningly successful operatic collaborations as *Der Rosenkavalier* and *Ariadne auf Naxos*. Schnitzler, most famous for his comedy of sexual manners, *Reigen* or *La Ronde,* was a psychiatrist as well as a writer of such psychological penetration that Freud claimed to see in Schnitzler his own double. "Whenever I get deeply absorbed in your beautiful creations," wrote Freud to Schnitzler in 1922, "I invariably seem to find beneath their poetic surface the very presuppositions, interests, and conclusions which I know to be my own." In addition to its literary brilliance, Vienna in the 1890s was also a city of musical and artistic genius. In 1897 Gustav Klimt created the Vienna "Secession" in art, and that same year Gustav Mahler became musical director of the Vienna Opera.

Zweig, remembering himself and his schoolmates in the nineties, tried to describe what the social diffusion of aestheticism could mean.

> If I look back today, then I must objectively confess that the sum of our knowledge, the refinement of our literary technique, and our artistic level were really astounding for seventeen-year-olds and only explicable by the inspiring example of Hofmannsthal's fantastic prematurity, which forced us towards a passionate exertion towards giving the very best in order to maintain some show of respect in each other's eyes. We were masters of all the tricks, the extravagances, the venturesomeness of the language; we possessed the technique of every verse form, and in countless attempts had tested every style from Pindaric pathos to the simple diction of the folk song. Each day we showed each other our work, mutually pointed out the slightest discrepancies, and discussed every metric detail.

Freud's eldest son, Martin, was not seventeen, but only ten years old in October 1899, and his father was writing thus to Fliess:

> At present my son Martin is not writing any poems. I believe I reported to you from Berchtesgaden that he said: "I do not actually believe that my so-called poems are really good." This pronouncement marked a turning away from the preceding creative period.

Was Freud slightly amused at the poetic concerns of his ten-year-old son? If so, he was certainly very serious when he wondered about the value of the book that he himself had just finished, *The Interpretation of Dreams,* and wrote to Fliess nervously about its stylistic merits. "Somewhere inside me," wrote Freud, "there is a feeling for form, an appreciation of beauty as a kind of perfection; and the tortuous sentences of my dream book, with their parading of indirect phrases and squinting at ideas, deeply offended one of my ideals."

It was Vienna's prevailing aestheticism that conditioned the oddly literary treatment of Hedwig Keplinger in the press. The fairy-tale frame, the catalog of colored garments, the outline for a "novel"—these were the formal and stylistic reflexes of a decade devoted to literature and art. But the next version of the story really showed what Zweig meant by an "overvaluation of the aesthetic carried to the point of absurdity." On October 15, the *Neue Freie Presse* featured a huge story under a prominent title: "Hedwig Keplinger: A Servant Girl's Fate."

### Hedwig Keplinger: A Servant Girl's Fate (Part I)

In the morgue at Mödling there lies a young woman of twenty-four years, and next to her a child whom she carried over with her into the land of the silent.

A life has found its end. It was never an exceptional life, sharply distinguished from many others. An accident pushed this existence into a brighter lighting, and all at once we feel something that emanates from this young and pretty dead girl, something that breathes upon us softly, coolly, painfully, with a tragic terror.

Of this one girl we happen to know by chance how it happened and how she was; by chance we see more clearly, and because we know about her this and that, so we have a little bit of the feeling that we have lived closely alongside her, and that she has died like a child of this big city. She was only one of the many drawn by that brilliant magnet "Vienna." Every year in the autumn, when people here return from the country, the provinces send their young blood to the big city.

And the big city needs that, because it devours those who were born in it, enervates them, exploits them, and discards them when they are no longer of use, and then reaches for warm blood from the country.

So a fresh person from out in Styria comes together with the city people. The city woman wants to have "someone from the coun-try," a strong person who can work and is honest, a dull, loyal child who will slave in blind obedience and knows nothing of claims and rights and has not yet been enlightened and ruined by the city servant girls. And when at home the girl encounters a city man, and he sees her laughing healthy youth, then he says to her firmly: You should see that you come to Vienna. For a girl like you it's just a shame to sit in the nest in the country. You can make your fortune in the city. When people see how you . . . When you come to Vienna, just write to me, and I'll look out for you a little.

And at these words the girl feels on her a gaze that makes her proud and nervous—such a fine city man, and he looks at her like that, but . . . And the girl starts to find country work distasteful, and she gets the feeling that in the city life is much easier, people have much less to do and live better, and people can make their fortunes too—and so she goes to Vienna to go into service. With ten guilders she arrives. She rents a bed for one guilder a week, including breakfast. At the servant agency she pays two guilders to register. And one day, in the morning around eight, she wanders from the outskirts, where she has her quarters, into the center of town, where the servant agency does its business. Amazed, with big eyes, she sees the shop displays and the crowds of people. The noise makes her dumb and dizzy. Sometimes a man addresses her with more or less clear intentions, but she doesn't understand him. "What do you want?"

He takes the time and trouble to make his intentions clear to her, but she shakes her head, meaning, "Well, well!" She buys herself bread and sausage, and eats it before the gates of a house.

At seven in the evenings she is back with the woman who rents her the bed, who explains, and enlightens, and warns. She mustn't get involved with anyone; there are pimps running around every-where in Vienna, and with a word she could find herself contracted to Bulgaria or to Turkey. To be sure, it also happens that a man who chases girls behaves respectably—deals with the girl nobly, takes care of her or marries her, but that happens so seldom. As a rule men are scoundrels and rascals who want only to exploit a poor girl, and then abandon her when they have achieved their goal.

And finally the girl from the country finds a job . . .

### "LITERATURE DEMOLISHED"

That was how it began, the newspaper story "Hedwig Keplinger: A Servant Girl's Fate." Her name appeared in the title, but not in the story itself. The opening paragraphs, beginning with the body in the morgue, clearly referred to Hedwig Keplinger, but she was not to be presented as an exceptional case. Instead, in this telling of the tale, she was just a nameless girl, a sociological archetype. "So a fresh person from out in Styria comes together with the city people." In fact, Hedwig Keplinger was from the province of Styria, but that detail let the reader know only that this could be Hedwig Kep-linger—though it could be many other girls as well. The inten-tions of the story were frankly sociological; its points were con-cerned with the cruel relations between the big city and the provinces, between men and women. Vienna devouring, enervat-ing, exploiting, discarding. City men as lechers, seducers, pimps. And the girl from the country was the sympathetic victim, the heroine of the story.

But if the story's intentions were sociological, its form and style suggested something else altogether. The country girl was neither strictly Hedwig Keplinger nor a sociological construction; she was a literary creation. Her story was full of imagined details and thoughts and even snatches of conversation. "When you come to Vienna, just write to me, and I'll look out for you a little." Authorial license from the very beginning allowed certain aspects of Hedwig Keplinger's story to be misrepresented or stylistically transformed. The "laughing healthy youth" of the country girl suggested that she was some kind of milkmaid on a farm, not the daughter of a man who worked in a provincial iron foundry. The dead child in the morgue was not murdered, but rather "carried over into the land of the silent." So, was this journalism at all? In fact, the format of the piece in the newspaper resembled nothing so much as the special fiction features which regularly accompanied the news. If the first two pieces on Hedwig Keplinger, "Murder and Suicide" and "A Big-City Novel," contained literary elements, this new and much longer piece actually presented the story recreated as literature. Unlike those two earlier pieces, this one was signed, and the author's name was one that the Viennese of 1899 would have recognized as a notable one in the cultural life of the city.

His name was Felix Dörmann. His was the most significant pen in shaping the story of Hedwig Keplinger in October, and he would be deeply and publicly involved again in the child abuse sensation of November. Felix Dörmann was one of the minor poets of Young Vienna in the nineties, one of the men who gathered at the famous Cafe Griensteidl, part of the circle that included Hofmannsthal and Schnitzler, the circle that gave the city its glorious place in Austrian literature. Besides Hofmannsthal and Schnitzler, however, the other figures of Young Vienna have generally not been counted as giants. There was the critic Hermann Bahr, who came from Linz to Vienna and presided over the creation of the circle. There were the poets Leopold von Andrian and Richard Beer-Hofmann. There was Felix Salten, who did many years later achieve international fame and, eventually, immortalization by Walt Disney, as the author of *Bambi*. And there was Felix Dörmann.

In 1891 Dörmann burst upon the scene as a twenty-one-year-old poetic prodigy, the author of a controversial volume of decadent poems, *Neurotica*. Sigmund Freud, the supreme Viennese poet of neurotica, was still completely unknown then; his first paper on hysteria, coauthored with Josef Breuer, would not be published until 1893. For appreciating Dörmann the crucial figure for comparison was Hofmannsthal, the Viennese poetic prodigy of the early nineties. The history of Dörmann's talent unfolded under the shadow of Hofmannsthal's genius.

The two poets came from rather similar social backgrounds. Dörmann was the son of a Jewish father, a big businessman in wholesale trade, and a Catholic mother. The mixed religious background was also the hallmark of Hofmannsthal's ancestry, which has been, naturally, much more carefully studied than Dörmann's. Hoffmanns-thal's great-grandfather was a highly successful Jewish silk mer-chant in Vienna, and was even ennobled by the grandfather of Franz Joseph in 1827. (The family coat of arms combined the silk-giving mulberry leaf with the tablets of Moses.) Hofmannsthal's grandfather married a Catholic woman from Austrian Milan.

Hermann Broch, like Stefan Zweig, was a Viennese writer intel-lectually spellbound by the European world as he remembered it from before World War I. That Europe was the subject of his remarkable novel *The Sleepwalkers,* published in the early 1930s, and it was again his subject in the late 1940s in America (he too had had to flee from the Nazis) when he wrote a cultural analysis of Vienna, *Hugo von Hofmannsthal and His Time.* For Broch, Vienna in the 1880s was the scene of a "gay apocalypse" and the "center of the European value vacuum." The aesthetic genius of Hoffmanns-thal could emerge from that vacuum precisely because it was nour-ished by a nexus of assimilations: between Judaism and Catholi-cism, between bourgeois commerce and the alluring beacon of aristocracy. In Broch's analysis it was ultimately art and aestheti-cism that bridged, assimilated, ennobled:

> In the end, not as a Jew—although he was the first Hofmannsthal in three generations to enter into a Jewish marriage—but as an artist and with the artist's claim to nobility, Hugo von Hofmannsthal renewed the mission of assimilation. The spirit of his great-grandfather, em-bodied in the mystically potent image of the tablets of the law in the family crest, received a brilliant post-facto apology, if not exactly the kind of brilliance he might have dreamed of for his great-grand-children.

Stefan Zweig also observed this phenomenon of assimilation through art, focusing especially on the Viennese Jews.

> It was the pride and ambition of the Jewish people to cooperate in the front ranks to carry on the former glory of the fame of Viennese culture. They had always loved this city, and had entered into its life wholeheartedly, but it was first of all by their love for Viennese art that they had actually become true Viennese . . . It was only in regard to art that all felt an equal right, because love of art was a communal duty in Vienna, and immeasurable is the part in Viennese culture the Jewish bourgeoisie took, by their cooperation and promo-tion. They were the real audience, they filled the theaters and the concerts, they visited the exhibitions . . .

Hofmannsthal, thus, was simply the paradigm: a mixed ancestry finding the most perfect assimilation in the most perfect artistry.

Dörmann, the son of a Jewish businessman and a Catholic mother, matched the paradigm, and found his place at the Cafe Griensteidl in the early nineties.

Dörmann was born in 1870, Hofmannsthal in 1874, fatefully four years younger, destined to be that much more astoundingly prodigious. Both poets were born in Vienna itself, thoroughly Viennese. The "discovery" of Hofmannsthal was one of the legendary moments in the history of Austrian literature. Hermann Bahr has recounted how, sitting in the Cafe Griensteidl, he came upon an essay by a certain "Loris," an essay of unmistakable genius. Bahr was desperate to know who this Loris could be, and did all he could to arrange a meeting. On the appointed day Bahr sat at the cafe, imagining Loris as someone who must have spent twenty years as part of the Austrian embassy in Paris to have gained such sophistication and refinement. Then a boy approached, a high school student, and, to Bahr's amazement, he held out his hand and introduced himself: "I am Loris." That was in 1891, the same year that Dörmann published his *Neurotica*; he was twenty-one, and Hofmannsthal was seventeen.

In 1893, not yet twenty years old, Hofmannsthal published his verse play *The Fool and Death,* which was instantly acclaimed a masterpiece, and Dörmann published his second volume of poems, entitled *Sensations*. These were considered his finest poems, and two verses will give an idea of the nature of his craft and sensibility. The first is taken from the title poem of the collection, and features the typically extravagant floral imagery that characterized Dörmann's aestheticism.

> O Silberlila, Deine weichen Wellen,
> Wie Kinderseelen lilienkeusch und klar,
> In meine flammenmüde Seele quellen,
> Und meine Seele wird zum Hochaltar . . .

> (Oh silver lilac, your soft waves
> Like souls of children lily-chaste and clear,
> In my flaming-tired soul are flowing,
> And my soul becomes the high altar . . . )

The following lines from Dörmann's "Prayer" suggest some of the "decadent" emotional extravagances that he did not hesitate to versify.

> Trostlos weinende Sehnsucht,
> Du geleitest
> Einzig meine verirrte,

Wundenblutige Seele,
Und Dein hilflos
Kindisch-thörichtes Weinen
Mehrt ihre Qualen.

(Inconsolable weeping longing,
You accompany
Alone my erring
Bloody wounded soul,
And your helpless
Childish-foolish weeping
Increases its tortures.)

Dörmann's verses, to a modern reader, are such self-consciously crafted exemplars of fin-de-siècle decadence and aestheticism that they have almost the ring of parody. In the nineties, however, his poetry was taken very seriously. *Sensations* came out in a second edition in 1897, and, in fact, cultured readers of 1899, who came upon Dörmann's piece on Hedwig Keplinger, would have recognized his name as that of a significant contemporary poet.

Judgment of Dörmann's poetry from within Young Vienna was surprisingly harsh, considering that these were Dörmann's coffee companions at the Cafe Griensteidl. Consider Hermann Bahr's view of Hofmannsthal, and compare it to his judgment of Dörmann:

[Hofmannsthal] is thoroughly new—by far the newest among the Germans I know, like a forward prophecy of the far distant future . . . He has the joy, the lightness, the dancing of which the longing of Nietzsche dreamed. Whatever he touches becomes grace, pleasure, and beauty.

[Dörmann] does not speak from life. He speaks always from foreign literatures. His sorrows are from Baudelaire, and his desires are from Swinburne. In himself he heralds nothing. So he is like the worst sort of epigone . . .

Or consider Schnitzler's reaction to hearing Hofmannsthal read for the first time, and compare it to his diary entry upon reading Dörmann's *Neurotica* that same year:

After a few minutes we riveted our attention on [Hofmannsthal] and exchanged astonished, almost frightened glances. We had never heard verses of such perfection, such faultless plasticity, such musical feeling, from any living being, nor had we thought them possible since Goethe . . . I had the feeling of having encountered a born genius for the first time in my life, and never again during my entire lifetime was I so overwhelmed.

A volume of poetry by Felix Dörmann has appeared, *Neurotica,* which alongside very pretty details of language and mood, contains brutalities and tastelessness, lyric falseness and sloppiness.

As for Hofmannsthal's own view of Dörmann's poetry, there was the following letter to Schnitzler, dated New Year's Day 1892: "Dear Friend. Dörmann wants to read us his new book and has asked me to invite you. So if you have nothing better to do, come Saturday morning . . ."

In 1897, the year of the second edition of *Sensations,* the Cafe Griensteidl was torn down, and this demolition signaled the passing of a literary age. The fin de siècle of the nineties was over; the twentieth century was about to begin. Karl Kraus, the brilliant Viennese satirist, went so far as to celebrate the destruction of the cafe in his scathing essay "Literature Demolished."

The demolition worker taps at the window. And it's about time. In a rush all the literary equipment is gathered together: lack of talent, premature self-possession, poses, megalomania, girls from the outskirts, cravats, mannerisms, false datives, monocles, and secret nerves. It all has to go. Hesitating poets will be gently led away. Taken out of gloomy corners, they shrink from the day whose light blinds them, shrink from life whose fullness will oppress them. Life will shatter the crutch of affectation.

Kraus hated the literary values of the fin de siècle, and what he hated most, its poses and affectations, he certainly saw in Dörmann. "Literature Demolished" also attacked the members of Young Vienna individually. Dörmann was mocked for his nerves and his ecstasies, for his decadence and his mannerisms, for discovering his own suffering in Baudelaire. But in "Literature Demolished" not even Hofmannsthal was spared: it was his legend, however, that Kraus satirized, not his talent—the legend of the high school Goethe. As for Felix Salten, the future creator of shy little Bambi and Perri the squirrel, he felt himself so grievously insulted that he physically attacked Kraus in the streets of Vienna.

"It's about time," Kraus declared, and in that he was prophetic; Young Vienna was ready to move on. Hofmannsthal, above all, was on the verge of the great intellectual and spiritual crisis of his life: he lost his faith in language. He regained that faith, recovered spiritually, but gave up lyric poetry; in the twentieth century his genius was devoted to drama and opera. Dörmann also gave up lyric poetry at about this time. His last volume, *Laughter,* was published in 1896. After that he wrote plays, librettos, stories, novels; he ended up writing for the early Viennese cinema. Typically, while Hofmannsthal composed librettos for grand opera and collaborated with Richard Strauss, Dörmann was writing librettos for Viennese operettas.

This then was Felix Dörmann, a poet of Young Vienna but never a great poet, a man whose poetic past included all the poses and excesses of fin-de-siècle aestheticism. This was the writer who in October 1899 was presenting to the Viennese public Hedwig Keplinger as literature. Dörmann had been involved with journalism through the nineties as a theater critic, so perhaps it was natural for him to try his hand at other subjects for the press. His piece on Hedwig Keplinger, written in 1899, was a product of the years that immediately followed the demolition of the Cafe Griensteidl. These were the years of literary reorientation, when the members of Young Vienna were setting out to seek new genres and new values. And if they were blinded by the light, as Kraus would have it, was it any wonder that they should sometimes have instinctively fallen back on "the crutch of affectation"? So it came about that Dörmann wrote about Hedwig Keplinger, but could not help feeling "something that emanates from this young and pretty dead girl, something that breathes upon us softly, coolly, painfully, with a tragic terror." Here, for a moment, he slipped back to the world of *Sensations,* the literary world of the early nineties. But "Hedwig Keplinger: A Servant Girl's Fate" was written on the very edge of the twentieth century, only months from the turn, and Dörmann was trying so emphatically to write about life, not about silver lilacs, that he took his subject from the news of the day. The story was a true one, and at the same time it became less true as he recreated it.

## Hedwig Keplinger: A Servant Girl's Fate (Part II)

And finally the girl from the country finds a job.

Eight guilders wages, no more. She will have to be trained. From the money she should send something home, since her family believes that now that she has a job she must be swimming in money. And from her wages she must pay back her former proprietress money that had been advanced. And finally she needs shoes and a dress—she is young, scarcely sixteen, and doesn't want always to be running around looking like a scarecrow.

So the winter passes and the spring. She has been in Vienna now almost ten months. On July 1, the woman of the house informs her that she must go in fourteen days. "We aren't rich people. We're going to the country, but over the holidays we can't keep a servant girl. My husband will eat in a restaurant."

She has saved nothing, and moves back to her old proprietress. Now in the summer she finds no work as a servant. She falls into debt with the proprietress, and it's unpleasant for her to be at home. She goes out as often as she can and for as long as possible. For hours she sits in the public garden and the municipal park. She is bored, she is filled with longing, she is so alone. She sends away the first man who sits down next to her on the bench and addresses her. But the third one she likes. She talks with him, more and more often and for longer and longer. He does not immediately come forth with brutal intentions. She develops confidence. She tolerates his pressing her hand. He is such a dear man. He can put himself in her situation. He knows her home province. She feels warm when she is near him. After eight days she allows him to kiss her. They have known each other for three weeks already and have never yet had an evening meal together. One evening however she is all at once sick with hunger. She had quarreled with her proprietress and didn't go back for lunch, and she has no money to buy herself something.

He is touched by her self-neglect and innerly satisfied. He knows he is near his goal. He knows these girls from the country are stubborn, and it takes a long time to vanquish them. He is sweet and good to her. He likes her too.

Finally, at the beginning of August, he attains the desired relation with her. For him it is a charming adventure. For her he is the first. And what happens, on her part, happens completely from love. She hangs on him with the blind devoted tenderness of an animal. Sometimes it is a little too much for him, and he thinks about the end, but most of the time it's fine with him. She is simply happy. Autumn comes, and at his insistence she goes back into service. She comes to him every fourteen days.

One day she announces to him that she can remain in service only for at most two or three months more . . . because . . . He behaves very properly, takes care of her for as long as the difficult time lasts, and does what he can. But then, when she returns after so and so many months, she finds she has been forgotten. He explains to her that he liked her a lot, but now it's over; he also can't risk the possibility that something like this will occur a second time—the child will be taken care of. She staggers away like a dying woman. The blow strikes her in the heart. How she had anticipated the reunion—how she had trembled for the moment!

Her finest feelings, her first young and powerful sentiment has been defiled and annihilated—and yet she still loves the man.

A suicide attempt fails, and she is saved. With dull resignation she goes back to her position. Her only joy is his child, and she suffers over the fact that the child is in the country. She fears that something will happen to it, she wants to have it with her, to be able to do more for the child.

In the house where she serves there is a young man who comes and goes. He likes her; she is indifferent to him. He presses, he besieges her; she is disgusted with service. She wants to escape from her memories. She wants to be able to do more for the child. She has nothing more to lose. She wants to encounter "him," the man she can't forget, on the same level. When he sees her again with an-other man, perhaps he will be jealous. She will make herself pretty so that he will regret—he will see—she acquiesces . . . The young man takes care of her in the noblest way. He is truly in love, and also proud to have such a pretty lover. He educates her and has her educated. She learns something. First she half reluctantly puts up with the tenderness of her new friend, but then she gets used to him. The image of the first man becomes clouded, and she begins to forget. Out of gratitude she even begins to love this friend who does so much for her, to love him with a pale, somewhat threadbare love, but nevertheless with a certain devotion. Truly there is nothing like the storm of the first time. She forgets her servant girl past, strips it away, both internally and externally, and becomes an elegant young lady. True, she is just the lover of a young man of the world, but nonetheless a lovely creature with a certain sentimentality and originality of sentiment from the past. The young man, her friend, perceives with terror how much he has become accustomed to her; he finds her already almost indispensable. And more than once he catches himself in thoughts of marriage connected to her, she whom he has raised up, his lover the former servant girl who before him has passed through God knows how many hands. For naturally he does not believe there has been only one.

And he ends their relationship with a heavy heart and in the noblest way . . .

## COUNTRY GIRL, PEASANT BOY

Thus Dörmann continues, developing his story toward its fateful resolution, which was not so much literarily inevitable as it was absolutely predictable—since it was yesterday's news. But exactly what kind of a story was this that Dörmann was telling? In what

genre did he think he was writing? With the denouement approaching, the formal nature and literary category of the piece remained still puzzlingly unclear. For Dörmann was definitely not
writing just a journalist's report on Hedwig Keplinger.

In fact, he moved even beyond the bounds of the Viennese feuilleton—the most characteristic phenomenon of journalism in fin-de-
siècle Vienna. The feuilleton was an extremely personal essay in
which the subject proper was subordinated to the cultivation of
sensibility and creation of mood. Above all, the feuilleton was an
expression of Viennese aestheticism, inasmuch as its stylistic qualities were valued beyond any concern for content; the essay became
a small, personal work of art. Karl Kraus, the enemy of the Cafe
Griensteidl, also detested the feuilleton as journalistically dishonest, pretentious, and inappropriate—a symptom of Vienna's essential affectation. He once summed up the fundamental falseness of
the genre thus: "If you want a window decorated, you don't call in
a lyric poet." This could certainly have been addressed to the inap-
propriateness of entrusting Hedwig Keplinger to Felix Dörmann,
and yet Dörmann's creation was not a feuilleton. True, it was as
personal a rendering of Hedwig Keplinger as one could possibly
imagine in a newspaper. But Dörmann's authorial presence was not
really directed toward exploring his own sensibility as a feuilleton-
ist. He was interested in creating his character, Hedwig Keplinger,
as if he were a writer of fiction.

For Dörmann did not hesitate to lay bare the thoughts and feelings of his characters, and such literary license was not limited only
to the central figure. The park bench seducer "knows he is near his
goal" and "knows these girls from the country are stubborn." The
young man of the world "perceives with terror how much he has
become accustomed to her" and "catches himself in thoughts of
marriage." If Dörmann was privy to the thoughts of even these
subordinate figures, in the case of his heroine he could actually step
inside her head as she surrendered to temptation: "He is such a dear
man."

With such freedom of narration Dörmann's piece could not, despite certain similarities of intention, belong to the genre of the
psychological case history. In fact, Vienna was about to revolution-
ize that genre; the psychological case history was to become an
instrument of the genius of Sigmund Freud. The following year
Freud would undertake the analysis of Dora, which would lead to
perhaps the most famous such study ever written. But Dörmann's
approach to explaining Hedwig Keplinger, even though her case
was a true one, was irrevocably literary; it was an imaginative

reconstruction, not a psychological explanation. Furthermore, though Freud may have admired Schnitzler as his own double, Dörmann's story was very far indeed from the psychoanalytic vision which was emerging at the same time in the same city.

In part this was due to Dörmann's limitations as a psychological writer; the thoughts and emotions attributed to Hedwig Keplinger rarely rose above the obvious, the sentimental, the cliché. "Her finest feelings, her first young and powerful sentiment has been defiled and annihilated—and yet she still loves the man." But the unpsychoanalytic nature of Dörmann's treatment was in part intentional, inasmuch as he eschewed the actual details of the case, the real meat of psychoanalysis. It is all too easy to imagine that for Freud the key to the case might have been that blue silk reticule and the catalog of its contents. ("Dora's reticule, which came apart at the top in the usual way, was nothing but a representation of the genitals.") Or perhaps the yellow hat with the dark blue ribbon and the veil. ("As regards articles of clothing, a woman's hat can very often be interpreted with certainty as a genital organ and, moreover, as a man's.") But Dörmann's "girl from the country" had neither blue silk reticule nor veiled yellow hat; in fact she had no face and no name. All of his characters—the girl, the park bench seducer, the young man of the world, the proprietress—were nameless, faceless types. Psychological exploration was subordinated to sociological category. "Hedwig Keplinger: A Servant Girl's Fate" could perhaps be described as a "sociological fictionalization," though the adoption of such a term would only underline the fundamental difficulty of resolving the question of genre.

Considered in the context of Viennese literature, Dörmann's characters seemed to belong to Schnitzler's fictional world. This was true especially of the male characters: the urban seducer and the young man of the world. Schnitzler, who narrated his own many conquests in his memoirs, who kept count of his acts of intercourse in his diary, kept coming back to the figure of the Viennese Don Juan in his plays and novels. In the Anatol series of the early nineties, Schnitzler presented the hero with a different woman in each scene. In *Liebelei,* his great dramatic success of 1895, the young man of the world broke the heart of the girl from the outskirts, thereafter the Schnitzler female archetype of *"das süsse Mädel"*—"the sweet young thing." In *Reigen,* published in 1900 but too scandalous to be performed until 1920, Schnitzler created a chain of sexual connections, ascending the social hierarchy in successive scenes, including all his favorite Viennese types. *Reigen,* in fact, was in certain respects related to Dörmann's almost exactly contemporary "Hedwig Keplinger." Not only did the Schnitzler play feature a servant girl who connected first with a soldier and then with the young man of the house, but furthermore all the Schnitzler characters were nameless figures. The servant girl was simply that, no more.

But Schnitzler's servant girl was hardly presented as a tragic victim. Actually she was rather lighthearted about her sexual encounters, and said things like, "Heavens, I'd no idea you could be so naughty, Herr Alfred." Certainly there was no hint of a terrible fate awaiting her in the end. On the other hand, Anatol's lovers included married ladies, an actress, a dancer, even a circus performer—but no servant girls. To find a counterpart in Schnitzler to Dörmann's heroine, one must look to a late novel, *Theresa: Chronicle of a Woman's Life,* published in 1928 but set in the Vienna of the turn of the century. Theresa was no country girl from Styria, but the daughter of an army officer in Salzburg; she was compelled by circumstances to come to Vienna and earn her living as a governess. This certainly ranked her above a servant girl, but left her in a very similar position of dependence. Theresa had a succession of lovers in Vienna, as well as an illegitimate child who had to be cared for in the country, and her life ended in tragic violence. Interestingly, it was not Theresa who killed her child, but her son who murdered her. For all their parallels, Schnitzler's heroine originated in the middle class, while Dörmann's was a country girl. In this respect, Dörmann's choice of subject could be seen as the more ambitious literary effort, an attempt to explore a figure outside his own social class. On the other hand, his psychological portrait was so lacking in insight that one could almost sense the bourgeois pen behind the caricature. Certainly no one ever suggested that Dörmann was Freud's double, but it is also true that Freud himself did not try to write case studies of country girls.

Dörmann in 1899 was attempting a rather unflattering transition. Having started the decade as a lesser poet in the shadow of Hofmannsthal, he was now—the worst sort of epigone, according to Hermann Bahr—writing lesser prose with an eye to Schnitzler. Trying to transcend the demolition of the Cafe Griensteidl, Dörmann was moving from the aestheticism of fin-de-siècle lyric poetry to the social and psychological naturalism of turn-of-the-century prose. But it was not just that his writing lacked the psychological subtlety of Schnitzler, the psychiatrist-turned-writer, but also that Dörmann's naturalism, the attempted scientific objectivity in representing a slice of urban life, was undermined by his own sentimentality. The fact that Dörmann took his story from the news made it a potentially interesting naturalist experiment, but the alterations he allowed himself revealed his irrepressibly sentimental instincts. For instance, while the news reports had suggested that it was her wealthy lover whose picture she took to her death, Dörmann was determined to make her true love her very first lover and the father of her child. And Dörmann's country girl was lovingly devoted to that child.

Neither the Viennese feuilleton, nor the Freudian case study, nor Schnitzler's psychological fiction provides a really satisfying answer to the problem of genre. In fact, the most striking literary comparison to Dörmann's "Hedwig Keplinger" may be found in what seems, at first thought, an unlikely place. When Adolf Hitler wrote *Mein Kampf,* in prison after the Munich beer hall putsch of 1923, he devoted the second chapter to "Years of Study and Suffering in Vienna." Adolf Hitler came to Vienna from Linz in 1908, after his mother's death; he was nineteen, a few years older than Hedwig Keplinger was when she came to Vienna in 1893.

Hitler came to art-obsessed Vienna to study painting at the Academy. His application, however, was rejected, his drawing judged insufficiently talented. What followed were several years of "hardship and misery" during which he struggled to earn his living in the big city; he valued these years later for having made him "hard." They also gave him the opportunity to study "the social question," to appreciate the economic inequality between Vienna's "dazzling riches and loathsome poverty."

> In hardly any German city could the social question have been studied better than in Vienna. But make no mistake. This studying can not be done from lofty heights. No one who has not been seized in the jaws of the murderous viper can know its poison fangs. Otherwise nothing results but superficial chatter and false sentimentality.

Hitler, no doubt, would have regarded Dörmann's empathetic exercise as falsely sentimental chatter, but his own presentation of the "social question" in Vienna contained startling similarities.

Hitler began in the autobiographical first person: "I soon learned that there was always some kind of work to be had, but equally soon I found out how easy it was to lose it." And then, strangely, Hitler switched into a sort of third-person parable.

> The peasant boy who goes to the big city, attracted by the easier nature of the work (real or imaginary), by shorter hours, but most of all by the dazzling light emanating from the metropolis, is accustomed to a certain security in the matter of livelihood . . . As a rule he arrives in the big city with a certain amount of money; he has no need

to lose heart on the very first day if he has the ill fortune to find no work for any length of time. But it is worse if, after finding a job, he soon loses it. To find a new one, especially in winter, is often difficult, if not impossible . . . Now he walks the streets hungry; often he pawns and sells his last possessions; his clothing becomes more and more wretched; and thus he sinks into external surroundings which, on top of his physical misfortune, also poison his soul . . . At length he finds some sort of job again. But the old story is repeated. The same thing happens a second time, the third time perhaps it is even worse, and little by little he learns to bear the eternal insecurity with greater and greater indifference. At last the repetition becomes a habit.

And so this man, who was formerly so hard-working, grows lax in his whole view of life and gradually becomes the instrument of those who use him only for their own base advantage.

From this third-person narrative, Hitler then reemerged into first-person testimony: "With open eyes I was able to follow this process in a thousand examples. The more I witnessed it, the greater grew my revulsion for the big city which first avidly sucked men in and then so cruelly crushed them." Finally Hitler made the full transition to first-person autobiography, revealing that he had been talking about himself all along: "I too had been tossed around by life in the metropolis; in my own skin I could feel the effects of this fate and taste them with my soul."

Thus it was that Hitler's peasant boy, like Dörmann's country girl, came to the big city. For the boy Vienna was a "dazzling light," for the girl a "brilliant magnet." For both it took time to find a job, and both soon lost the jobs they found; both walked the streets unemployed. Both became "instruments," exploited by others for "base advantage." Both were "sucked in" and then "cruelly crushed" by the big city. Hitler's "social question" and Dörmann's "servant girl's fate" were one and the same, and the similarities went far deeper than details of plot; the crucial convergences were matters of form and style.

Both authors were clearly trying for the simple but powerful effect of urban naturalism; both were undermined by their own weakness for the sentimental cliché. They were deeply, sentimentally attached to the idea of the peasant violated by the city. Just as Dörmann eliminated Hedwig Keplinger's proletarian father so that she could be a country girl, so Hitler put aside his own civil servant father and preferred to write about a peasant boy. Certainly neither Dörmann nor Hitler could have known from experience the peasant perspective; they were merely enamored of the myth. Surprisingly, in Hitler's postwar prose there were the same fin-de-siècle intrusions that Dörmann brought to journalism from his poetic past. When Hitler wrote of "poisoned" souls and "tasting with his soul," he could have taken his phrases from Dörmann's early "decadent" poems—poems that Hitler would probably later have regarded as Jewish degenerate art. However, the two most striking formal devices, which both writers obviously cherished, were, first, the nameless third-person protagonist who gave each piece the air of sociological fiction, and, second, the unconventional immediacy of the present tense. "He walks the streets hungry." "She sits in the public garden."

There could be no stronger demonstration of the pervasiveness of certain stylistic and thematic preoccupations in turn-of-the-century Vienna. The city distinctly left its cultural mark both on Dörmann, the minor Viennese poet, and on Hitler, who would eventually return to Vienna as its master in 1938. For Hitler's poor peasant boy there was the possibility of salvation in national socialism. For Dörmann's country girl the tragedy could only move on to its inevitable conclusion.

## Hedwig Keplinger: A Servant Girl's Fate (Part III)

And he ends their relationship with a heavy heart and in the noblest way. He gives her 20,000 guilders as quittance. And even more: he discovers and introduces to her a young engineer who wants to marry if he can thereby get some money to make himself independent.

Then he travels in order to forget his lover whom he almost married.

She withstands the blow and is ready to take refuge in this tired gray marriage. She wants finally to have peace and to be taken care of. She knows why he is taking her, but she is likewise not taking him out of love. She wants a better man. She has become accustomed to a more refined life. With the 20,000 guilders she could go home to her parents. That would be a fortune at home in the Styrian nest. She would be the richest and most esteemed lady there. But she doesn't want to go back, doesn't care to return home to the peasants. She has other pretensions in life.

Then at the last hour the marriage plan is wrecked. The engineer knew nothing about the child. If there is also a child who comes with the marriage, then 20,000 guilders is too little.

She does not reply much to the cool and clever speech of the engineer. She agrees that he is quite right, and lets him go peacefully.

What now! Slowly to consume the money she has. To look for another man, again a man whom she also won't love. Another disillusionment. Is all this really worth the effort? Should she perhaps look for a position as a prostitute—or just go out in the streets to make connections. She is so disgusted! And an inertia creeps over her. To have peace. To know nothing. That is the only thing worth the effort. She is seized by infinite pity for her little girl! What is your fate, you poor little worm! A man will come whom you'll like, and then many will come whom you'll have to put up with in order to live. No, no, it musn't come to that. It is enough that I have had such a life, but not you, my poor little worm.

And then she set out for Mödling to the Liechtenstein woods, and shot the child and herself. But before that, for one last time she took up the memories of the first man, who also remained the only one she ever really liked, and who loved her also, approximately from the twelfth of July until the end of September.

## INSIDE HEDWIG KEPLINGER

Dörmann's interpretation of the murder of the child by her mother was absolutely unequivocal: Hedwig Keplinger murdered her child out of love. "She is seized by infinite pity for her little girl! What is your fate, you poor little worm!" The child was murdered to save her from the fate of her mother, from economic misery and sexual exploitation, from the fate of inevitable prostitution. "It is enough that I have had such a life, but not you, my poor little worm." Whereas the previous day's article had allowed for the unsentimental, even Freudian possibility of "a certain hatred" by the mother for her daughter, Dörmann totally revised the psychological explanation. Murder and suicide now bound together mother and daughter in love. It was just as at Mayerling ten years before; in fact it harkened back to that anthem of German romanticism, the Wagnerian *Liebestod* or love-death.

From the beginning of his piece, when the child was not murdered but "carried over into the land of the silent," through the country girl's reiterated longing to do more for her child, to the final mercy killing, Dörmann would have nothing to do with the possibility of hatred between parent and child. For him the problem of a mother who murdered her child was, morally and psychologically, no problem at all. And it was his huge story, featured in the most important newspaper in the city, that attempted to resolve the problem for the Viennese public. Here was the triumph of nine-teenth-century sentimentalism over twentieth-century psychology. To be sure, Dörmann would not be able to resolve things so neatly when it came to child abuse in November, but with the case of Hedwig Keplinger in October it was still possible to cling to one's sentimental ideals.

And at the same time, in the very same lines where Dörmann vindicated the sanctity of parental love, he also risked the final flourish in his stylistic concoction, his experiment in genre. Throughout the piece he allowed himself the literary license of imagining the thoughts of his characters, but at the climactic mo-ment he actually slipped into full and unmistakable stream of con-sciousness. When he wrote "She is seized by infinite pity for her little girl!" that was still narrated consciousness; he narrated what "she" was thinking. In the next sentence though—"What is your fate, you poor little worm!"—the "she" was gone, and the narra-tive became internal, from within her consciousness. And there the narrative remained: "A man will come whom you'll like, and then many will come whom you'll have to put up with in order to live. No, no, it musn't come to that." And then, to conclude the internal monologue, Dörmann took the very last step and presented his servant girl in the first person: "It is enough that I have had such a life, but not you, my poor little worm." This was the final stylistic transformation in which the nonfictional Hedwig Keplinger was presented in hopelessly fictional first-person stream of conscious-ness.

Considering that all this was appearing in the guise of journalism, the transformation was nothing less than preposterous. On the other hand, considering the piece as literature, the narrative shift was entirely consistent with Dörmann's apparent interest in Schnitzler's psychological naturalism. The very next year, in the special Christmas issue of the very same newspaper, Schnitzler would make literary history with the publication of "Lieutenant Gustl," written entirely as an interior monologue in stream of con-sciousness. What was most striking about Dörmann's use of this form was that he adopted it at precisely the same moment that he made his final interpretive point. That is, at the same time that the murder of the child was conjured away and transformed into a sort of *Liebestod*, the character of Hedwig Keplinger was totally trans-formed into literary fiction. It was a simultaneous triumph of both aestheticism and sentimentality, the perfect fin-de-siècle Viennese climax.

## "SUBSCRIBER TO THE *NEUE FREIE PRESSE*"

In order to appreciate the historical significance of Dörmann's extraordinary piece, one must understand that it appeared, not in an obscure literary review, and not in a sensational mass tabloid, but rather in the most respectable, most distinguished, and most influential newspaper of turn-of-the-century Vienna. Founded with the Revolution of 1848, closed down by the Nazis after the Anschluss of 1938, at the turn of the century the *Neue Freie Presse* was the unrivaled, unchallengeable oracle of Viennese cultured bourgeois liberalism. Stefan Zweig remembered it thus:

> In Vienna there was really only one journal of high grade, the *Neue Freie Presse,* which, because of its dignified principles, its cultural endeavors, and its political prestige, assumed in the Austro-Hungarian monarchy a role not unlike that of the *Times* in England.

In fact, Henry Wickham Steed, the future editor of the London *Times,* was, at the turn of the century, the *Times* correspondent in Vienna, and he too later recorded his professional opinion of the *Neue Freie Presse*:

> One and all read it from day to day, or, rather, twice a day, unconsciously adopt its standpoint and allow it to colour their views of public affairs. The greater part of what does duty for "Austrian opinion" is dictated or suggested to the public by the editor-proprietor of the *Neue Freie Presse,* of whom it has jokingly, but, in a sense, not untruthfully been said that "next to him the Emperor is the most important man in the country."

Dörmann's interpretation of Hedwig Keplinger, then, was appearing in the newspaper which was perhaps the single most powerful force in defining and shaping Viennese public opinion.

At the outbreak of World War I, the circulation of the *Neue Freie Presse* was well over 100,000, but its power and influence were not determined by numbers alone. What counted was its position as cultural arbiter for the liberal middle classes, and their cultural hegemony over Viennese society as a whole—the "hegemony" that Antonio Gramsci identified as a pervasive domination of values, quite apart from holding political power. The liberals in Austria had their interlude of real power between the Austro-Hungarian compromise of 1867 and the great economic crash of 1873. If thereafter, as Schorske has suggested, they consoled themselves for political disappointment by seeking refuge in art and intellect, the *Neue Freie Presse* both led and followed (as newspapers do) in this reorientation. The editor-in-chief, Moritz Benedikt ("next to him the Emperor is the most important man in the country"), was always completely loyal to the aging Emperor, despite their differences in political perspective; Benedikt was even seen as a sort of "great vassal." At the same time, the newspaper achieved for itself a position of cultural overlordship in the empire, and there the conservative Emperor could not even compete for influence. Indeed, the liberal "renunciation" of politics might be seen as historically vindicated, for politically the empire was on the edge of disintegration and extinction, while Viennese art and thought was destined for a brilliant and enduring future in the twentieth century. Schorske has argued that "the writers of the nineties were children of this threatened liberal culture." The *Neue Freie Presse* was the undisputed arbiter and guardian of that culture, and it is there that we must look to find out what it meant, culturally, for a mother to murder her child in fin-de-siècle Vienna. Similarly, the newspaper can show us how Vienna formulated and interpreted the horrors of child abuse.

For if the *Neue Freie Presse* was the newpaper of the parents of the writers of the nineties, it nevertheless tried not to be left behind by the intellectual innovations of that decade. It was, according to Zweig, a newspaper dedicated to preserving its own preeminence:

> Its editor, Moritz Benedikt, a man of phenomenal powers of organization and untiring industry, put his entire, almost daemonic energy into excelling all the German papers in the fields of culture and literature. No expense was spared if he wanted something from a noted author; he would send telegram after telegram, and would agree in advance to any fee. The holiday numbers at Christmas and New Year were complete volumes with their literary supplements and included the greatest names of the time: Anatole France, Gerhart Hauptmann, Ibsen, Zola, Strindberg, and Shaw found themselves associated in this paper which accomplished so immeasurably much for the literary orientation of the city and the whole country.

If Benedikt wanted a distinguished literary figure like Felix Dörmann to write about Hedwig Keplinger in October 1899, that could be arranged. If he wanted stories by Hofmannsthal and Schnitzler for the Christmas issue in December, that too could be arranged, and it was. By 1899 the newspaper had proudly adopted the innovative geniuses of the early nineties, but beyond such purposeful sponsorship of individual writers, the paper was thoroughly and implicitly imbued with the prevailing aesthetic values. Even before Dörmann was writing about Hedwig Keplinger, the editors had already conceived of the story as "A Big-City Novel."

The *Neue Freie Presse* was powerful enough to determine that this, of the many potential sensations of October, was to be the outstanding one. When Stefan Zweig had his first feuilleton accepted by the *Neue Freie Presse,* at about the same time, he found that he suddenly existed as a literary figure in the eyes of his parents' generation.

> My parents occupied themselves but little with literature and laid no claims to any judgment of it. For them, as well as for the entire Viennese bourgeoisie, only that was of importance which was praised in the *Neue Freie Presse,* and only what was ignored or attacked there was inconsequential.

It was this power, not only to interpret the world for its readers, but to decide what was to be noticed and what ignored, that focused public attention on Hedwig Keplinger. The same power would be even more significant the following month when the paper chose to take notice of something that almost no one was willing to notice in nineteenth-century Europe: the problem of child abuse. For the *Neue Freie Presse* marked its subjects, and made them a part of Viennese culture, just as it marked its readers as members of that culture. Those in the Austrian provinces who subscribed to the paper were known to have printed on their visiting cards the proud credential "Subscriber to the *Neue Freie Presse.*" Thus the provincial promoted himself to the cultural level of the capital.

Even that troubled provincial boy Adolf Hitler, when he came to Vienna, "zealously" read the *Neue Freie Presse:* "I respected the exalted tone, though the flamboyance of the style sometimes caused me inner dissatisfaction." And eventually Hitler was able to put his finger on just what it was that dissatisfied him, for Vienna brought to his attention "the Jewish question."

> And I now began to examine my beloved "world press" from this point of view.
>
> And the deeper I probed, the more the object of my former admiration shriveled. The style became more and more unbearable; I could not help rejecting the content as inwardly shallow and banal; the objectivity of exposition now seemed to me more akin to lies than honest truth; and the writers were—Jews.

Moritz Benedikt was Jewish, as was Eduard Bacher, who shared the powers of editor-in-chief. The leading cultural figure at the paper was the feuilleton editor, and in 1899 this was none other than Theodor Herzl, the founding father of Zionism. Herzl began life as a well-dressed, well-assimilated Viennese dandy, a Schnitzler hero perhaps. In 1891 he was sent to Paris as the correspondent for the *Neue Freie Presse,* and there he witnessed the anti-Semitism aroused by the Dreyfus affair. In 1896 he published *The Jewish State.* As feuilleton editor in Vienna in 1899, his concern was not, like Hitler's, that the paper was too Jewish, but rather that it was not Jewish enough. For Benedikt and Bacher refused to permit the paper to have anything to do with Herzl's Zionism, and Herzl was seriously thinking of resigning. As Hitler saw it, "The so-called liberal Jews did not reject the Zionists as non-Jews, but only as Jews with an impractical, perhaps even dangerous, way of publicly avowing their Jewishness."

Since Dörmann's piece on Hedwig Keplinger was not properly a feuilleton, Herzl was probably not the one who personally commissioned and oversaw its publication. Certainly his diary entry for the next day, October 16, revealed no trace of the two bodies in the woods.

> The Boer War may be Pandora's box for the Jews of England. If the English troops should fare badly, the repercussions can hit the Jews. The mine speculators will be accused of having plunged England into this misfortune.
> Am I seeing things aright?

Herzl was in Vienna at the *Neue Freie Presse* during the days of the murder and suicide sensation, and yet he, like Freud, like the Emperor, clearly had other matters uppermost in his mind. Still, there was a certain parallelism between Herzl and Dörmann: two literary aesthetes of the early nineties who, in the late nineties, turned their attention to social questions. Dörmann addressed himself to a servant girl's fate, in a very small way, and Herzl to the fate of the Jews, with tremendous consequences. Hitler's evolution was similar, a decade later and at an accelerated pace, from student of painting and architecture to student of "the social question" and "the Jewish question."

Hitler in 1899 was still a ten-year-old boy in Linz, but there were plenty of anti-Semites in Vienna to raise anti-Semitic objections to the *Neue Freie Presse.* While Hitler rejected the editors and writers simply because they were Jews, his more substantive objections to the newspaper were not without a certain partial validity. After studying the case of Hedwig Keplinger in the *Neue Freie Presse,* one might well understand how the style could be first disturbing and eventually "unbearable." The content could indeed be "shallow and banal," and above all, as Hitler insisted, there was something decidedly false about the presentation of the news. These same objections were raised by Vienna's most penetrating cultural critic,

Karl Kraus, himself a Jew, though not untouched by a certain Jewish anti-Semitism. Kraus, the satirist, was one of the most brilliant haters in intellectual history. He hated literary aestheticism and the Cafe Griensteidl, he hated Herzl and Zionism, he hated psychoanalysis and World War I. But his deepest and most obsessive lifelong hatred was reserved for the *Neue Freie Presse*. The newspaper stood for everything that he hated about Vienna, everything sentimental, hypocritical, and false.

Kraus began his career as a journalist in the nineties at the *Neue Freie Presse,* the only Viennese newspaper where it was possible to begin a career as a distinguished journalist. At the beginning of 1899 Benedikt offered him a position as the paper's leading satirist; it was even said that he was being considered as a successor to Herzl as feuilleton editor, since Herzl's Zionism was creating tensions between him and Benedikt. Kraus refused the position. "There are two fine things in the world," remarked Kraus, "to be part of the *Neue Freie Presse* or to despise it. I did not hesitate for one moment as to what my choice had to be." Herzl longed to break with the paper but, in fact, remained at his post until he died in 1904. In December 1899 he threatened Benedikt with secession: "I am going to start a distinguished paper on the largest scale." But Benedikt was absolutely confident in his reply: "There is not room in Vienna for two such papers." That same year Kraus founded a small independent review, *Die Fackel* (*The Torch*); he wrote it almost entirely himself, he financed it almost entirely himself, and he brought it out until his death in 1936.

The collected issues of *Die Fackel* constitute a body of satirical work of unique genius, and a devastating indictment of Viennese and Austrian society and culture. While Kraus and *Die Fackel* were purposefully never mentioned in the *Neue Freie Presse*—his defection was not forgiven—Kraus in his little paper devoted pages and pages to an obsessive, though uncontested, war against the big paper and its presentation of the news. In Kraus's paper the *Neue Freie Presse* was quoted at length in its most preposterous excesses; it was ridiculed, parodied, and denounced. In 1910, with Freud present, a paper was presented to the Vienna Psychoanalytic Society entitled "The *Fackel* Neurosis." The author diagnosed in Kraus a neurotic oedipal attitude toward the *Neue Freie Presse*, and especially linked Kraus's own father Jacob, "the blessed one" in Hebrew, to the editor Benedikt, "the blessed one" in Latin. Kraus was interpreted as seeking to prove that his own little organ (*Die Fackel*) was equal to that of his father (the *Neue Freie Presse*). This identification of names and anatomical organs may seem psychoanalytically tenuous, but the oedipal suggestion was not so farfetched. Herzl, for instance, was quite capable of remarking in 1899: "I have given my best to the *Neue Freie Presse* for ten years now. I am a son of the firm." The point of importance is that Kraus, who probably hated the newspaper more than anyone in Vienna, was also very possibly its most fanatically, neurotically attentive reader.

It was this intensity of power and influence, even over its enemies, that made Dörmann's piece in the *Neue Freie Presse* so important. For in the *Neue Freie Presse,* far more than anywhere else, the case of Hedwig Keplinger and her daughter Olga was deemed worthy of attention, was interpreted according to the cultural values of fin-de-siècle Vienna, and was then presented to the cultured Viennese bourgeoisie in a definitive interpretation.

## THE SOCIALIST PERSPECTIVE

The *Neue Freie Presse* was the most important newspaper in Vienna in 1899, but it was not the only one. Other papers, which represented different social and political perspectives, could also look at Hedwig Keplinger quite differently. For instance, while the *Neue Freie Presse* was the organ of bourgeois liberalism, the *Arbeiter-Zeitung* (*Worker's Newspaper*) was the organ of Austrian socialism. Its editor, also the founding father of the Social Democratic Party of Austria, was Viktor Adler; Adler was a Jew born in Prague, a doctor trained at the University of Vienna, a friend of Gustav Mahler, a friend of Friedrich Engels, and one of the preeminent figures in the socialist Second International. For Adler and the *Arbeiter-Zeitung,* the great subject of the day in October 1899 was one that was barely mentioned in the *Neue Freie Presse.* This was a landmark year in the history of European socialism, the year that Eduard Bernstein published his reevaluation of Marxism, a work on "evolutionary socialism," the fountainhead of twentieth-century socialist revisionism. Despite the polemical intensity of this issue, on October 14 the *Arbeiter-Zeitung* found space for a story on "Murder and Suicide." There was even space for most of the catalog of clothing, though these details, together with the tale of the shoemaker assistant's daughter and the mushroom hunt, here followed the narration of Hedwig Keplinger's story, rather than introducing it as they did in the *Neue Freie Presse.* The *Arbeiter-Zeitung* was too much a part of fin-de-siècle Vienna to omit such literary and aesthetic details altogether, and yet not so utterly under the influence as to subordinate content to literary and aesthetic form.

The content of the story, however, also had a distinctly different tone in the *Arbeiter-Zeitung,* a rather less tragic tone. Little Olga was a "charming blonde," and Hedwig Keplinger was both "elegantly dressed" and "strikingly pretty." Her most recent lover had "jilted" her, as did the previous one. This lightness of tone was in obvious contrast to the report on the industrial accidents of that same day, stories that the *Neue Freie Presse* had, for its part, taken rather lightly. The accidental shooting of one worker by another in the cement factory was termed by the *Arbeiter-Zeitung* "a terrible misfortune," even though the shot was not fatal. The case of the man who was killed in the sheet metal factory, which in the *Neue Freie Presse* was called "Misfortune with a Rolling Machine," in the *Arbeiter-Zeitung* was given much more dignity under the title "A Worker's Death." It was described as a "horrible misfortune." Hedwig Keplinger's case was not deemed worthy of such strong adjectives—*schrecklich, grässlich*—in the *Arbeiter-Zeitung.*

The next day, October 15, this implicit lack of sympathy for Hedwig Keplinger became explicit. On the same day that Felix Dörmann in the *Neue Freie Presse* was making Hedwig Keplinger into the sympathetic servant girl heroine of bourgeois Vienna, the *Arbeiter-Zeitung* offered a dissenting opinion which really could not hope to prevail. From the socialist point of view, Hedwig Keplinger was the daughter of a worker who betrayed her class. She came to Vienna and there, instead of working for her bread, she chose the "nonworking existence of the lover of a rich man who surrounded her with unfamiliar luxury." Her story was narrated in the paper, though without the fictional forms that Dörmann adopted. And whereas for Dörmann, Hedwig Keplinger was above all a tragic victim of society and the big city, for the *Arbeiter-Zeitung* she was basically a lazy girl with no one to blame but herself. "The luxurious life of a do-nothing became for her the source of the tragic conflict." This socialist perspective brought sharply into focus the bourgeois-liberal nature of Dörmann's treatment in the *Neue Freie Presse.* Although Dörmann seemed, on the surface, to recognize that the servant girl had been exploited by men of the upper class, really his was a characteristically sentimental conception of class conflict and social exploitation. For Hedwig Keplinger was just the sort of lower-class figure that bourgeois Vienna could take to its heart, a servant girl from the provinces who wanted only to marry a middle-class man and dress elegantly. Dörmann even went so far as to eliminate her proletarian origin, lest it intrude upon his benignly sentimental class conceptions. And that is why the *Arbeiter-Zeitung* had to reject her as a representative figure of the oppressed classes; sympthy for Hedwig Keplinger could only distort and detract from an honest appreciation of class struggle in capitalist society. Perhaps the battle against Bernstein's evolutionary revisionism even added a certain sharpness to the socialist rejection of Hedwig Keplinger's vain aspiring toward the well-dressed bourgeoisie.

As in Dörmann's piece, the *Arbeiter-Zeitung* built to a psychological explanation of why Hedwig Keplinger finally did what she did. As with Dörmann, there was a hint of penetrating her consciousness, though for the most part the narration was more straightforwardly speculative and analytical. In the end, after telling how the engineer refused to marry her, the *Arbeiter-Zeitung* concluded:

> What then? Then she would have had to work again, she who was no longer accustomed to working. The fear of it terrified her. Why did she take her child with her into death? She loved it idolatrously . . .

On that ellipsis, the article ended, and the ellipsis was also probably the only "literary" device in the article that seriously violated the conventions of journalism. The reconstruction of her motivation was not only far less literary than Dörmann's, but also much less flattering and sympathetic. However, on the crucial point that is most of interest to us, the murder of the child—the *Arbeiter-Zeitung* absolutely agreed that this was an act of love. True, the word "idolatrously" (*abgöttisch*) suggested that this love might have been taken too far. But nevertheless, while the *Arbeiter-Zeitung* refused to accept bourgeois sentimentalism about Hedwig Keplinger's own unfortunate fate, socialist and liberal Viennese perspectives entirely agreed on a sentimental interpretation of the murder of the child.

## HEDWIG KEPLINGER AND SARAH BERNHARDT

On October 15, Dörmann published his deeply sympathetic fictionalization of Hedwig Keplinger, and that marked the high point of the sensation in the press. On the next day, it moved out of the newspapers and into the open air, with the funeral of the dead woman and her dead child. Inspired, or perhaps only titillated, by Dörmann and the press in general, the public attended the funeral in great numbers. The coffins were covered with flowers and buried together in one grave, appropriate for two supposedly united in love and death. A telling—and pathetic—detail was that the *Neue Freie Presse* reported the dead child's name as Leopoldine, not Olga. Perhaps the editors carelessly erred in the notice of the funeral, or perhaps they had never taken the trouble to get the name right during the previous days of the sensation. That the name should have been left finally in doubt—Olga or Leopoldine—was entirely characteristic of the newspaper's implicit unwillingness to examine too closely the murder of the child. The most telling detail of all, however, was the heading under which the funeral notice appeared: "The Last Act of a Drama." The story thus completed its diverse metamorphoses from genre to genre, finding its final literary form in the one the Viennese always loved best, the theater.

As if this heading were not clear enough to make its point, "The Last Act of a Drama" was placed facing the theater page for additional emphasis. This also made the funeral notice more prominent since, according to Zweig, "The first glance of the average Viennese into his morning paper was not at the events in parliament, or world affairs, but at the repertoire of the theater, which assumed so important a role in public life as hardly was possible in any other city." On this particular day, the theater review facing the funeral notice was not without a certain relevance. It was a review of Sarah Bernhardt in Sardou's *Tosca*. And Tosca, more familiar to us from the Puccini opera, was both murderess and suicide. Indeed Tosca the murderess made for an interesting counterpart to Hedwig Keplinger, since she murdered, not a child, but the man who tried to coerce and exploit her sexually. In 1899 Sarah Bernhardt was at the peak of her magical powers—earlier that year she had introduced in London her legendary Hamlet—and the Viennese reviewer lingered over her particular electricity as Tosca committing murder.

> Her silence as the murderess is stirring and convulsing. And she has so much to keep silent . . . Just trembling with terror she secretly prepares the dagger for the man who will be her victim; when she faces him, she waits with a veiled gaze for the opportunity to strike; and when he sinks down, struck, she cries at him in a hate-filled tone, almost celebrating in his ear, that he finds this end now for his misdeeds.

As written, this could almost be Hedwig Keplinger's fantasy revenge, the murder she did not commit. It would not have been a difficult connection to make with the review directly facing the funeral notice, with the funeral billed as "The Last Act of a Drama."

The presentation of the funeral as drama was the fitting final touch to conclude a sensation that, from the beginning three days before, had been formulated and interpreted with a relentless array of literary devices and aesthetic effects. It was a case of "Murder and Suicide," and, as a woman driven to kill herself, Hedwig Keplinger was the sympathetic heroine of her own story. But her role as murderess was not just conveniently ignored. Dörmann narrated the very moment of the murder—and sought to render it as sympathetic as the suicide. The convergence of form and message was unmistakable in the climax of the piece, when the explosion into literary stream of consciousness coincided with insistence on murder motivated by love. In *Civilization and Its Discontents* Freud suggested the following relation between art and human misery.

> People who are receptive to the influence of art can not set too high a value on it as a source of pleasure and consolation in life. Nevertheless the mild narcosis induced in us by art can do no more than bring about a transient withdrawal from the pressure of vital needs, and it is not strong enough to make us forget real misery.

Freud believed that art was not strong enough to make us forget our own misery, but in the case of Hedwig Keplinger we can see how in Freud's Vienna the appeal to the aesthetic sensibility could indeed help the public accept that a child had been murdered. But the narcotic of aestheticism would not work nearly so well when, a month later, it came time to deal with the horrors of child abuse.

## CHAPTER TWO

# The Hummel Case:
# Child Abuse and the Omnipotence
# of Maternal Love

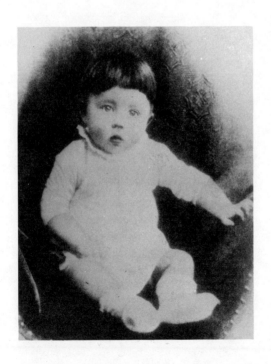

*Hitler as a baby*
*(Reproduced by courtesy of Superstock)*

## INCIDENTS AND SENSATIONS

FROM the funeral of Hedwig Keplinger in mid-October till the explosion of the child abuse sensation in mid-November, there were a succession of incidents reported in the press that were thematically related to the murder and suicide in the woods. Yet none of these incidents were presented as major stories, and so the case of Hedwig Keplinger and the child abuse cases occurred as two peaks of public interest, standing out together over the valley of related incidents that occurred in between. These incidents, however, are of considerable interest, both for constructing the social history of Vienna during these final months of the nineteenth century, and for appreciating the mysterious distinction between what was merely newsworthy and what was fully sensational.

The day of Hedwig Keplinger's funeral, October 16, there was also a report in the *Neue Freie Presse* of a young man, a twenty-five-year-old butcher's assistant, who jumped from a bridge into the Danube, leaving behind on the bridge a brown overcoat and a soft black hat; his suicide, like hers, was motivated by "unfortunate love," but those two words were deemed sufficient to satisfy the public in his case. The next day "an elegantly dressed woman in black" shot herself in the head; she was the fifty-two-year-old wife of an official, and she killed herself out of grief for her son who had killed himself exactly one year before. A few days later, a Viennese twelve-year-old schoolgirl, Frieda W., jumped from a fourth-floor window for fear of having her truancy reported to her father; according to the report, when she was not in school she "went around in the streets."

On October 22 the memory of Mayerling was raised with the formal announcement in the *Neue Freie Presse* that Princess Stephanie, the Dowager Crown Princess, was to remarry. Two days later there was a report from Bohemia of two young lovers who were found dead together, each shot through the temple. A few days later, when two elderly Viennese ladies (ages seventy-two

53

and seventy-three) were found mysteriously dead after dining together, it was immediately suspected that this was a double suicide
by poisoning. At the same time, two fifteen-year-old Czech boys
committed suicide together; they had run away from home to Vienna, hoping to go from there to South Africa to enlist in the Boer
army, but were sent back home to their parents and decided to kill
themselves. On November 2, the Emperor Franz Joseph visited the
imperial crypt to pray at the sarcophaguses of the murdered Empress Elisabeth and the suicide Crown Prince Rudolf.

That same day, a twenty-four-year-old seamstress took poison
and died, out of grief over the recent death of her lover. Two days
later there was a report from Hungary of two dead brothers, who
had left a note declaring their intention to commit suicide together;
actually it was the nineteen-year-old who shot his seventeen-year-
old younger brother, and then himself. On November 6, the story
"Father and Daughter Found Shot" received slightly more attention. The fifty-eight-year-old bookbinder Leopold Goberitz and his
sixteen-year-old daughter Wilhelmine had disappeared from Vienna a month before, rumored to have fled to America on account
of an incestuous relationship between them. Now a Viennese hat
label made it possible to identify them in two bodies found dead
near Budapest; he had shot her in the temple, and then himself.

On November 9, the heading "A Scene on the Danube" presented the story of a young woman sighted on the Emperor Franz
Joseph Bridge with four little children, all of them ready to jump.
The reason was extreme poverty (her husband was in prison), but,
fortunately, "At the last moment the love of her children held her
back from the ultimate step." She was brought to the police, and
released with a strong warning and a little money. The same day, at
the other end of the social spectrum, likewise outdoors, the Baron
Ludwig von Pereira-Arnstein went out and shot himself in the
Prater for no reason that anyone could guess at; before leaving
home he inquired whether his father had come looking for him. The
baron had served in the Austrian administration of occupied Bosnia
and Herzegovina, at Sarajevo. On November 11, a butcher's assistant, in love with a certain Leopoldine Zipperer, a cook who rejected
his affections, tried (and failed) to butcher her and shoot himself.

Judging from the amount of space they occupied in the newspapers, one can see that none of these incidents of violence captured
the Viennese imagination as Hedwig Keplinger did. At the same
time, this sampling from the press suggests that there were any
number of cases during that month whose themes were distinctly

related to the most sensational aspects of her story. These were incidents of murder and suicide, of parents and children, of desper-ate adolescence and hopelessly frustrated romance. That these cases should have been simply reported without much fuss gives some idea of what the Viennese of 1899 accepted in their society as a not too extraordinary kind or degree of violence. Felix Dörmann had declared, rhetorically, that even Hedwig Keplinger, for all the at-tention she received, was never "exceptional," was merely "a child of this big city," a simple illustration of a servant girl's fate. The incidents that occurred in the month after her funeral seemed to support Dörmann's contention. They suggested that the signifi-cance of Hedwig Keplinger was precisely the way her story summed up the thematic preoccupations of fin-de-siècle Vienna, from the bizarre tragedies of the imperial family to the pathetic romances of a Schnitzler play.

It was not until November 12, a full month after Hedwig Kep-linger's murder and suicide, that a new sensation emerged, which not only echoed some of the notes of her tragedy, but also provided so many completely new twists that it could not be reported and dismissed in an easy paragraph. The *Neue Freie Presse,* in a long article entitled "Parents Who Murder Their Children," announced the imminence of two court cases, and this article marked the begin-ning of the unique Viennese child abuse sensation of 1899. On November 14, the first of the two cases came to trial, the case of Juliane and Joseph Hummel, who murdered their five-year-old daughter Anna.

## "LIFE DOES NOT FOLLOW POETRY"

The bodies in the woods had been presented to the public in a catalog of clothing that was almost absurd in its insistence on de-tailed completeness. The body of Anna Hummel—examined by the authorities after her death, six months before—was now described for the public in another catalog of scrupulous detail. There was a tear wound on the left ear with bloody tissue, and another lacera-tion cutting through the entire thickness of the upper lip. Corre-spondingly, in the upper jaw the front teeth were missing. The collarbone was broken. The seventh rib was broken with festering suppuration at the break, and the third, fourth, and fifth fingers of both hands were deformed. And there were countless abrasions and bruises at the forehead, temples, cheeks, ears, chin, nose, thighs, arms, and back. The emaciated body of the five-year-old measured

88 centimeters (35 inches) and weighed 8,850 grams (under 20 pounds). Death was attributed to blood poisoning from tissue inflammation on the head and face.

Nothing could more dramatically illustrate the contrast in imagery between the two cases than the two different descriptive lists. The dead body of five-year-old Anna Hummel was described as a catalog of wounds and lacerations, while the body of six-year-old Olga (a.k.a. Leopoldine) Keplinger was a catalog of garments with even the single bullet hole at the temple covered by a white lace hat. One case was susceptible to aesthetic treatment, and the other was not. But in both cases there was this almost compulsive detailing of items which suggests a virtually Freudian sensibility, a conviction that within the details might lurk unsuspected meanings, and that no omission, however trifling, would be insignificant. The public could not be spared the grisly and unrelenting enumeration of wounds on the child's body.

The *Neue Freie Presse* actually heralded the court case with a big article two days before the trial, including the catalog of the wounds. The article alerted the attention of the city to the coming trial; the paper had decided to make this story an important one. And it began, peculiarly, with a paragraph about "Hannele"—the heroine of the naturalist drama of 1894, *Hannele,* by the German playwright Gerhart Hauptmann. For this was the drama, according to the *Neue Freie Presse,* that was about to be enacted in the courtroom. It was an odd theatrical intrusion, reminiscent of Hedwig Keplinger's funeral, which, in the same newspaper, became "The Last Act of a Drama" and was implicitly juxtaposed with Sarah Bernhardt's Tosca. This was the Vienna whose passion for theater Stefan Zweig characterized as "fanaticism" and "mania." For Hermann Broch Vienna was "a dominating theater culture" where "the entire texture of life [was] interwoven with that of the theater." This notion of "interweaving" was not altogether abstract, for it perfectly fit the newspaper's observation that "Hannele" was about to come to the courtroom.

Hauptmann's Hannele is a fourteen-year-old girl in a mountain village who has been so badly beaten and mistreated by her father (before the play begins) that she dies (at the end of the last act). It was thoroughly typical of the Viennese sensibility immediately to set the child abuse issue in a literary context. But whereas Hedwig Keplinger, the sentimentalized heroine, was linked to Sardou's *Tosca* of 1887, definitely a traditional melodrama of the nineteenth century, the brutal child abuse case of Anna Hummel, so much more difficult to sentimentalize, was linked to a naturalist work of

1894 which was very much a forerunner of twentieth-century modern drama.

Hannele expires in the final scene in a delirium which offers her a chorus of angels to carry her to heaven. The Viennese commentator in November 1899, obviously recalling a particular performance, noted that Hannele dies "with a smile of joyous bliss." If, however, it was possible to watch the play and be caught up in the blissfulness of Hannele's delirium, the *Neue Freie Presse* assured its readers that they would be able to follow the child abuse cases only "with terror and horror." The significant conclusion was this: "Life does not follow poetry." This cliché could not be taken for granted in a culture where art and literature were such a pervasive "interwoven" part of life. The literary reference had to be proposed in order to be rejected.

Life does not follow poetry, for child abuse is a matter of children "tortured, martyred, mistreated [*gequält, gemartert, misshandelt*] until death takes pity on them." It is something "barbaric" that "reminds one of medieval tortures." (The term "misshandeln"—to mistreat, to abuse—used in the press and in the courtroom in 1899, lacked the clinical specificity it has today; here, for instance, torture and martyrdom took precedence in the aggregate summation.) The newspaper listed not only the wounds on the body in excruciating detail, but also the cruelties practiced by the abusive parents: how they starved the child on a little bread and coffee, how they tied her down hungry with food in sight, how they made her eat her own excrement when she lost control of her bowels, how they burned her hands in hot water and beat her with iron pokers and thick canes. And the commentator who declared that life does not follow poetry, a little further along in the same article, could not help remarking that in these cases, "There are episodes that would make a great impression in a sociological novel." Here, just as with Hedwig Keplinger whose story was billed as "A Big-City Novel," the Viennese sensibility still could not resist the compulsion to interpret sociological reality by exploring the possibilities of literary genre.

This then was the announcement on November 12 of the great child abuse sensation. The next day, November 13, the day before the trial began, the *Neue Freie Presse* published its news item about "Postcards from the End of the World." After the news of the day before, the catalog of wounds and tortures, there may have been something more than irony in the editorial hypothetical—"If in the coming days the world really does come to an end . . ." For the details of the child abuse sensation were virtually apocalyptic in their unprecedented horror. Of the image on the postcard of the apocalypse we are told only that it was one of "fear and anxiety," and that the cards all sold out immediately. In the notice of the Hummel case the day before, the parents were described, in an odd phrasing, as "dedicated to the destruction [*Untergang*] of their five-year-old girl." The next day's notice of the anticipated apocalypse used the usual term, "Weltuntergang," for "the end of the world." The destruction of the child—"Untergang"—may have held certain subliminal apocalyptic connotations, with the end of the century only six weeks away. What the Viennese of 1899 could not have known, of course, was that the unprecedented brutalities of child abuse they read about in the newspapers would eventually be recognized as a not uncommon sociological syndrome in the twentieth century.

## "AS FAR BACK AS MEMORY REACHES"

Just as the *Neue Freie Presse* chose to signal the coming of the child abuse trials in advance with the article "Parents Who Murder Their Children," so the paper was also first to present to the public the Hummel trial itself. The publication of an evening edition allowed for a first installment on the opening day of the trial. Merely from the article headings one could see how different was the presentation of the Hummel case from that of Hedwig Keplinger. In October, the first heading of "Murder and Suicide" was quickly followed by "A Big-City Novel." Now, in November, "Parents Who Murder Their Children" was followed by "A Slowly Murdered Child." Whereas in the case of Hedwig Keplinger the murder of the child was played down and conjured away, in the Hummel case it remained irrevocably central.

In the revealing editorial introduction to the account of the trial, the opening sentences referred unmistakably to the great case of the previous month.

> Mothers who murder their children appear every year repeatedly before the court. It is then perhaps a murder committed out of hot tenderness towards the child whom the mother, in her despair, wants to spare the limitless distress to which she herself is abandoned. Or the mother has carried out the murder of the child at the moment when she brought it into the world, when love of her little sprout has not yet been awakened in her—a deed whose motive was deep shame before the public or also the painful concern of not being able to afford the means of subsistence for the child. But a murder by parents committed in slow cruelty out of hatred—of that there is scarcely an

example here in the judicial chronicle as far back as memory reaches. Will we from this trial discover the deeper motives that would make comprehensible to us this deed which is horrible beyond all measure?

The final question was left hanging—proclaiming Freud's Vienna as a city of psychological explorers. And yet the way that the question hung, unanswered, also suggested perhaps something rhetorical in the way it was formulated. The ambivalence of the question—its psychological boldness together with its rhetorical bluff—might draw the reader's attention back to the previous sentence. There were no ready answers, for this was a question which had not been posed "as far back as memory reaches."

The case for comparison was Hedwig Keplinger, and the article here virtually quoted from Dörmann's piece of the previous month: "a murder committed out of hot tenderness toward the child whom the mother, in her despair, wants to spare the limitless distress to which she herself is abandoned." The murder of a child by its mother was here described as something morally neutral, even admirable in necessity, committed either in "hot tenderness' or "painful concern." And above all, it was not uncommon—for such mothers "appear every year repeatedly before the court."

In fact, there had been a case of this sort only days before, when a report of strange smells led the police to an attic where, in a laundry basket, wrapped up in rags, they found the skeleton of an infant. The mother, a twenty-six-year-old servant who had come to Vienna from Hungary, had killed the child a few months before, when its birth created difficulties in her relationship with the man who was both her lover and her employer; he was not the child's father, and had been given to understand that the child was being cared for in the country. This woman, whose story was news but not sensational news, provided an example of the kind of mother who "repeatedly" appeared before the court. The case fit somewhere in between that of Hedwig Keplinger and that of the Hummel child, lacking the romance of the mother's suicide in the former, lacking the brutally lacerated corpse of the latter. If this too was a murder "committed in slow cruelty out of hatred," there was at least no insistent evidence to force that view on the public. And so this case was noted and passed over, just as the child abuse sensation was beginning, for the Hummel case was seen as something quite new.

It was this newness that the *Neue Freie Presse* couldn't help coming back to as the case proceeded. When the account of the trial was completed in the newspaper the morning after, the same editorial voice developed the same theme.

That which otherwise drives murderers to their terrible and wicked deeds—wild greed and implacable, insane vengeance—even these would be motives with a mitigating effect, compared to what came to light today. Has it ever before come out that parents together took their five-year-old child, who never did them any harm—and didn't kill her, no, but by devising tortures which remind one at times of Dante's Hell, slowly led her to her death? That with a certain satisfaction, with a passionate zeal, they prepared for their child unheard of sufferings? All day long to have to listen to the details of a deed of unprecedented crudeness! But one's indignation is finally dulled, because one can't apply a human standard of measurement to such dreadful behavior.

In the commentary of the previous evening there had been at least a rhetorical willingness to explore this new phenomenon, but now the commentator was already exhausted from having to listen to the story. It could not be conjured away, to be sure, but the earlier readiness to confront the case had been "dulled."

Whereas in the first article murderous child abuse had been judged far more culpable than mere infanticide, now it was declared worse than murder in general. The comparison to the murderer motivated by greed or vengeance was, in fact, a reference to another dramatic case of violence which at first seemed likely to rival the child abuse sensation for public attention. A few days before the Hummel trial, an eighty-six-year-old Viennese factory owner and his seventy-five-year-old housekeeper were found murdered in his villa near the city. The police had no idea who could have murdered them, but the hypothesized motives were theft or vengeance. That there were two victims no doubt made the murder more intriguing to a public whose fantasies of violent death were nourished on memories of Mayerling. The editorial comment weighed the crimes, the murder of the old man and woman and the "destruction" of the child, and at the same time thus weighed the two potential sensations. And the Hummel case was deemed the more remarkable, the more horrible of the two.

The reason for this judgment was that murder was familiar, its motives all too familiar, whereas child abuse was "unprecedented" and therefore unfathomable. "Has it ever before come out . . ." Here the newspaper took up the same note that had been sounded the evening before; "There is scarcely an example here in the judicial chronicle as far back as memory reaches." This child abuse sensation of 1899 opened up a subject that had simply not been opened up before in Vienna; it represented a breakthrough in contemporary sociological awareness. For all the horrified amazement, however, the press was not so naive as to assert that no child had ever before been abused. But it had not previously been recorded in the judicial chronicle; it had never before "come out." The Viennese child abuse sensation of 1899 is historically rare and valuable, because for a brief moment in history, at the turn of the century, the submerged phenomenon of child abuse "came out."

## "A NIGHTMARE FROM WHICH WE HAVE ONLY RECENTLY BEGUN TO AWAKEN"

If child abuse came out in Vienna in 1899, it was soon buried and forgotten again. The true and lasting "discovery" of child abuse was quite recent. In 1961 the subject was presented to the American Academy of Pediatrics, and in 1962 the article "The Battered-Child Syndrome" was published in the *Journal of the American Medical Association*. It marked a revolutionary change in public consciousness, the beginning of real recognition that child abuse was a serious social problem, the signal for the most urgent social, psychological, medical, and legal attention. For a world in which most people hardly thought about child abuse, let alone believed that it existed as a widespread phenomenon, "The Battered-Child Syndrome" was a startling revelation. The issues that it raised are still painfully prominent and unresolved a generation later.

The reason that child abuse remained for so long unrecognized was not only that a prevailing sentimental myth of the loving parent made the idea both offensive and incredible. The very idea of child abuse could not exist as long as children were regarded as the virtual property of their parents, subject to parental discipline without appeal. What was generally (though not universally, even then) recognized as child abuse after 1962, was once very likely to have been viewed as just the exercise of the legitimate parental prerogatives of power and punishment. That the concept itself was so problematically ambiguous and unrecognized has made it all the more difficult to try to study the nature and significance of child abuse in past centuries.

The history of childhood, as a special field of study, developed only recently; the seminal work of the French historian Philippe Ariès, *Centuries of Childhood*, was published in 1960. The book's controversial central argument was that the very idea of childhood just did not exist before the Renaissance, that is, "an awareness of the particular nature of childhood, that particular nature which distinguishes the child from the adult." This thesis still remains at the center of historical debate over children, and the controversies in the field suggest one fundamental reason why the field itself took such a long time to emerge: The sources for the history of childhood tend to be either scant or oblique. An important part of the Ariès thesis, for instance, was based on the special place of children in the paintings of the seventeenth-century Dutch masters—the thesis assumed a connection between the position of children in art and the position of children in society.

If the concept of childhood was indeed of such historically recent origin, a new phenomenon of the sixteenth, seventeenth, and eighteenth centuries, then it was perfectly plausible that the discovery of child abuse should have had to wait until the twentieth century. Without a concept of childhood, there could really be no concept of child abuse. Ariès, in fact, argued that while the discovery of childhood created the characteristic coddling of the modern family, it also led to much stricter social and parental pressure on children. There was, he suggested, an ominous side to this discovery of childhood.

*Centuries of Childhood,* however, was published just before "The Battered-Child Syndrome," and after 1962 it was possible for historians to see more deeply into those ominous shadows. When a collection of historical essays was published in 1974 as *The History of Childhood,* a conscious attempt to consolidate and reorient the field, "The Battered-Child Syndrome" was a crucial factor in the formulation of the fundamental issues. The eminent historian William Langer wrote the Foreword to the collection:

> Unhappily the results of these investigations are most depressing. They tell a long and mournful story of the abuse of children from the earliest times even to the present day . . . Children, being physically unable to resist aggression, were the victims of forces over which they had no control, and they were abused in many imaginable and some almost unimaginable ways . . . The story is monotonously painful, but it is high time that it should be told, and that it should be taken into account not only by psychiatrists and sociologists, but also by historians. So large and crucial a segment of human existence should not forever remain veiled and neglected by those whose mission it is to recover man's past.

Here the whole history of childhood was virtually reconceived as the history of child abuse.

The editor of the book, Lloyd deMause, who the year before was the founding editor of a new journal, *The History of Childhood Quarterly,* wrote the lead essay for the collection, and set up both a conceptual framework and an emphatic tone.

The history of childhood is a nightmare from which we have only recently begun to awaken. The further back in history one goes, the lower the level of child care, and the more likely children are to be killed, abandoned, beaten, terrorized, and sexually abused. It is our task here to see how much of this childhood history can be recaptured from the evidence that remains to us.

DeMause sketched a chronological schema that showed the history of childhood slowly changing for the better, from the infanticide of the ancient world and child abandonment of the Middle Ages, to the "socialization mode" of the nineteenth century and a new "helping mode" dating from the mid-twentieth century. It was as if all past history had been building toward "The Battered-Child Syndrome." Such a sweeping thesis was rendered controversial not only by its own teleological optimism, but again by the scarcity and limitations of the historical evidence. For if the history of childhood is difficult to trace in the sources, the history of child abuse is that much more difficult.

In 1977 Lawrence Stone published *The Family, Sex, and Marriage: In England 1500–1800*, marshaling a vast array of sources and constructing an appropriate theoretical framework. In parent-child relations he discerned a development from "the utter subordination of the child" in an age of reinforced patriarchy ("more children were being beaten in the sixteenth and early seventeenth centuries than ever before") to the emergence of an "affectionate and permissive mode." The author of an eighteenth-century handbook on child rearing pronounced: "Severe and frequent whipping is, I think, a very bad practice: it inflames the skin, it puts the blood in a ferment; and there is besides, meanness, a degree of ignominy attending it, which makes it very unbecoming." Stone, however, recognized the more affectionate eighteenth century as historically defined in contrast to both "the harsh and remote seventeenth-century upper-class domestic relations" and "the cloyingly pious and morally oppressive Victorian ones."

For it was above all the nineteenth century, the century that was drawing to a close in Vienna during those final months of 1899, that was most problematic for any theory of progressive benevolence in the history of childhood. Industrialization and urbanization created more brutal conditions for the children of the poor, while the children of the middle classes were "socialized" according to the obsessive values of Victorian morality and propriety. So though parents certainly took an interest in their children in the nineteenth century, though children received care and attention, the attention often took forms that, to the twentieth-century sensibility, resemble child abuse. There were, for example, the tortures that the Victorians devised to prevent their children from masturbating: binding them to their beds, locking them into contraptions that served as underwear, prescribing punitive circumcision for girls as well as boys. In 1855 Celestine Doudet, a French governess and teacher, stood trial for torturing five English sisters under her care (and killing one of them), in order to stop them from masturbating. The girls' father, it seemed, had encouraged the governess to do whatever she could to put a stop to such a troubling practice among his daughters. Celestine Doudet was sent to prison for three years, and after her release she continued to work as a governess.

While the intensified attentions of the nineteenth century sometimes resulted in unprecedented cruelties, it was also true that there were the beginnings of an awareness and even indignation over the sufferings of children. Though the evidence of English poetry may be subject to the same methodological limitations as that of Dutch painting, William Blake's poor chimney sweeper seemed to signal a new level of consciousness. In Blake's "Holy Thursday," one of the *Songs of Experience* of the 1790s, the poet also spoke of children.

> Is this a holy thing to see
> In a rich and fruitful land,
> Babes reduc'd to misery,
> Fed with cold and usurous hand?

Blake's was a lone prophetic vision in the late eighteenth century, but the nineteenth-century novels of Charles Dickens were passionately consumed by Victorian readers, and Dickens was highly conscious of cruelty to children. The beating of David Copperfield by his stepfather Mr. Murdstone and the institutional starvation of Oliver Twist in the workhouse remain legendary moments in Victorian literature. Charlotte Brontë's Jane Eyre, of course, received the full treatment: first cruelly beaten by her stepmother, and then sent off to be institutionally mistreated at school. The Victorian novelists, however, as these famous examples suggest, rarely went so far as to discover and denounce the physical abuse of children by their own natural parents. To find that in the nineteenth-century novel, one might turn to *Huckleberry Finn,* for Huck was a victim of the battered-child syndrome.

> But by-and-by pap got too handy with his hick'ry, and I couldn't stand it. I was all over welts. He got to going away so much, too, and locking me in. Once he locked me in and was gone three days. It was dreadful lonesome.

Huck's tone here was surprisingly matter of fact, and if readers have often failed to take note of the fact that he was an abused child, it was because the concept didn't yet exist distinctly for Mark Twain in 1885. It was not until pap actually tried to kill Huck with a knife that the boy ran away, the first move in his Mississippi odyssey.

Beyond literary awareness there was some philanthropic concern about cruelty to children in both England and America, beginning in the 1870s. Organizations were founded, but the problem of parental abuse received only limited and tenuous public recognition. When Jacob Riis published in 1890 his landmark account of New York slum conditions, *How the Other Half Lives,* he included chapters on "The Problem of the Children" and "Waifs of the City's Slums." He knew that slum life was related to infant mortality, child abandonment, murderous "baby-farming"—and even abuse. He was aware of the activity of America's Society for the Prevention of Cruelty to Children, and wrote about the importance of asylums.

> It is one of the most touching sights in the world to see a score of babies, rescued from homes of brutality and desolation, where no other blessing than a drunken curse was ever heard, saying their prayers in the nursery at bedtime. Too often their white night-gowns hide tortured little bodies and limbs cruelly bruised by inhuman hands.

While Riis thus seemed to confront the problem of child abuse, his wording was at the same time tellingly characteristic of nineteenth-century evasion. The word that was never mentioned was "parents," and the "inhuman hands" remained detached, unidentified. Circumlocutions like this showed why Victorian reformers failed to bring child abuse clearly and lastingly before the public. A recent study of the English Society for the Prevention of Cruelty to Children observed that even Victorian concern gave way to "the curious decline of public interest in child abuse between 1914 and the early 1960s."

On the European continent there was still less public airing of the issue. As it happens, there was a French doctor, Ambroise Tardieu, president of the Academy of Medicine in Paris, who published in 1860 an article that substantially anticipated, by a whole century, the findings of "The Battered-Child Syndrome." An analysis of the evidence in certain court cases, taken together with his own experience of performing autopsies in the Paris morgue, produced very definite conclusions:

Among the numerous and very diverse facts which make up the med-
ico-legal history of blows and wounds, there is one that forms a group
completely separate from the rest. These facts, which until now have
remained in total obscurity, deserve, for more than one reason, to be
brought to the light of day. I am speaking of the facts of cruelty and
brutal treatment of which children are particularly the victims and
which derive from their parents, their teachers, from those, in a word,
who exercise more or less direct authority over them . . . The inflexi-
ble severity of a teacher, the harshness of an avid master, the aversion
of a step-mother may explain even excessive corporal punishments
inflicted on young children. But that from the most tender age, those
defenseless unfortunate children should have to experience, every day
and even every hour, the most severe cruelty, be subjected to the most
dire privations, that their lives, hardly begun, should be nothing but a
long agony, that severe corporal punishments, tortures before which
even our imagination recoils in horror, should consume their bodies
and extinguish the first rays of reason, shorten their lives, and, finally,
the most unbelievable thing of all, that the executioners of these
children should more often than not be the very people who gave
them life—this is one of the most terrifying problems that can trouble
the heart of man.

Tardieu's presentation was heartbreakingly passionate, absolutely
explicit, and thoroughly documented—but it excited no response
and was completely ignored. A century passed before advances in
the field of radiology made it possible to produce again the evidence
that Tardieu found in his autopsies at the Paris morgue. And it was
destined to be the radiologists (doctors who examine X-rays, not
patients) who made it impossible to avoid recognizing the battered-
child syndrome.

Tardieu, however, has recently taken on a special significance for
Freud's Vienna. Jeffrey Moussaieff Masson, in his attempt to show
that Freud could not have been utterly naive about the physical and
sexual abuse of children, has drawn attention to Tardieu. For
Freud, studying in Paris in 1885 (six years after the death of Tardieu), attended autopsies at the Paris morgue. Furthermore, Masson has discovered that at least one book by Tardieu (which dis-
cusses the sexual abuse of children) was present in Freud's library
in Vienna. The possibility that Freud was familiar with the work of
Tardieu meant that there could have been at least one man in
Vienna in 1899 who had some inkling of what child abuse meant.

The Viennese press, however, was clearly unaware that child
abuse had been medically discovered in Paris thirty years before—
discovered and forgotten. Now in Vienna it was to be discovered

again. And if Tardieu never got any public response to his article, the Viennese cases of 1899 received the most intensive attention of the press. The case of Tardieu confirms for the historian what was already confidently supposed: that there was indeed child abuse in France in the nineteenth century. The Viennese press sensation can tell us much more: not only that there was child abuse in Vienna, but also the meaning of child abuse for the nineteenth-century mentality. Thus child abuse was discovered again—and extensively discussed—before being again forgotten.

## "A LOW LEVEL OF CIVILIZATION"

Joseph Hummel, age thirty-three, was a day laborer who worked in a laundry, and Juliane Hummel, age twenty-nine, did washing and ironing. He appeared at the trial as a powerful man, blond, with a twisted mustache. He spoke with equanimity, and the *Arbeiter-Zeitung* described him as the typical "Viennese from the bottom." Juliane Hummel, feeble and pale, was no such Viennese type. Like Hedwig Keplinger, she had come from the provinces; Juliane Hummel came to Vienna at the age of fifteen. It was there that she met the Viennese laundry worker. In 1894 they had an illegitimate child, Anna, who was sent away to be cared for at a fee. Then Joseph and Juliane Hummel decided to marry, and another child was born, in wedlock, a little boy named Max. Finally Anna was brought to live with her parents, and legitimized, in 1896. On March 9, 1899, she died, just before her fifth birthday.

The case of Hedwig Keplinger involved certain titillating connections to the world of bourgeois Vienna; she had been the domestic servant of middle-class ladies, the lover of middle-class gentlemen. The Hummel case, on the other hand, was set in a world very much apart. Hedwig Keplinger the bourgeois public could even take to its heart; Joseph and Juliane Hummel, who evoked no such sympathies, had to be studied from the reassuring security of absolute social separation. A man who was employed by the day in a laundry was not even an industrial proletarian; the Hummel parents were part of a great Viennese urban underclass. Far more than Dörmann's vision of a servant girl's fate, the Hummel story revealed a dark and ugly corner of life in a big city at the turn of the century.

With a population of a million and a half, Vienna was the third city in Europe after London and Paris. A study published in 1894, by an economist at the University of Vienna, suggested that the living conditions of the Viennese poor were even worse than in

those other two larger cities. In 1890 Vienna had annexed its sub-
urbs, thus extending the city limits and almost doubling its population all at once; the new districts included both factories and slums.
Furthermore, as a great imperial capital, Vienna was attracting
provincials—like Hedwig Keplinger and Juliane Hummel—at a socially unassimilable rate. In 1891 only a third of Vienna's population was actually Viennese in origin. By the turn of the century the
socioeconomic imbalances of the big city were staggering, and the
young Adolf Hitler was enraged by the contrast between "dazzling
riches and loathsome poverty."

Hitler deplored the general "inattention to social misery" in Vienna, and Viennese aestheticism, both a refuge and a distraction,
seemed to encourage that inattention. Hofmannsthal's verse-play
The Death of Titian described the young aesthetes around the Renaissance master who had fled from the big city (sixteenth-century
Venice) to escape the ugliness of urban life. One of the aesthetes
looked toward the city in the distance and commented:

> There dwells hatefulness and vulgarity,
> And the madmen dwell among the beasts,
> And what the distance wisely veils from you,
> Is disgusting and dreary and spiritlessly filled
> With beings who do not recognize beauty,
> And name their world with our words . . .
> For our joy or our pain
> Has with theirs only the word in common . . .

> (Da wohnt die Hässlichkeit und die Gemeinheit,
> Und bei den Tieren wohnen dort die Tollen;
> Und was die Ferne weise dir verhüllt,
> Ist ekelhaft und trüb und schal erfüllt
> Von Wesen, die die Schönheit nicht erkennen
> Und ihre Welt mit unsren Worten nennen . . .
> Denn unsre Wonne oder unsre Pein
> Hat mit der ihren nur das Wort gemein . . .)

Hofmannsthal wrote this in 1892, and certainly intended it as a
reflection on the attitude of his Viennese contemporaries toward
"the social question" in an alienating metropolis. The aesthetically
oriented bourgeoisie of 1899, for whom the world of the poor was
already hateful, vulgar, and disgusting, could set the behavior of
Joseph and Juliane Hummel in a social context. Child abuse and
laundry labor could both be kept at a safe distance.

For Hofmannsthal's Renaissance aesthetes, the ugly urban world
was completely separate, linked only by a common vocabulary,
since the vulgar masses "name their world with our words." The

*Neue Freie Presse* showed a similar sensibility at the Hummel trial: "All day long to have to listen to the details of a deed of unprecedented crudeness!" This sense of social distance and cultural distaste allowed the paper to formulate a sweeping judgment upon the Hummel case by emphasizing its social and cultural context. The case was "crass" and "bestial," and the monstrosity of the Hummel parents could be partly explained, even partly excused, on the grounds that they were "without education, people on a low level of civilization." This, obviously, was no explanation, but rather a repudiation, encouraging the paper's cultured liberal bourgeois readers to dissociate themselves from a world almost anthropologically distinct.

In the *Arbeiter-Zeitung,* where one might have expected to find a more serious treatment of the social context of the Hummel case, there was on the contrary an even more absolute dismissal. Workers and socialists were also encouraged to separate themselves from Joseph and Juliane Hummel. That they too were among the economically oppressed meant that their world was much less alien here than in the *Neue Freie Presse,* and it was therefore all the more urgent to set them apart. "Such a deed is so abominable, so unhuman, so contrary to all natural instincts, that one cannot explain it by any social oppression or other external circumstances." This absolute refusal to consider the socioeconomic circumstances went contrary to the determinist orthodoxy of Marxist theory, and betrayed the purposefulness and urgency of dissociation. For especially in this period of the struggle against Bernstein's revisionism, there could be no careless qualifications of Marxism.

The liberal press thus insisted that the social context had everything to do with the Hummel case, while the socialist press declared that the social context meant nothing. Neither provided any sociological analysis, the one because the level was too low, the other because it was irrelevant. Felix Dörmann did not even try to recreate imaginatively the world of Joseph and Juliane Hummel, but for some idea of how the problem might have been formulated, we may turn again to those remarkable Viennese social parables of Adolf Hitler. For Hitler, though he did not consider the issue of child abuse, was deeply conscious of the sufferings of children amidst the social misery of Viennese poverty.

Imagine, for instance, the following scene:
In a basement apartment consisting of two stuffy rooms, dwells a worker's family of seven. Among the five children there is a boy of, let us assume, three years. This is the age in which the first impressions are made on the consciousness of the child. Talented persons retain

traces of memory from this period down to advanced old age. The very narrowness and overcrowding of the room does not lead to favorable conditions. Quarreling and wrangling will very frequently arise as a result. In these circumstances, people do not live with one another, they press against one another. Every argument, even the most trifling, which in a spacious apartment can be reconciled by a mild segregation, thus solving itself, here leads to loathsome wrangling without end. Among the children, of course, this is still bearable; they always fight under such circumstances, and among themselves they quickly and thoroughly forget about it. But if this battle is carried on between the parents themselves, and almost every day in forms which for vulgarity often leave nothing to be desired, then, if only very gradually, the results of such visual instruction must ultimately become apparent in the children. The character they will inevitably assume if this mutual quarrel takes the form of brutal attacks of the father against the mother, of drunken beatings, is hard for anyone who does not know this milieu to imagine. At the age of six the pitiable little boy suspects the existence of things which can inspire even an adult with nothing but horror.

Again with unnamed protagonists and the same present tense which characterized the story of the peasant boy in the big city, Hitler explored the social question by creating a family scene. A nameless child stood clearly at the center, his situation evoked with Dickensian sentimentality and indignation. There was no child abuse here, of course, but Hitler came close to suggesting it. There were "drunken beatings" and "loathsome wrangling." There was fighting among the children, and "brutal attacks of the father against the mother." It was precisely the same sociological reconstruction that might have been used to account for child abuse. Indeed, if Hitler had been somewhat less sentimental, those children might not have been merely observers of the drunken beatings. The sinister final sentence even suggested that Hitler had not told all that he knew.

In another Viennese scene from *Mein Kampf,* Hitler began with the problem of hunger, instead of overcrowding, and again lamented that "the little children, in their earliest beginnings, are made familiar with this misery." Hunger too leads to domestic fighting and drunken brutality, and when the father comes home, "such scenes often occur that God have mercy!" In the Hummel trial, when Juliane Hummel was asked why her husband beat the child, she replied, "He was given to drinking, and when the child was disobedient he punished it." Joseph Hummel could have been a figure in one of Hitler's literary illustrations of the social question, the typical "Viennese from the bottom." He and his wife belonged to the world that Hitler would call upon his readers to imagine. The Viennese press in 1899 preferred to keep that world at a distance, and with it the monstrosities of child abuse. Neither the editors nor the readers of the *Neue Freie Presse* were eager to imagine the social context of the Hummel case. A day laborer in a laundry belonged to a separate world, to a different "level of civilization."

## "THE RECIPE FOR DOING AWAY WITH THE CHILD"

In June 1898, when Anna Hummel was four, her parents had received a judicial warning for "excess of domestic discipline." There had been reports to the police that they were mistreating their child. According to Christine Hummel, the wife of Joseph Hummel's brother, the officially reprimanded parents were not greatly distressed. Juliane Hummel was quoted as saying, "My husband and I bought ourselves some pork, and the worrying was over." Furthermore, she allegedly confided in her sister-in-law that from then on they would beat the child in such a way as to avoid visible bruises. The prosecution contended that, from this moment, the parents were intent upon murdering their child, and finally achieved their end in 1899. Monstrous mistreatment was not difficult to establish, but the intention to murder was a trickier thing to prove in a case where the medical cause of death was blood poisoning from tissue inflammation. Two court doctors further attributed the child's death to undernourishment and spiritual suffering, both connected in this case to parental abuse, but neither a rare condition for the children of the poor in the nineteenth century. It was perfectly clear that were it not for the actual death of the child, the issue of abuse, however horrendous, would never have come to trial and thus to the attention of the public. But was this an act of premeditated murder which called for the death penalty? The issues of sensational child abuse and legal murder were very significantly entangled from the beginning.

One witness testified that Joseph Hummel actually struck the little corpse in the coffin, and said: "Wretch, hold your head up straight." As for Juliane Hummel, she was supposed to have said this after the death: "For a while there will be some gossip, but the child is gone, and we're free of the thieving bastard." Such remarks showed the parents as monsters, showed that they did not regret their child's death, but did not necessarily prove that they murdered her. As for the actual moment of dying, the most the prosecution could do was make much out of the fact that no doctor was called to the deathbed. Juliane Hummel testified that they did not go to doctors anyway; doctors cost too much. When Anna was very sick, her parents took her to an old lady who prepared herbal potions that included bits of the child's hair and nails. If the public was expected to regard as proof of murder the fact that the urban poor did not avail themselves of medical doctors, that showed only again how very set apart was the economic reality and popular culture of the underclass.

One circumstance that made a great impression, in the courtroom and in the press, was that the parents held shut the mouth of the child, so that she could not cry out when they beat her—"could only in suppressed weeping and soft whimpering give expression to her great spiritual and physical suffering." The point of this brutal muzzling was, presumably, to prevent the child's cries from drawing the attention of the neighbors. And yet, just as the resolution to beat but not bruise her resulted nevertheless in a mutilated corpse, so, despite the parents' efforts to abuse their child in silence, there was no lack of firsthand testimony against them at the trial. This case of child abuse was not exactly a private affair, and any number of neighbors and relatives turned out to have witnessed the brutalization of the child. They were witnesses from the same social world as the Hummel parents themselves; the jury that heard the case against the laundry laborer and his wife considered also the testimony of a gardener's wife, an ironing lady, and a custodian, among others. The only bourgeois witnesses were the doctors of the court, who testified to the condition of the corpse and the likely causes of death. It was evident that doctors of their standing would never have come into contact with the body of Anna Hummel when it was still alive. In the same way, the death of this child brought the world of the lower classes to the attention of the public at large.

Magdalena Kronberger was a neighbor, the wife of a gardener. She testified that Anna Hummel was often left home alone all day long without food, and the neighbors used to slip her bread and sweets through a crack in the door. Then the parents realized what was happening, and nailed the crack shut with a board so the child could not receive such offerings. In this way they insisted that the abuse of their child was their own business. And yet Magdalena Kronberger could also testify to having seen with her own eyes Juliane Hummel smearing excrement into the child's mouth. She also saw the mother beating her child on the fingers with a hot poker, while saying, "Does that hurt, Annerl?" When this was related in court, Juliane Hummel jumped to her feet to cry out her objection: "If you're going to lie, you should lie right! But there's another who will judge!" Magdalena Kronberger was not shaken by this interruption, though her next remark about Juliane Hummel was rather more discreet: "She said things to me about the child that I cannot repeat." The witness then told that she had four times reported the child's situation to the police, but nothing had happened. Clearly, only the death of the child brought attention to the case of abuse.

The custodian Franz Keszeg saw just as much as the gardener's wife. Anna had told him that the burns on her hands came from her mother putting them in hot water, and he saw with his own eyes the child bound half naked to a trunk with her food for the day just out of reach. "The brat deserves the punishment because she's so bad," said Joseph Hummel on that occasion, but he had brought sweets and chestnuts for the little boy Max. The witness also claimed to know that in the middle of winter Anna had been forced to spend an entire day standing barefoot in cold water. The custodian and his wife offered to take the child and raise her as their own, but Joseph and Juliane Hummel refused the offer, just as they had nailed shut the crack in the door. Juliane Hummel also interrupted the custodian's testimony to tell the courtroom: "That's not true. Whatever a Bohemian says is a lie." In 1899 the Badeni language laws for Bohemia remained heatedly controversial. For two years there had been riots and demonstrations by Czechs and Germans in Vienna, a violent upsurge of national antagonisms which could even surface momentarily at the Hummel trial.

The testimony of Magdalena Kronberger and Franz Keszeg was confirmed and extended by a dozen other witnesses, and the accused parents themselves essentially admitted to most of the specific atrocities that had been witnessed. That the abuse of the child was so open to observation suggested a social environment without domestic privacy. But it also suggested that despite the police warning, and although they tried to keep their child silent as they beat her, the Hummel parents were not fully aware that what they were doing was an outrage—if not a crime—and should be kept from everyone's eyes. The explanation lay in Joseph Hummel's casual explanation to the custodian—"The brat deserves the punishment because she's so bad." Both parents repeatedly protested at the trial that they had only been punishing a bad child, and it was precisely that distinction which made child abuse a fundamentally unrecognizable concept until "The Battered-Child Syndrome." If the Hummel parents were partly aware that what they were doing should be kept quiet, they also obviously felt that their behavior, conceived as

discipline, was at worst an excessive exercise of their parental prerogatives.

While the Hummel parents miserably insisted that abuse was no
more than discipline, the lawyers wrestled with the question of
whether it was anything less than murder. The defense attorney
told the jury that the evidence made this a case of manslaughter at
the worst, perhaps only "serious bodily injury with a fatal result."
The prosecutor, however, declared that systematic torture was evidence of a murderous intention. The child was "murdered, no, not
murdered, but butchered with horrible tortures." The *Arbeiter-
Zeitung* picked up the phrase and used it to introduce the whole
story—"not murdered, but butchered"—seemingly unaware that
the rhetorical device of the prosecutor actually helped make the
point of the defense: that whatever this crime was, it was not
exactly legal murder. For at the same time the paper declared,
"There can only have been one prevailing intention for the accused:
out of inexplicable hatred, by continued inhuman abuse, to do away
with their poor child." Similarly, in the *Neue Freie Presse,* hunger
and abuse were cited together as "the recipe for doing away with
the child." But here again, the paper unwittingly undermined the
charge of murder with its own rhetorical extravagance. The parents
"didn't kill her, no, but by devising tortures which remind one of
Dante's Hell, slowly led her to her death." It was the same pattern
of semantic uncertainty: not murdered but butchered, not killed but
led to her death. For the crime was unfamiliar, the case unprecedented: "there is scarcely an example here in the judicial chronicle
as far back as memory reaches." So naturally there was no obvious
formula at hand for articulating the atrocity, and at the same time
no legal precedent for punishment. The jury, however, unani-
mously agreed to the charge of murder, and Joseph and Juliane
Hummel were condemned to death by hanging.

### "FAITH IN THE MOTHER"

The heart of the trial was the examination on the witness stand of
the accused parents, and, for the press and the public, this really
amounted to a spotlight on Juliane Hummel, the mother. Joseph
Hummel, that typical "Viennese from the bottom" with his twisted
blond mustache, never drew an equal share of emphasis and outrage
in the courtroom and in the press. He himself, under examination,
attempted to shift responsibility for the abuse and death of the child
onto his wife.

JUDGE: Was Anna a good child?

JOSEPH HUMMEL: No, she was very bad.

JUDGE: We'll see about that. You are supposed to have been drunk often.

JOSEPH HUMMEL: Not often, only sometimes.

JUDGE: Did your wife complain about the child?

JOSEPH HUMMEL: Every evening when I came home. So I punished Anna.

JUDGE: Did you yourself see that the child was bad?

JOSEPH HUMMEL: I didn't have any time for that.

JUDGE: So just because your wife complained, you disciplined the child. In what way then?

JOSEPH HUMMEL: Only with my hand, I beat the child from behind.

JUDGE: How was the child fed?

JOSEPH HUMMEL: When I was home the child had the same food that we had. But I came home for dinner at most once a week.

JUDGE: Were both children, Anna and little Max, treated just the same?

JOSEPH HUMMEL: By me they were.

JUDGE: Did little Max also get beatings?

JOSEPH HUMMEL: No, because he was good.

Joseph Hummel first of all blamed the dead child, whose behavior brought upon her the punishments she deserved. But second, he pointed to his wife as the responsible figure behind the abuse of the child; it was she who demanded that Anna be punished. As for himself, his day labor in the laundry was so long that he was never at home; in that sense, he could claim to have been no father at all to his child, and therefore certainly not an abusive father.

Hitler, exploring the social question in one of his parables of the laborer in the big city, believed that nothing was more poisonous and demoralizing than the "eternal insecurity" whereby the laborer found a job only to lose it inevitably before long. Joseph Hummel lost his job, such as it was, in the period preceding his daughter's death. Today a social worker would surely note the father's unemployment as one of the stress factors that probably aggravated abuse of the child. In the courtroom in 1899, however, this circumstance was given a different emphasis: It undermined the father's special pleading, his claim that he had no idea what was happening to his child while he was at work.

JUDGE: In the time right before the death of the child you were unemployed and almost always at home. During this time did you mistreat the child?

JOSEPH HUMMEL: I didn't, my wife did.

JUDGE: So only your wife, why?

JOSEPH HUMMEL: Because she loved the boy more.

JUDGE: And you tolerated this mistreatment, you the father, who ought to have protected his child?

JOSEPH HUMMEL: I didn't get involved, because I didn't want any quarreling.

JUDGE: So, for the sake of sweet peace you allowed the child to be slowly killed. Do you know how the child's injuries were inflicted?

JOSEPH HUMMEL: No. When I asked my wife how the child burned herself, she said it was from coming too close to the oven.

The judge seemed ready to accept the shifting of primary responsibility to the mother. He scolded Joseph Hummel for having "tolerated" the abuse, for not having "protected" Anna, for having "allowed the child to be slowly killed." But Joseph Hummel, in blaming his wife and blaming the dead child, did not succeed in absolving himself before the court. He was found guilty of murder, and condemned to death along with his wife. The final verdict, however, specified that he was to be hung first, in odd token of the fact that she was deemed more guilty than he.

If the judge, examining Joseph Hummel, reproached "the father who ought to have protected his child," the prosecutor, in his summation for the jury, centered his emotional appeal on the role of the mother. This was Dr. R. von Kleeborn, and as the prosecutor of both of the great child abuse cases of November, his was a crucial voice in the formulation of the whole issue.

> In our times, eaten away by doubt and the mania for mockery, if there is still something of value, then it is faith in the mother. Everything gives way before the power of maternal love. It is the purest sentiment, but it is also stronger than anything else; it overpowers everything. This mother also had a child, and she murdered it, no, not murdered, but butchered it with horrible tortures. Her deed makes a mockery of everything that is holy to human beings; one could almost doubt the omnipotence of maternal love.

Juliane Hummel had to be executed in order to preserve the purity of society's faith in motherhood. There could be no clearer statement of the sentimental Victorian family ideal. It was just this dogmatic sentimentalism that made people so reluctant to recognize the existence of child abuse, and which now, after a case had been recognized, left them determined to preserve the dogma by executing the offender. One could "almost" doubt, but one did not actually doubt; the Hummel case would itself "give way" to the "omnipotence of maternal love." The myth would live on. This was the essential ideological and sentimental context for the Viennese child abuse sensation, and one aspect of that context was expressed in the overwhelming sexual imbalance of the prosecutor's pitch: both parents stood accused of murder, but his rhetorical appeal was only to faith in the mother, to maternal love. One wonders whether paternal abuse was still more impossible to contemplate, or, alternatively, whether paternal brutality was rather taken for granted.

And in fact, though the judge, the lawyers, and the jury were all men, the courtroom spectators were predominantly women. The reporters took note:

> It was a parquet of mothers before whom these images of atrocities unfolded, and one could often see in the horror that painted itself on the features of these women, how personally near to them went the fate of the girl tormented to death.

To speak of a "parquet" of mothers, as if the courtroom were a theater, occurred naturally to the same Viennese journalistic sensibility that initially explained the child abuse case by a reference to Hauptmann's Hannele. At the same time, a parquet of "mothers" confirmed the emphasis of the prosecutor's summation: the issues of the case were seen as women's issues, reflections on motherhood. The men who controlled Viennese journalism and Viennese law were not unwilling to help make women and mothers the focus of the case. Furthermore, just as the prosecutor's tribute to motherhood seemed flagrantly to neglect fatherhood, the reporter's parquet of mothers, as a descriptive phrase, was chosen over the at least equally valid alternative: a parquet of daughters. The psychological center of the case concerned not the protection of daughters, but rather the protection of the ideal of motherhood by the condemnation of an abusive mother. It was these crucial emphases, on motherhood rather than fatherhood, and again on mothers rather than daughters, that made the examination of Juliane Hummel the true heart of the trial.

## LAUGHTER AND MERRIMENT

Juliane Hummel, like her husband, did not have the appearance of a monster. She was feeble, quiet, and pale; her face was plain and narrow. At twenty-nine she seemed prematurely aged—which was hardly surprising, since she had come to Vienna from the provinces at fifteen, worked at washing and ironing, and had two children under rather uncertain economic and marital circumstances. The contrast between her unassuming appearance and her tremendous crime was disconcerting. How was one to understand her "soft voice, suppressed weeping, and mild tone"? Could this be the same woman who tortured her child to death? Giving testimony, her voice was so soft that the judge constantly had to ask her to speak up. This repeated injunction betrayed the half-conscious effort to induce her to reveal herself, to get her to appear as the monster she had to be.

The opening questions immediately established the court's legal dilemma, that murder and child abuse were not necessarily the same thing.

> JUDGE: Do you admit to being guilty?
> JULIANE HUMMEL: No.
> JUDGE: Did you mistreat your child?
> JULIANE HUMMEL: Yes.

It was not essential to deny abusive mistreatment in court, any more than it had to be concealed from the neighbors all along. The judge then went on to lecture the witness in a tone of oddly inappropriate righteousness.

> JUDGE: Do you remember how you were treated by your mother?
> JULIANE HUMMEL: I was treated well.
> JUDGE: And did that do you good?
> JULIANE HUMMEL: Yes.
> JUDGE: I just wanted to confirm that the accused hadn't had before her eyes a bad example.

If the judge's remarks seemed legally pointless, they were nevertheless relevant to the fact that the case was "unprecedented." By isolating Juliane Hummel even from her own mother, the courtroom examination attempted to redeem "the omnipotence of maternal love" and "faith in the mother."

After this introduction, there occurred in the examination of Juliane Hummel the first manifestation of what was to become its characteristic peculiarity. The judge was taking the witness through the period of her "concubinage," that is, the period before her legal marriage—when Anna was born. The baby had been sent away to receive foster care for a fee. The judge now asked Juliane Hummel whether the fee had been a burden.

> JUDGE: Was that hard on you?
> JULIANE HUMMEL: Oh, for a child one does everything.
> JUDGE: In your mouth that sounds like the most frightful irony.

This comment by the judge might have been simply another instance of pointless lecturing, and yet the spectators in the courtroom responded in a striking manner. According to the *Neue Freie*

*Presse,* there was a "sustained commotion in the public" and "signs of indignation and ironic merriment."

Commotion and indignation do not surprise us under the circumstances; it is the "ironic merriment" that strikes us as strange and disturbing. Certainly it is not difficult to see the ironic contrast between the motherly platitude—"for a child one does everything"—and the evidence of what Juliane Hummel actually did for her child. "Everything" involved hot pokers, excrement, beating, binding, burning, starving, and ultimately death; those were the images that must have occurred to the spectators in the courtroom, forcing the irony upon them. But merriment? This odd response was not entirely spontaneous, for it was the judge who drew everyone's attention to the irony, and thus provoked the general merriment in the courtroom. Indeed, this merriment was as much in response to his "joke," as to her platitude. In short, this bizarrely inappropriate relishing of the "humor" of the case was no accidental eruption, but, on the contrary, was pointedly emphasized and encouraged. Furthermore, just as the judge brought the irony to the attention of the courtroom, the newspapers brought it to the attention of the general public. The merriment in the courtroom was faithfully noted in a parenthetic addition to the transcript of the interrogation.

If this were merely an exceptional outburst, we would be inclined to pass it over as a freakish moment of uneasy, possibly desperate, emotional excitement. It was, however, the first of many such moments of merriment that punctuated the trial, so many that comedy became almost a regular emotional counterpoint to the grisly tragedy of child abuse. Soon after the first outburst, the judge and witness reached the point in the history of the case when Anna Hummel returned to live with her parents after their marriage.

JULIANE HUMMEL: She was healthy and looked well.
JUDGE: How did you all live?
JULIANE HUMMEL: Quite well. We had meat and vegetables to eat almost every day.
JUDGE: Did your husband drink?
JULIANE HUMMEL: A lot.
JUDGE: You too?
JULIANE HUMMEL: No.
JUDGE: So how did it go with Anna at home?
JULIANE HUMMEL: I always took care of the child.

At this point, in response to that last platitude of motherhood, the courtroom broke into laughter. Again the irony was plain enough: Anna Hummel was indeed "taken care of" by her mother, that is, tortured to death. The spectators were certainly very quick to seize upon this irony—this second time without having the judge point it out. In fact, they almost seem to have been poised to appreciate a remark that might have been passed over as tediously banal. That the "funny" lines were so essentially trite and platitudinous suggests that what the spectators were relishing was something like what Hannah Arendt identified in the Austrian Adolf Eichmann as "the banality of evil." The same emotional dynamic was behind the courtroom's merry response to Juliane Hummel's final plea: "I can't help it. I did what I could."

If the spectators were quick to perceive a titillating irony within such declarations, they were also extreme in the tone of their reaction. It is not so hard for us to imagine responding to that irony with a grimace or a shudder or a groan, but it is less easy to understand emotionally how Juliane Hummel provoked frank merriment and loud laughter. The historian Robert Darnton, in his celebrated essay on "The Great Cat Massacre," described a group of eighteenth-century French workmen who massacred a lot of cats and found the episode riotously funny. It was the peculiar humor of the situation that became for Darnton the point of departure for historical analysis:

> It strikes the modern reader as unfunny, if not downright repulsive
> . . . Our own inability to get the joke is an indication of the distance
> that separates us from the workers of preindustrial Europe. The perception of that distance may serve as the starting point of an investigation, for anthropologists have found that the best points of entry in an attempt to penetrate an alien culture can be those where it seems to be the most opaque. When you realize that you are not getting something—a joke, a proverb, a ceremony—that is particularly meaningful to the natives, you can see where to grasp a foreign system of meaning in order to unravel it.

This whole approach is very well suited to a discussion of the horribly unfunny Hummel trial. For the laughter and merriment in the courtroom constitute for us the most opaque, least comprehensible aspect of the case. This, more than anything else, gives us a sense that we are exploring an alien culture in fin-de-siècle Vienna, for even if we are capable of perceiving the irony, it could hardly be said that we get the joke.

To be sure, the Vienna of 1899 is much closer to us historically than is eighteenth-century France. Indeed what is most historically exciting about the fin de siècle is its delicate position, on the threshold of our own century, yet still very much the culmination of the

Victorian age which was coming to an end. Musil in 1930 already wrote of "the good old days when there was still such a place as Imperial Austria," and Zweig ten years later, in the preface to his Viennese memoirs, already lamented that "all the bridges between our today and our yesterday and our yesteryears have been burnt." In this sense, the alien humor of fin-de-siècle Vienna could also be considered as culturally remote, requiring anthropological exploration. The very recent twentieth-century breakthrough in our appreciation of child abuse makes 1899 virtually still the ancien régime in the history of childhood.

Hermann Broch, in his discussion of Vienna's "gay apocalypse," remarked that the city was "merry, often idiotically merry." The word that he used for merry, "heiter," was the same one used to describe the merriment—"Heiterkeit"—at the Hummel trial. Another brilliant Viennese intellectual observed: "We do not know what is giving us enjoyment and what we are laughing at." That was Sigmund Freud, and the line came from his book on *Jokes and Their Relation to the Unconscious*, published in Vienna in 1905. Freud tended to present his psychological observations as universally, scientifically valid, but here too, as in so many of his works, one may take his observations as particularly relevant to their Viennese cultural context. Indeed the jokes that Freud analyzed were the jokes that he heard in Vienna at the turn of the century. The ʰᵃᵗ we sometimes do not know what we are laughing at, ⁻ᵗ that we are idiots, but rather because ted to unconscious materials and pro- Hummel trial, the idiotic merriment, nprehensible even to those who were laughing in ...

## "WERE YOU FOND OF THE CHILD?"

When the spectators broke into laughter, the judge demanded silence in the courtroom, and this happened so many times that the laughter, the irrational response of the crowd, seemed to stand in opposition to the rational legal process of the trial itself. It was, however, the judge himself who had given the general merriment its first encouragement. Juliane Hummel was unquestionably the comic object of the laughter in the courtroom, and the spectators were the laughing audience for the joke. The judge in the Hummel case was Dr. Johann Feigl, a man who was soon after to become a target for the merciless satirical denunciations of Karl Kraus. For

Kraus, Feigl came to represent the monstrosity of Austrian justice, and his handling of the Hummel trial may give some idea of why he was later cast in that role.

Perhaps Feigl's most flagrant intervention in the examination was in confronting Juliane Hummel with the story of the crack in the door which was nailed shut so the starving child could not receive scraps of food from the neighbors. As ever at a loss to equate abuse with legal murder, the judge suggested to the defendant that she nailed up the crack because she wanted her child to starve to death. She did not deny the story, but neither did she admit to the murderous motivation.

JULIANE HUMMEL: Please, I never had a hostile intention.
JUDGE: Then what kind of intention did you have?
JULIANE HUMMEL: I didn't want the child to be given any sweets.
JUDGE: Naturally—so she wouldn't ruin her stomach.

This was probably the most remarkable of all the judge's ironic intrusions, remarkable because the explicit anatomical reference called to mind the little mutilated corpse which had been described in the courtroom in such excruciating detail. Again his irony was provoked by a cliché of conventional motherhood, the concern about sweets—which did indeed sound outrageous in the mouth of a woman who had deliberately starved her daughter. The comment of the judge, however, was very nearly as inappropriate as that of the witness, and the crudeness of his response suggested the extreme nature of his provocation. For it was not only his parental sensibility that was offended in the exchange, but also his judicial design. Her incidental comment about sweets followed immediately upon a confrontation over the central issue of intention to murder. Juliane Hummel had freely admitted to nailing shut the crack in the door, but emphatically refused to admit hostile, let alone murderous, intentions. His horrible joke was a mark of his frustration at the legal tenuousness of an unprecedented case. It was furthermore a manifestation of the generally undefined nature of child abuse: The judge was reduced to crude irony in his concern to emphasize that Juliane Hummel was definitely different from all the other Viennese mothers who didn't want their children to eat sweets.

The frustration of the judge and the spectators with Juliane Hummel was aggravated throughout the examination by her "soft voice" and "mild tone." Just as she clung to the platitudes of motherhood, at the same time she presented herself in a manner distinctly unmonstrous. This incongruity was eventually articulated by the judge with his characteristic ironic touch. At that particular point, she was attempting to shift the responsibility for the crime to her husband.

JULIANE HUMMEL: He was given to drinking, and when the child was disobedient he punished it.
JUDGE: Did you watch?
JULIANE HUMMEL: Yes. I told him it was enough already.
JUDGE: And did you not harm the child?
JULIANE HUMMEL: Yes.
JUDGE: Why?
JULIANE HUMMEL: The child was disobedient, and I was irritated. Please, I am so bad-tempered.
JUDGE: As you seem so soft today, one doesn't notice it at all.

Here again the accused woman was clinging to the fine line between child abuse and traditional nineteenth-century parental discipline, and the judge could do no more than respond with a pointless comment about her manner. Indeed, while she was softly pleading her own bad temper, it was the judge who was actually losing his. In essence, he accused her of presenting herself falsely, for the central problem the court was wrestling with, the dilemma that could be resolved only with irony, was the disturbing incongruity between what she admitted to doing and how she accounted for it on the witness stand.

The irony of the judge played an unmistakable part in the most baffling and, at the same time, the most fascinating eruption of laughter in the examination of Juliane Hummel. She had just admitted to forcing her daughter's hands into boiling water, not a very funny subject.

JUDGE: Doesn't that suggest a hatred of the child?
JULIANE HUMMEL: No.
JUDGE: What must hatred look like, if that's love! Were you fond of the child?
JULIANE HUMMEL: Yes. (Laughter)
JUDGE: (To the spectators) That is much too sad for one to be able to laugh at it. (To the defendant) Why then did you mistreat the child?
JULIANE HUMMEL: Because she was disobedient.
JUDGE: One punishes a disobedient child, but one does not mistreat it.

Here the cue to laughter was her single word of affirmation. The judge's question—"Were you fond of the child?"—also offered ironic provocation to the spectators. Considering his style, it is not difficult to imagine that he put the question in a provocative tone. Her one word in reply constituted a summation of all those other maternal platitudes that had amused the court: Yes, I was fond of the child. This, however, was no platitude, but a very simple affirmation, the emotional essence of motherhood. The joke here was no matter of word play, but rather the very notion of parental ambivalence and psychopathological complexity.

"What must hatred look like, if that's love!" exclaimed the judge, and the point, dramatically emphasized by the laughter of the spectators, was that hatred and love could not possibly have anything to do with each other in a case like this one. Just as in the case of Hedwig Keplinger the possibility of "a certain hatred" toward her child was quickly resolved into murder out of love, so the Hummel case had to be resolved definitively in the other direction. For Juliane Hummel to say that she was fond of her child could only be a joke. It was sufficiently oppressive for turn-of-the-century Vienna to accept that a mother could hate her child; to go further and accept the possibility of psychological ambivalence in such a case was inconceivable. It was just such ambivalence that Freud feared his readers would refuse to accept in the Oedipus complex. As for the judge's lame insistence that "that is much too sad for one to be able to laugh at it," it almost seems that the sad thing he referred to was not the fate of the child, but rather the reply of the mother to his question.

From the very beginning of the trial there had been those who had protested against having to hear about the details of child abuse.

> All day long to have to listen to the details of a deed of unprecedented crudeness! But one's indignation is finally dulled because one can't apply a human standard of measurement to such dreadful behavior.

To a certain extent, the laughter in the courtroom came from spectators like this one, who could not bear to listen to the reiterated details, whose indignation and sense of horror finally gave way. Laughter offered an emotional release. This release, however, was by no means random in occurrence; it came in response to certain particular aspects and patterns of the trial. For the emotionally overloaded reporter, the case was almost beyond judgment, beyond measurement, but for the prosecuting attorney it had an emotional logic of its own:

> In our times, eaten away by doubt and the mania for mockery, if there is still something of value, then it is faith in the mother . . . Her deed makes a mockery of everything that is holy to human beings; one could almost doubt the omnipotence of maternal love.

The repeated word "mockery" was perhaps no mere rhetorical device. If there was indeed a "mania for mockery" in turn-of-the-century Vienna—perhaps related to Broch's sense of the city as

"merry, often idiotically merry"—then nothing could have illustrated that mania more emphatically than the Hummel trial.

According to the prosecutor, the deed made a mockery of motherhood, and in the examination of Juliane Hummel her words also
seemed to mock, albeit unintentionally, as she mouthed the platitudes of motherhood. Her concern that her daughter should not eat
sweets seemed to be the most outrageous mockery of Viennese
mothers who didn't want their own daughters to eat sweets; her
concern about punishing her disobedient child reflected on all those
parents with the same concern. And the spectators who felt that
she was making a mockery out of them reacted by making a mockery
out of her, by laughing at her pathetic efforts to defend herself. In
this sense, laughter was the perfectly appropriate revenge of the
"parquet of mothers."

In his book on jokes, Freud raised the issue of jokes and hostility,
and the special significance of jokes when hostile impulses were
subject to restriction and repression.

> By making our enemy small, inferior, despicable, or comic, we achieve
> in a roundabout way the enjoyment of overcoming him . . . A joke
> will allow us to exploit something ridiculous in our enemy which we
> could not, on account of obstacles in the way, bring forward openly or
> consciously.

The humor directed at Juliane Hummel was certainly hostile: she
was perceived as the enemy. But what were the "obstacles" to
expressing hostility more directly? Why was it necessary to use the
"roundabout way" of laughter? Freud's analysis of the jokes of his
Viennese contemporaries suggested the possibility of unconscious
psychological obstacles, and in the case of Juliane Hummel these
emerged from the ominous undefined issues that linked her case to
the position of parents in general.


## "THE KINGDOM OF HUMOUR"

Freud, in his book on jokes, offered an intriguing account of how
humor might come to be found in unlikely places.

> The species of humour are extraordinarily variegated according to the
> nature of the emotion which is economized in favour of the humour:
> pity, anger, pain, tenderness, and so on. Their number seems to remain
> uncompleted, because the kingdom of humour is constantly being
> enlarged whenever an artist or writer succeeds in submitting some
> hitherto unconquered emotions to the control of humour, in making

them, by devices like those in the examples we have given, into
sources of humorous pleasure.

Freud then went on to cite as the frontier of this kingdom of humor
a particular Munich journal which had "astonishing results in
achieving humour at the cost of horror and disgust." Thus Freud
gave an unusual twist to the optimistic nineteenth-century faith in
the progress and expansion of civilization; here it was humor that
was forever advancing to newer and greater "conquests." In this
view the Hummel trial could have been viewed as the vanguard of
contemporary humor, even the *dernier cri*—"achieving humour at
the cost of horror and disgust." Freud seemed almost to take for
granted that humorous pleasure was a desirable alternative to the
unpleasant emotions on which it fed. This fit, in a characteristically
Viennese way, with the discussion of art in *Civilization and Its
Discontents:* Freud's one misgiving about the "mild narcosis in-
duced in us by art" was that it was "not strong enough to make us
forget real misery." Humor in the Hummel trial played something
like the narcotic role of aestheticism in the case of Hedwig Keplinger. In both cases, the most disturbing aspects were partly dis-
armed and transformed. Hedwig Keplinger underwent a literary
apotheosis, while Juliane Hummel became the object of laughter
and merriment.

There were ironic contrasts and conflicts that underlay the moments of merriment at the trial, but there must also have been
another element—something almost impossible to discern from the
transcripts—that made those moments so irresistibly comical for
those who were present. What was it about the tone and bearing of
the woman that enabled irony and incongruity to find their expression in frank laughter? That is more than a court transcript can
convey to the historian a century later, but there are certain clues to
be found in those moments when the trial broke away from the
formal, conventional pattern of courtroom testimony. In the judge's
examination of Juliane Hummel, his presence and personality overwhelmed hers, and this was only natural since the courtroom was
his sphere and he was in control. Juliane Hummel, however, could
appear as much more of a personality when addressing people from
her own sphere, interrupting the other witnesses. She cried out at
the gardener's wife, "If you're going to lie, you should lie right."
She broke into the custodian's testimony to insist, "Whatever a
Bohemian says is a lie." Perhaps the most comical scene of the
whole trial, the scene that received the most laughs and caused the
most merriment, was another such interruption—when Juliane

Hummel reacted to the testimony of her sister-in-law, the coach-
man's wife.

Christine Hummel was the wife of the brother of Joseph Hummel, and she was one of the most important witnesses at the trial.
She had taken care of Anna for some time when her sister-in-law
was working, and was able to assure the court that the little girl
was "a pretty, healthy child whom everyone liked." She described
how angry Juliane Hummel became when she came to see Anna
and the child did not run to kiss her. She told how Anna would
come to her and say, "Auntie, Mother doesn't like me." She described seeing her sister-in-law throw the little girl in the street,
breaking the child's leg. It was she who quoted Juliane Hummel's
lack of contrition after the first police warning ("my husband and I
bought ourselves some pork, and the worrying was over"), she who
quoted the mother's resolution to beat the child without bruising it.
Christine Hummel claimed to have heard Juliane Hummel determine to get rid of Anna, and also insisted to the court that it was
the mother, much more than the father, who brutalized the child.

Juliane Hummel at last interrupted to denounce her sister-in-law
as a liar, to tell the courtroom that Christine Hummel had had an
affair with Joseph Hummel, her brother-in-law, and that therefore
her testimony was an act of jealous revenge. "What, not true what
I say?" exclaimed Christine Hummel on the witness stand to Juliane Hummel, the defendant. "If you say that, I'll knock you one."
Then both women erupted into violent insults and threats, and,
according to the *Neue Freie Presse,* "In the public and among the
jurors there reigned merriment."

Here the trial broke away from the conventional form of examination and testimony, and instead of the witnesses replying to questions they were reacting to each other in direct exchange. The form
became less that of a trial, and much more something like drama.
The *Neue Freie Presse* had originally presented the Hummel case as
an adaptation of Gerhart Hauptmann's tragic *Hannele,* appealing to
the city's fanaticism for the theater. But the exchange between
Juliane Hummel and Christine Hummel was not a scene of tragedy.
The trial, taking a dramatic turn, had become comic drama, and the
spectators, including the jurors, responded as an appreciative audience. In this scene, perhaps for the first time, one can almost see the
comedy, imagine oneself laughing in the audience—always supposing that one could keep from thinking about the mutilated corpse of
the five-year-old girl which lay at the bottom of the drama.

What then was the special comic ingredient that here, and
throughout the trial, spiced the lines of the transcript and made the

audience laugh? When Juliane Hummel was testifying, her husband and codefendant was removed from the courtroom according
to legal form. Reciprocally, when he testified she was removed.
After they had both testified, however, they were brought face to
face, and confronted with each other's testimony—a difficult moment since each had tried to shift responsibility to the other. Here
again was the same sort of transformation from a strictly judicial to
a loosely dramatic form. Consider this fragment from the miserable
exchange between husband and wife.

> JULIANE HUMMEL: You were drunk when you beat the girl.
> (Du warst ja besoffen, wie du's Mädel g'haut hast.)
> JOSEPH HUMMEL: I didn't do it.
> (I hab's nit 'than.)

Even if one does not understand German, one cannot fail to notice
the explosion of punctuation marks. Those marks indicate contractions from the full proper German, and that is how the transcript
rendered in print the dialect in which the laundry laborer and his
wife addressed each other. This transcription of dialect offers the
key to the comic element in the Hummel trial, and the slangy use of
besoffen for "drunk" adds the final point of confirmation. As in the
scene between Christine Hummel and Juliane Hummel ("I'll knock
you one!"), the comic drama was of a particular kind—it was comedy of the lower classes.

This was the comic element which was present throughout the
trial, which is so difficult for us to discern a hundred years later
from the transcripts, but was always immediately present for the
spectators in the courtroom in 1899. That element was in the voices
of the witnesses and the defendants, in their dialects, no doubt also
in their carriage and gestures, all of which marked them irredeemably as from the separate world of Vienna's lower classes. That
dialect was less immediately apparent in the testimony of Juliane
Hummel to the judge, because he was asking the questions and
setting the tone, so that she responded by trying to match his proper
speech. As soon as she addressed her husband, however, she spoke
in her normal dialect, and it was scrupulously, even cruelly, transliterated in print.

Though she may have tried to control her language while answering the questions of the judge, the wife of the laundry laborer
would not have actually managed to speak proper bourgeois German. The spectators would not have failed to note the inflections
that betrayed her best efforts. And when they laughed, those in

flections must have been a part of what they laughed at. The maternal platitudes that provoked their merriment contrasted ironically
with the torture of the child, but there was a further contrast that
added comedy to irony: between her conventionally proper bourgeois sentiments and her lower-class dialect. When she told of her
concern that Anna would eat too many sweets, the irony of the fact
that she starved her child was supplemented by the comedy of
hearing such a bourgeois concern expressed by the wife of the
laundry laborer. Hofmannsthal's Renaissance aesthetes found that
the "disgusting" urban masses "name their world with our words."
In spite of such imitation, however, the difference between the two
worlds remained clear enough.

The *Neue Freie Presse,* the newspaper of cultured bourgeois Vienna, from the very beginning, even before the opening of the trial,
noted that the defendants were "without education, people on a
low level of civilization." Their crime was "crass" and "bestial,"
one of "unprecedented crudeness." The *Neue Freie Presse* took
special care to note parenthetically the outbreaks of laughter and
merriment in the courtroom, for it was bourgeois Vienna that could
best appreciate the lower-class comedy. Just as the judge signaled
the "joke" to the spectators, so the leading newspaper signaled it to
the middle-class public, the larger audience.

Laughter, merriment, and irony were thus the most striking features of the Viennese response to the Hummel trial. Laughter
served as a refuge from the horrors of child abuse, and, at the same
time, from the troubling issues raised by its undefined nature. The
platitudes of motherhood that Juliane Hummel recited on the witness stand were treated as jokes, and motherhood itself was pre-
served from mockery by making mock of her. The issues of child
abuse were trivialized and evaded; above all, humor made it unnecessary to take those issues seriously. At the same time, the class
implications of this particular humor made the whole phenomenon
of child abuse into something reassuringly remote for bourgeois
Vienna.

Freud, in his analysis of what was comic, considered the case of a
man who could waggle his ears, and concluded that "a good deal of
the comic effect produced on us by animals comes from our perceiving in them movements such as these which we cannot imitate
ourselves." Were there also people who could communicate by
such expressive movements and gestures? Freud suggested "a child,
or a man from the common people, or a member of certain races."
The fundamental origin of comic pleasure, according to Freud, lay

in "a comparison of another person with ourself." The spectators in the courtroom watched Juliane Hummel "waggle her ears," that is, defend herself in the dialect and manner of "the common people." They compared her to themselves, found her incomparably different, and therefore they laughed. The reporter for the *Neue Freie Presse,* after all, found that his indignation was waning because it became impossible to apply "a human standard of measurement."

## "IN AN AGE OF CIVILIZATION"

"Why this deeply rooted aversion toward the little girl for whose existence they themselves were responsible?" wondered the *Neue Freie Presse* before the opening of the trial. And then again, after the opening, "Will we discover from this trial the deeper motives that would make comprehensible to us this deed that is horrible beyond all measure?" These weighty psychological questions had to be posed, but as the case proceeded, they were so resolutely evaded as to be rendered largely rhetorical. At the trial, the psychological probing of the accused parents was so scant and so crude that, a century later, one is almost left with more interesting material for analyzing the judge and the spectators than for analyzing the parents themselves. In fact, it was never suggested in the courtroom that this was a problem in psychopathology, and at the awful moment when Juliane Hummel claimed to be fond of her child, the spectators simply laughed. The judge was interested in the inner motivations of the parents only to the extent that these could be plausibly presented as something resembling first-degree murder. And the newspapers did not develop the psychological side of the case much further than the limited observations that were made at the trial.

Felix Dörmann's rendering of Hedwig Keplinger's inner psychological motivation was hopelessly sentimental; in the case of Juliane Hummel, where sentimentality had been so seemingly ripped to shreds, psychology was unable to say anything at all. Dörmann had managed to redeem "the omnipotence of maternal love" in his literary treatment of Hedwig Keplinger, and it was precisely that which in the Hummel case, according to the prosecutor, could be redeemed only at the scaffold. "Psychology is confronted by a mystery just as great as that which confronts sociology," proclaimed the *Arbeiter-Zeitung,* and here there was at least some awareness that Vienna had stumbled upon something new and important. Nothing

in the experience of the nineteenth century had prepared the Viennese of 1899 to understand and deal with this. And, in fact, when
the *Arbeiter-Zeitung* did try to write about the character of Juliane
Hummel, the paper succeeded only in showing that it was indeed
quite incapable of dealing with the problem psychologically.

> Her wild cruelty and satanic wickedness did not prevent her from
> being a religious woman—another proof of how superficial and how
> unfelt is that which the clericals call piety, and of how often these
> gentlemen see good Christianity where there can only be crude super-
> stition.

This eager anticlerical swipe went beyond the obvious accusation
of religious hypocrisy, virtually to imply that "crude superstition"
helped make Juliane Hummel the monster that she was. Her so-
called piety was seen as significant—in some vague and undefined
way—and the *Arbeiter-Zeitung* gave special boldface emphasis to
the summation by Christine Hummel of the defendants: "He had to
do washing, and she ran to the churches and read prayerbooks."
The emphatic subheading was "The Beast as Devotee."

The *Neue Freie Presse* also frankly declared that the abusive
parents were a psychological mystery: "It remains mysterious how
with such passion and such horrible means they pursued their goal.
And it is a mystery that they loved one child and hated the other."
In the press, as in the courtroom, it was the ambivalent aspects of
the case that were most disturbing and least considered. The *Neue
Freie Presse* was, however, prepared to hint at a solution to the
mystery: "A complete explanation is not to be found. With painful
surprise, one says to oneself that in an age of civilization there can
be such people only by an atavism."

This pseudo-anthropological suggestion came, of course, from the
newspaper of cultured Vienna: the Hummel case represented not
only a threat to motherhood, but also to civilization itself. The
notion of "an atavism" certainly fit with the paper's previous as-
signment of the Hummel parents to "a low level of civilization." If
the factor of social class put them at a safe remove from bourgeois
Vienna, the notion of "atavism" served to make child abuse historically as well as socially remote. Perhaps no one was bothered by the
logical contradiction of projecting into the past something that, by
common agreement, no one could remember ever having happened
before. Or perhaps the term "atavism" was intended to relegate
child abuse to the even safer realm of time immemorial. At any rate,
neither "atavism" nor "crude superstition" constituted a serious
psychological explanation.

## "A WORLD OF NEW PROBLEMS"

If the newspapers of Freud's Vienna were so disappointing in their psychological insights, one can't help wondering how Freud himself interpreted the actions and motivations of Joseph and Juliane Hummel. In October, when Hedwig Keplinger killed herself and her daughter, Freud was anxiously awaiting the publication of *The Interpretation of Dreams*, especially concerned that readers would reject as "monstrous" his analysis of "Dreams of the Death of Persons of Whom the Dreamer Is Fond." He urged his readers to turn from sentimental ideals to "everyday observation," to recognize the hostility that lay "concealed in the relations between parents and children." The murder of Anna Hummel by her parents should have demonstrated even more emphatically than the case of Hedwig Keplinger that such hostilities were by no means too monstrous to be true. Furthermore, while it would have been of interest to know what Freud saw in Hedwig Keplinger's reticule, it would have been of historic significance to know how he interpreted one of the few cases of child abuse to emerge before the public eye of the nineteenth century. Yet Freud left no sign that he took note of Hedwig Keplinger in October, and neither did he leave any word about the Hummel trial in November.

Though the Fliess correspondence from those weeks showed not a trace of Anna Hummel, Freud's letters were full of thoughts connected to the mortality of children. On October 27, Freud wrote about his concern over the "epidemic of colds" among his children, and his special concern about his seven-year-old son Ernst. The news that Fliess's infant daughter Pauline was also very seriously ill set Freud to thinking and writing on November 9, the week before the Hummel trial, about the terrifying dangers of pediatric illness.

So, poor Paulinchen is suffering so much, and I do not even know her. My sister's little one, who was so wretched and run down half a year ago, is now full of vigor and mischief; and so, in a case like this one, our first and foremost thought is that children get over most things. When Mathilde had diphtheria for the second time, a medical university colleague came to the house at number 19. He inquired, as the concierge told us later, whether the Freud girl was already dead. That was very Christian. But the girl is still alive and is growing appropriately in length and fortunately also in width. An epidemic of feverish colds raged through all the others, and some of them had diarrhea. The worst of it was that a few did not have enough with one attack. Just

today Sophie once again began to have diarrhea and a fever, while the
sore throats and colds of the others are on the wane. For the past two
weeks, moreover, Ernst has had an elevated temperature in the afternoon for no apparent reason. The two mothers insist—just to make
me anxious—that he resembles too closely their brother Isaac, who
died of tuberculosis.

Childhood mortality was still tragically unpredictable at the end of
the nineteenth century, and Freud was thinking anxiously about
the frailty of his own children, at the same time that all Vienna was
reading about the death of Anna Hummel. Thus parental anxiety,
as well as professional interest, might have conditioned Freud's
receptivity to the child abuse sensation of the moment. The "parquet of mothers" at the trial suggests that the case was gruesomely
compelling for Viennese parents, and yet, in Freud's case, thoughts
of his own children may have rendered the Hummel trial impossible
to follow. This was not because of twelve-year-old Mathilde, and
not because of seven-year-old Ernst, nor even because of six-year-
old Sophie. "An epidemic of feverish colds raged through all the
others," wrote Freud, and "the others" included four-year-old
Anna Freud. The feverish little Anna Freud, who would one day
grow up to be the grande dame of psychoanalysis, was in 1899 the
same age with the same name as little Anna Hummel. Many factors
may have contributed to Freud's failure to note the child abuse
sensation, but this coincidence of names and ages was precisely the
sort of "Freudian" explanation that would have most appealed to
Freud himself.

His general mood at the moment of the trial was described in a
letter to Fliess of November 19:

> On Sunday, the 12th, in the afternoon I again fell ill, for reasons
> unknown to me, with ill humor that continued, intensified with heart
> and head migraines, and terminated completely with a head migraine
> on Thursday, so that since then I have not only been well but down-
> right merry. I want to keep this periodic mild depression under obser-
> vation; its meaning is entirely unclear to me.

The day Freud fell ill, November 12, was the day that the *Neue
Freie Presse* (Freud's newspaper, naturally) inaugurated the child
abuse sensation with the article "Parents Who Murder Their Children." The migraines then continued through the day of the trial on
the fourteenth, and the days of most intensive press coverage on the
fourteenth and fifteenth, culminating and then clearing up on the
following day, leaving Freud "merry."

The Fliess correspondence would seem to suggest that what was weighing on Freud most at the time, even more than the illnesses of his children, was the publication of his book. For *The Interpretation of Dreams* was published during the first week of November, and he was bracing himself for the reaction. The same letter of November 19, which described the mysterious bout of migraines, also commented bitterly on the book.

> It is a thankless task to enlighten mankind a little. No one has yet told me that he feels indebted to me for having learned something new from the dream book and for having been introduced to a world of new problems.

Freud's intellectual energies were focused on the book he had just published. As for new work, on October 27 he wrote to Fliess, "I am lazy again and have no ideas," while on November 19 he wrote that "the science is resting." It was clearly not the moment for him to address himself to an altogether new problem, such as child abuse, when he had just that month brought forth "a world of new problems" and awaited the response of "mankind."

The Freud of the letters, who found it a thankless task to have enlightened mankind, did not take quite the same tone as the Freud who, in his book, wrote of his fear that his ideas would be utterly dismissed. A yearning for recognition certainly complemented his fear of rejection. On November 26, he wrote to Fliess, "The dream book has not yet occasioned any outcries," and one senses that, in this sentiment, regret overshadowed relief. As it happened, the great outcry of November 26 was over child abuse, for on that day the *Neue Freie Presse* published an "Appeal to All Feeling People." This was not the outcry that Freud was listening for. On December 9, he replied to the good news from Fliess that the book on dreams had perhaps a dozen readers in Berlin. "I must have some readers here as well," wrote Freud. "The time is not yet ripe for followers. There is too much that is new and unbelievable, and too little strict proof." Hoping for readers, yearning for followers, Freud was not attuned to something else "new and unbelievable" that had come to light in Vienna.

The fact that Freud was looking out for any attention to his book points to an unmistakable conclusion about his life during these months. One more passage from the Fliess correspondence will bring this into focus, this passage from a letter of December 21, already the end of the year.

> The book has had one single review, in the *Gegenwart*; as a critical evaluation it is empty, and as a review it is inadequate. It is just a bad

patchwork of my own fragments. However I am willing to forgive everything because of the one word "path-breaking." Otherwise the attitude of people in Vienna is quite negative; I do not believe that I shall succeed in getting a review published here. We are, after all, terribly far ahead of our time.

This shows us the Freud who yearned for the glory that he knew he deserved, but the passage, almost incidentally, also tells us that Freud, awaiting reactions, was above all looking for reviews—especially in Vienna. That means that, from the date of the publication at the beginning of November, right through to the end of the year, precisely the period of the child abuse sensation, Freud was paying the most careful attention to the newspapers and journals of the city. Through his children's illnesses, through his own migraines, Freud did not fail to read the newspapers, hoping for a review, longing for some attention to his book. He was not looking for child abuse, but if he was reading the newspapers in Vienna after the first week in November, he could not possibly have remained unaware of it.

## "A SPLENDID MONUMENT"

Magdalena Kronberger, the gardener's wife, told the court that she had gone to the police four times to report that Anna Hummel was being tortured by her parents—but nothing happened. Actually the police did present Joseph and Juliane Hummel with an offical warning against "excess of domestic discipline"—a warning that probably intensified the abuse of the child and hastened her death. On the other hand, if the parents had stopped short of actually killing the child, they might have gone on torturing her well into the new century, without any official intervention, let alone public sensation. The imperial and municipal authorities were poorly prepared to deal with a social problem that was not yet recognized as a social problem. If academic issues of psychology could be left unexplored and "mysterious," it was rather more pressing to consider child abuse as a social problem—as a problem that called for some sort of more effective social response and control.

The *Arbeiter-Zeitung,* though reluctant to see in the Hummel case a consequence of "social oppression," did not hesitate to turn the issue of child abuse into an attack on the Austrian state. In so doing, the editors frankly recognized child abuse as a serious social problem, and set forth a social analysis immediately, even before recounting the trial.

However much one may wonder at it, as incomprehensible as one may find it—there are really mothers who, without compelling external motive, furiously hate their children, and with satanic malice torture them to death. Besides these fortunately rare spiritual cripples, there are however many other women whose hearts, although they become mothers, remain empty, and never glow with maternal love. Few of these sad mothers would do what Juliane Hummel has done, but something of the wild cruelty of that beast also stirs in them, and so it is an ominous danger for those poor creatures who have the misfortune to be the children of unloving women. The mother who does not love her child should have no right to that child! Reason demands it, and the interest of society demands it. Society however—at least the present one—disavows this interest. Under no circumstances does it want to decide to deny any mother the right to her child, because, though by means of its deputies—that is, the state—it watches domineeringly over every movement of the individual, and encumbers him with countless burdensome fetters, it stops before the family. There it wants to exercise no control, because otherwise one would arrive at the perspective of the wicked revolutionary who does not respect the holiness of the family, and who wants to give up to the collectivity an influence over child rearing.

This analysis came very close to suggesting that child abuse was a widespread problem, even a syndrome, though it was presented more benignly as a problem of "unloving" rather than abusive parents. (In the press, as at the trial, everything was a matter of mothers, and fathers were played down and conjured out of the picture.) The *Arbeiter-Zeitung* sharply identified that sentimental reverence for the "holiness of the family," which made child abuse inconceivable, which required the execution of the Hummel parents, and which here was named almost sarcastically as the obstacle to any effective social reform. Society and the state, as defenders of the family, were enemies of childhood, and child abuse was ingeniously transformed into a reason for collective "communism"—as it was understood by the socialists of the turn of the century. While the bourgeois *Neue Freie Presse* regarded child abuse as an atavism, the socialist *Arbeiter-Zeitung* managed to suggest that child abuse was a necessary and integral part of contemporary bourgeois society. The "wicked revolutionary" was all the more justified in wanting to overthrow a state and society that would not protect Anna Hummel from her parents.

This socialist analysis was published as a confident introduction to the account of the trial itself on November 15. The *Neue Freie Presse*, however, took rather longer to come to terms with child abuse as a social problem, and to recommend a response. In the heralding article of November 12, the liberal paper had made the

obvious suggestion that the police should do a better job of following up on parents who received official warnings. There was also a
less obvious suggestion that the warning should perhaps be made
not for "excess of domestic discipline," but rather for "injury with
hostile intent." A few days after the trial, on November 19, there
were some brief retrospective reflections again on the need to follow
up on warnings, and even to remove the child from the home if
abuse continued. These limited remarks were finally superseded on
November 26, on the eve of the second great child abuse trial, by
the dramatic "Appeal to All Feeling People"—written and signed
by a group of concerned citizens, sponsored and published by the
editors of the newspaper. The opinion of the "revolutionary" Arbeiter-Zeitung counted for very little in the government of Vienna
and of Austria, but the Neue Freie Presse was the most powerful
and influential newspaper in the empire.

The "Appeal" began with a bizarre flourish, tellingly characteristic of turn-of-the-century Vienna. Readers were reminded of the
great fire of 1881 at the Ring Theater, which killed hundreds in
the audience. The Ringstrasse was the monumental boulevard of
the city: "an enchantment out of the Thousand-and-One Nights,"
as it seemed to the impressionable young Adolf Hitler. Schorske has
analyzed the Ringstrasse as the cherished creation of Austrian liberalism in its mid-nineteenth-century moment of ascendancy; how
much liberal Vienna cherished its theaters has already been suggested. So, beginning with this traumatic reminiscence, the liberal
Appeal of 1899 then observed that the fire of 1881 was followed by
the foundation of the city's Volunteer Rescue Society. Since the
torture and murder of children by their parents was "no less terrible" than the fire in the theater twenty years before, since all at
once child abuse was becoming a "constant rubric" in the press, this
was surely the moment to create a Children's Rescue Society.

Therefore a group of men had gathered together—men, naturally, to deal with the problem of "unloving women"—to form a
nonpolitical humanitarian union called Treue—that is, "Fidelity."
And their Appeal to Vienna was not merely an appeal for kindness
to children, but rather an appeal for contributions of money toward
the construction of an asylum for abused children. The heart of the
appeal was aimed at municipal pride:

> Vienna will hear us. Vienna will soon be able to point with pride to a
> completely new humanitarian creation, that has grown out of the time
> and its needs—to point to a splendid monument to the long-famous,
> and in spite of the confusion of the day, still unspoiled, Viennese sense
> of nobility.

This appeal to "nobility" was not formulated by men of the noble class; it was signed by a businessman, a banker, a writer, an editor, a lawyer, a wine merchant, a cafe proprietor, and a Romanian court conductor. The editors of the *Neue Freie Presse* would provide further information, and receive donations on behalf of the new venture.

It perfectly fit Schorske's historical paradigm for Viennese culture: bourgeois liberalism seeking spiritual nobility in the creation of a monument. And yet this passionately self-congratulatory humanitarian vision was, at best, an awkward response to the gruesome Hummel case. For Schorske, the buildings of the Ringstrasse provided "an iconographic index to the mind of ascendant Austrian liberalism." But what was the iconographic significance of a monument to (or rather against) child abuse? Perhaps it was to affirm "the omnipotence of maternal love" or "the holiness of the family"—and also to memorialize the condemnation and annihilation of Juliane and Joseph Hummel. Yet, at the same time, as an asylum for abused children, it had to be also a reminder of unloving parents and suffering children, not a very attractive focus for Viennese pride. In the rhetoric of the Appeal, the ceremonial significance of the construction predominated over its functional significance as an asylum, but, to the extent that both aspects coexisted, there must have been a certain tension within the grand conception, an ambivalent iconography. And what of the analogy to the theater fire of 1881? Was this just nostalgia for the less alienating urban past, when Vienna was not yet a metropolis on the brink of the twentieth century, not yet a really "big city" with really big social problems? Or was the burning theater of 1881 also an iconographic metaphor for the child abuse sensation of 1899, a tragedy in which the victims could only be memorialized by a work of reconstruction? If the asylum—that "completely new humanitarian creation"—was in fact intended as a work of rebuilding, not just building, then it was certainly the Viennese family, symbolically burned, that was to be restored as a splendid monument. In fin-de-siècle Vienna, even a new and horrible social problem could find an architectural, aesthetic solution.

The same sort of architectural approach to social problems would make a real mark on cultural history in 1902, when Otto Wagner won the design competition that set him to building the splendid Steinhof Church, the architectural ornament of a new insane asylum. Wagner, another innovative genius of fin-de-siècle Vienna, had renounced the Ringstrasse style to become a modernist pioneer; the Steinhof Church, with its gilded dome, was one of his masterpieces, an important work of modern church architecture. Thus it was entirely characteristic that Vienna should have considered constructing an architectural monument as an asylum for abused children, and three years later, the same sort of aesthetic scheme would be approved for a different sort of asylum and a different social problem.

The nature of the Appeal was symbolically rich and potent, but the practical proposal for an asylum revealed a social vision rather more limited than the architectural vision. The Viennese child abuse sensation of 1899 was so fleeting that it was over long before it could be commemorated in brick or stone. In that brief moment, however, the *Neue Freie Presse* was much more concerned with the proposed monument than with the problem it was supposed to express and address. The Appeal had nothing to say about how abused children were to be rescued from their parents, how they were to find their way to this imagined asylum. The businessman and the banker and the wine merchant and the court conductor, no doubt, thrilled to the inspirational rhythms of their manifesto. Perhaps they believed that if they could just build the right building, all the details of program and procedure would somehow take care of themselves. But those details found no place in their Appeal. Where the socialist *Arbeiter-Zeitung* challenged the state to intervene in the life of the family, the liberal *Neue Freie Presse* was most unmistakably silent. Instead, it sponsored a liberal solution, offering to collect private contributions on behalf of a group of private "nonpolitical" bourgeois citizens, who sought to establish a private project of architecture and philanthropy.

In 1899, despite the glaring contempt of the socialists, despite Hitler's belief that Vienna was "socially speaking, one of the most backward cities in Europe," despite the survival of an aged Emperor who read only the army register, Austria and Vienna were relatively advanced in terms of government social welfare. In the 1880s, the conservative minister president, Count Edward Taafe, had imitated in Austria much of Bismarck's pioneering German social welfare program—including the regulation of child labor. In 1897 the Christian Socialist mayor of Vienna, Karl Lueger, famous for his shrewd political manipulation of anti-Semitism, inaugurated a period of remarkable municipal socialism with broad new welfare services. These included schools, playgrounds, and orphanages for Viennese children. The socialist call for state involvement in protecting children from abuse was not so extremely advanced as to be out of the question in turn-of-the-century Vienna. On the contrary, it was the liberal response, in the vastly more influential *Neue Freie*

*Presse* that was backward and timid, incapable of reacting to the social problem of child abuse with anything more than a symbolic vision.

The hollowness of the Appeal of November 26 was even a step backwards from the paper's previous scant and tentative suggestions regarding more efficacious social control. It was certainly a retreat from the notice of the week before, on November 19, when the paper spoke of society's obligations to children, and of the need for better supervision after official warnings to parents. That notice also contained one of the most crucial formulations of the whole child abuse sensation of 1899, though at first glance it is hard to know what to make of it. There was a mention of the possibility of some sort of government intervention in the matter of child abuse. And then this is what followed:

> At any rate the population of Vienna would be more grateful for some action of this kind by its elected representatives, than for the eternal senseless vilification of the Jews.

The first half of the sentence, introduced by the phrase "at any rate," perfectly illustrated the highly uncertain tone of the newspaper in the matter of government intervention. It is the second half of the sentence that is bizarre and mysterious: For what on earth did child abuse have to do with the Jews? This seemingly inexplicable juxtaposition leads us deeper into the iconographic symbols and associations of the Viennese child abuse sensation of 1899.

## "THE ETERNAL SENSELESS VILIFICATION OF THE JEWS"

It was Freud's Vienna, Mahler's Vienna, Klimt's Vienna—but it was also Hitler's Vienna. If the capital of the declining Habsburg empire was a sort of cultural crucible for the twentieth century, it was that same vessel that first submitted to high heat the explosive elements of twentieth-century anti-Semitism. Hitler came to Vienna in 1908, at the age of nineteen, and in *Mein Kampf* his discovery of "the Jewish question" complemented his study of "the social question" as the central aspects of his Viennese experience. As a boy in Linz, he had known nothing about Jews, and the few that there were had even "taken on a human look." Hitler's account of his discovery of Jews and anti-Semitism was dramatically introduced by the one-sentence paragraph: "Then I came to Vienna."

In Vienna Jews constituted 10 percent of the city's population, and many were highly recognizable in the distinctive kaftans that marked their recent migration from Eastern Europe. "Once as I was strolling through the Inner City," noted the naive young Hitler, "I suddenly encountered an apparition in a black kaftan and black hair locks. Is this a Jew? was my first thought." Other Jews were not visibly distinct in dress, but were notably prominent in the cultural life of the city, because, in Zweig's words, "it was the pride and ambition of the Jewish people to cooperate in the front ranks to carry on the former glory of the fame of Viennese culture." Hitler noticed this too: "Was there any form of filth or profligacy, particularly in cultural life, without at least one Jew involved in it?" In fact, in this matter, the Viennese memoirs of Zweig and Hitler provide an almost perfect counterpoint. Zweig proudly pointed to the Jews behind "nine-tenths of what the world celebrated as Viennese culture," while Hitler furiously held the Jews to account for "nine-tenths of all literary filth, artistic trash, and theatrical idiocy."

Hitler's discovery of anti-Semitism was very much a part of his experience of Vienna. "Since I had begun to concern myself with this question and to take cognizance of the Jews," he recorded, "Vienna appeared to me in a different light than before. Wherever I went I began to see Jews." The young Hitler was, as in the social question, ever the studious urban sociologist: "The relation of the Jews to prostitution and, even more, to the white-slave traffic, could be studied in Vienna as perhaps in no other city of Western Europe." In short, in turn-of-the-century Vienna Hitler concluded that the Jews constituted a "pestilence, spiritual pestilence, worse than the Black Death of olden times."

But Hitler's conclusions did not come only from his personal researches. In Vienna he found already developed an anti-Semitic political tradition that dated back to before he was born. In particular, Georg von Schönerer and Karl Lueger were men who pioneered the political exploitation of violent anti-Semitism, men whom Hitler recognized as political role models and ideological mentors. For in this respect turn-of-the-century Habsburg Austria was a cultural progenitor of twentieth-century Nazi Germany. Hitler, in *Mein Kampf,* wrote thus about Schönerer and Lueger: "they both tower far above the scope and stature of so-called parliamentary figures." In a corrupt political world, he looked to them as "pure and unassailable."

Schönerer in the 1880s creatively combined passionate German nationalism with violent anti-Semitism, and brought them to bear on political campaigns against the Rothschild railroads and against Jewish immigration to Austria. He was a pioneer of anti-Semitic thuggery, and his political slogans declared that Jews were pigs; Hitler revered him as a "profound thinker." Karl Lueger, "Handsome Karl" to his devoted Viennese constituents, made far more subtle and politically effective use of anti-Semitism, a paragon in an Austrian political tradition that showed itself still alive a century later in the Austrian presidential campaign of Kurt Waldheim in 1986. Karl Lueger was the mayor of Vienna at the time of the child abuse sensation of 1899, and he was still mayor in 1908 when Hitler came to Vienna. For Hitler he was "the greatest German mayor of all times." Lueger's political brew of Catholic clericalism, municipal socialism, blond-bearded good looks, and demagogic anti-Semitism was so frighteningly potent that the Emperor Franz Joseph at first vetoed his election as mayor in 1895. Freud recorded that he "overindulged out of joy only, on the day of Lueger's non-confirmation," meaning that he smoked a cigar. But in 1897 the Emperor surrendered to the insistence of the electorate, and Lueger became mayor. He always appreciated anti-Semitism as a political asset, and exploited it freely in the spirit of his proverbial confession: "I decide who's a Jew." The political careers of Schönerer and Lueger, and also the formative experiences in the Viennese metropolis of their heir and pupil Adolf Hitler, suggest the special significance of fin-de-siècle Vienna in the history of anti-Semitism. But what could anti-Semitism have to do with the child abuse sensation of 1899?

As it happens, a landmark event in the history of Austrian anti-Semitism took place in 1899. The location was the province of Bohemia, but, as with the controversial Bohemian language laws, the reverberations were felt with special intensity in Vienna, the capital. On April 1, 1899 (three weeks after the death of Anna Hummel, six months before her parents stood trial), a dead body had been found in the woods near the little town of Polna in Bohemia—another body in the woods to haunt the decline of the Habsburg empire. It was a nineteen-year-old village girl, Agnes Hruza. She had been murdered, her throat cut, and the doctors who examined her body found that it contained curiously little blood. A vagrant Jew, Leopold Hilsner, was arrested. It was springtime, the season of Easter and Passover, and in Polna, and then in Bohemia, and then in the whole Habsburg empire, there were accusations of Jewish ritual murder, the notorious blood ritual. In September (a month before the bodies of Hedwig Keplinger and her daughter were found in the woods), Leopold Hilsner was tried for murder and—on the dubious testimony of a witness who claimed to have seen him, from a distance of half a mile, near where the body was found—he was condemned to death. The trial, however, was invalidated on legal technicalities, and a new trial was promised the following year.

This postponement only broadened and intensified the anti-Semitic agitation throughout the empire, and on October 27 the long-dead body of another Bohemian girl was found near Polna, and Hilsner found himself charged with a second ritual murder. Meanwhile, he had been trapped into a confession which he retracted on September 29, fell into again on October 7, and retracted once again on November 20 (at the height of the child abuse sensation). Such confusion enhanced the nasty agitation all the more, and the organized anti-Semites of Vienna even sent a reporter to Polna to "investigate" and bring the case to the Viennese public. The mastermind of the Viennese agitation was a certain Ernst Schneider, one of Lueger's carefully controlled henchmen, whom Zweig especially remembered for his political exploitation of "legends of ritual murders and similar vulgarities." By December the anti-Semitic denunciation had penetrated into the Reichsrat, the parliament in Vienna.

"Is there no Zola?" was the challenge of one Viennese Jewish community leader, for by the autumn of 1899 the anti-Semitic agitation had reached such proportions in the capital that it seemed comparable to the Dreyfus affair, then raging in Paris. Alfred Dreyfus was a French Jew and a captain in the French army accused in 1894 of selling secrets to the Germans, convicted of treason on questionable evidence, and sentenced to the French penal colony on Devil's Island. The French military command refused to admit to judicial error and would not reconsider the case; at the same time anti-Semitic appeals rallied Frenchmen of the right to the support of the army. In 1898 the French novelist Emile Zola began to turn the tide of public opinion with the courageous publication of the open letter, J'accuse, denouncing the army and defending Dreyfus.

> Since they have dared, I too shall dare. I shall tell the truth because I pledged myself to tell it if justice, regularly empowered, did not do so fully, unmitigatedly. My duty is to speak; I have no wish to be an accomplice. My nights would be haunted by the specter of the innocent being expiating, under the most frightful torture, a crime he never committed.

The controversy became so intense that it almost destroyed the French government, but finally in September 1899 Dreyfus received a presidential pardon. The Hilsner affair in Austria in 1899, with its dubious court conviction and the arousal of mass anti-Semitism, naturally reminded people of the Dreyfus affair in France. It was not hard to follow the analogy in the appeal: "Is there no Zola?"

As it happens, there was a Zola figure who emerged to defend Hilsner and the Jews—but not in Vienna. In Prague Thomas Masaryk, then a professor of philosophy, risked his career and braved the fury of the mob, to argue publicly that Hilsner was innocent, that ritual murder was mere superstition, and that "this superstition is the shame of our times." Masaryk, born in Moravia, had studied at the University of Vienna, written a book about suicide, and settled in Prague with his American wife. He had already been elected to the Reichsrat in Vienna in the 1890s, and he was soon to be elected again on his way to becoming the most important political leader in Bohemia and the intellectual interpreter of the Czech national heritage. It was he who negotiated with Woodrow Wilson the terms of independence for Czechoslovakia during World War I, and he became the first president of Czechoslovakia. As much as anyone else he was responsible for the destruction of the Habsburg empire at the end of the war, its dissolution into national states. Throughout his career as a scholar and a statesman he was known for his courageous integrity, and in 1899 he was the one public figure who dared to speak out on behalf of Hilsner, to denounce the anti-Semitic hysteria.

Masaryk in Prague was unquestionably the Zola of the Hilsner affair, but there was also at least one supremely powerful person in Vienna who found the affair disgusting. The old Emperor Franz Joseph did not believe in ritual murder, and did not approve of demagogic anti-Semitism. He let the case run its ugly course, and then, when Hilsner was once again condemned to death on November 14, 1900 (coincidentally, the anniversary of the Hummel trial), Franz Joseph intervened to save the man's life by commuting the sentence to life imprisonment.

The Emperor was thus able to step in at the last minute to rescue Hilsner from the gallows, but in the meantime the Jews of the empire had to fend for themselves against the horrible implications of the alleged crime. By the beginning of October 1899, the controversy was raging in Vienna, and three thousand Viennese Jews gathered in the concert hall to denounce the disgusting blood libel. That they should have chosen the concert hall was, of course, highly characteristic of fin-de-siècle Vienna, a city in which even such a controversy as this could take on the air of a cultural event. Theodor Herzl found the gathering distasteful precisely because of its exclusively bourgeois nature. He had been asked by the organizers please not to disrupt the gathering by sending Zionist students.

Herzl asked whether they would at least discuss at the concert hall the fate of the Jews who were being driven out of Bohemia by the anti-Semitic hysteria, but he was "implored" not to raise this issue. He could see clearly, as he noted in his diary on October 13 (the day that Hedwig Keplinger shot herself and her daughter), that the "upper Jews" of Vienna were afraid of a mass migration to the city, a migration of poor Jews from Bohemia.

Karl Kraus, who despised Herzl and hated Zionism, was no less cynical about the gathering in the concert hall. In their eagerness to refute the charge of ritual murder, Kraus found the Viennese Jews ludicrously ready to do battle on the "terrain" chosen by the anti-Semites. It was "tasteless," wrote Kraus in *Die Fackel,* to demand that non-Jews "take a position," and to expect a respectable person to clap his Jewish neighbor on the shoulder and whisper reassuringly in his ear, "No, I don't believe you're capable of committing a ritual murder." For Kraus ritual murder became a matter of tastelessness, just as for Zweig it was a "vulgarity." Kraus cynically expressed his confidence that the whole controversy would not affect bourgeois business relations, and that even if a case of ritual murder were definitively proven, Austrian Catholics would still do business with the Rothschilds. Like Herzl, Kraus was put off by the prosperous air of the Viennese Jews in the concert hall, but Kraus went further in his insistence that the Jews who responded to the charge of ritual murder were almost as tasteless and hypocritical as the anti-Semites who initiated and spread the libel.

In October the controversy in Vienna reached the concert hall, and in November it penetrated still further into the opera house. This was to become a legendary moment in the history of Viennese anti-Semitism. On the evening of November 27, 1899 (on the eve of the second child abuse trial of the month), Gustav Mahler was conducting the premiere performance of his new production of Wagner's *Die Meistersinger.* "If the whole of German art were to disappear, it could be recognized and reconstructed from this one work," commented Mahler. "It almost makes everything else seem worthless and superfluous." The opera house was sold out. After the famous prelude there was wild applause, but there was also some hissing from anti-Semites, protesting against a Jew conducting Wagner. Mahler immediately began the first act, to end the demonstration, but the same hissing returned hours later at the sublime prelude to the third act. An observer recorded Mahler's reaction:

> He had no defense against the commotion. For, whenever he raised his arms to quell the uproar so that the performance could resume, the

storm broke out afresh in the audience. At last, he resigned himself to letting it pass over him. He sat there with head bowed, as if it all had nothing to do with him, looking as if he were quietly waiting for an unavoidably heavy rain-shower to stop pelting down on his back.

What was not recorded was that this incident in the opera house was not an isolated outburst of anti-Semitism; it took place in the context of the agitation that followed upon the ritual murder trial in Bohemia. Furthermore, Mahler's resignation—"head bowed, as if it all had nothing to do with him"—was very much what Karl Kraus was counseling when he mocked the Jews in the concert hall for tastelessly responding to the ritual murder charge.

As for the *Neue Freie Presse*, Karl Kraus, much as he detested that newspaper, really could not have found in its pages the sort of "tasteless" refutation that seemed to him so offensive in the ritual murder controversy. The newspaper that dictated "the greater part of what does duty for Austrian opinion," the newspaper of cultured Viennese liberalism, was curiously elliptical in its coverage of the Hilsner affair and the consequent agitation in Vienna. The meeting in the concert hall was comprehensively reported, without apparent irony, but in October 1899 the *Neue Freie Presse* expressed its own opinion only indirectly by publishing two letters to the editor. There was one, on October 1, from an indignantly sarcastic rabbi— "Yes, what a shame that it is so infinitely difficult, yes, even quite impossible, to prove a ritual murder!" There was another, on October 17, from a Jewish shopkeeper in Cracow, who was almost strung up by a Polish crowd when a six-year-old girl couldn't be found by her mother.

References to the anti-Semitic agitation in Vienna were even scanter and more indirect than references to the Hilsner case itself. On October 11, there was an account of the trial of a Jewish stockbroker who was charged with driving his servant girl to suicide by accusing her of theft; she jumped out a window, survived the fall, and said she had jumped on account of "wounded honor." It was reported that the case was exciting "eine kleine Judenhetze"—a little Jew-baiting agitation. On November 6, the *Neue Freie Presse* touched on these matters even more elliptically, almost jokingly, under the heading "A Victim of the Anti-Semitic Agitation." A certain Viennese embroiderer was struck by the delusion that he was the intimate confidant of the mayor, Karl Lueger, and was so obstreperously intent on paying a friendly visit at the town hall that he had to be taken to the hospital for psychiatric observation. The embroiderer was the "victim." The point of the

story, one supposes, was that anti-Semitism was not so far from
insanity, but the tone of light amusement made this a rather curious
and strangely allusive vehicle for commenting on the anti-Semitic
agitation. Most remarkable of all was that such a story was not
printed as a supplementary footnote to fuller reports, but rather
instead of them.

When Hitler first came to Vienna, before he underwent his con-
version to anti-Semitism, he was favorably impressed by the way
the *Neue Freie Presse* reported anti-Semitic incidents. He admired
the "dignified form in which the really big papers answered all
these attacks, or, what seemed to me even more praiseworthy, failed
to mention them; in other words, simply killed them with silence."
After he had completed his study of the Jewish question, however,
Hitler found this same approach not admirable but infuriating:

> I now saw the liberal attitude of this press in a different light; the lofty
> tone in which it answered attacks, and its method of killing them with
> silence, now revealed itself to me as a trick as clever as it was treach-
> erous.

This killing silence was clearly what was going on in the pages of
the *Neue Freie Presse* during the fall of 1899. The newspaper of the
cultured bourgeoisie responded to the Hilsner affair and the anti-
Semitic agitation not with "tasteless" indignation and refutation,
but rather, like Mahler at the podium, waiting for the storm to pass
"as if it all had nothing to do with him." Readers of the *Neue Freie
Presse* in November 1899 would have learned little from their daily
paper about the anti-Semitism that was raging in their city. We
know what they were reading about instead: they were reading
about child abuse. They would have known far better than we can
know how to interpret that cryptic call for action against child
abuse: "At any rate the population of Vienna would be more grate-
ful for some action of this kind by its elected representatives, than
for the eternal senseless vilification of the Jews." For during that
month of November 1899 there was good cause to propose a weighing of child abuse against anti-Semitism—especially if one was conscious of their relative weights in the press.

Moritz Benedikt and Eduard Bacher, the chief editors of the
*Neue Freie Presse,* were German Jews who came from the Czech
provinces of Moravia and Bohemia respectively, that is, from the
turbulent center of the empire's nationalities crisis and also of the
ritual murder hysteria. This category of German Jews born in Bohemia and Moravia who became great men in Vienna also included
Sigmund Freud, Gustav Mahler, Karl Kraus, and Viktor Adler.

Benedikt and Bacher regarded their newspaper as the organ of German liberalism. The meaning of this liberalism was summarized by the historian Adam Wandruszka, who wrote a history of the newspaper: "Uncompromising advocacy of the principles of freedom and progress, law and justice, of the close alliance with Germany and the cultural predomination of the German element within the monarchy, assured the newspaper its monopoly of the German liberal population of the monarchy." Carl Schorske defined Austrian liberal culture more generally as "centered upon rational man, whose scientific domination of nature and whose moral control of himself were expected to create the good society." Nineteenth-century European liberals, according to one standard history textbook, "believed in what was modern, enlightened, efficient, reasonable, and fair." With values such as these, the editors of the *Neue Freie Presse* and their liberal readers could only have been horrified to find their faith in reason and progress shattered by hysterical accusations of ritual murder. But these editors were also Jews, and for them the hysteria was particularly menacing. They regarded their paper as an organ of German liberalism, but to anti-Semites and other enemies the *Neue Freie Presse* was easily stigmatized as a "Jewish paper." Moritz Benedikt especially resented this, for he considered himself a German, and his liberalism envisioned a hopeful future of social assimilation among Germans, Christian and Jewish. Theodor Herzl, though he was the cultural editor of the *Neue Freie Presse,* and thus one of its most powerful figures, could not persuade Benedikt even to mention Zionism in the newspaper. According to Henry Wickham Steed, future editor of the London *Times,* Benedikt was "fanatically devoted to the propagation of Jewish-German 'Liberal' assimilationist doctrine," and "ready to sacrifice journalistic and other advantages on the altar of his peculiar politico-racial faith." This faith could have received no more grievous blow than the explosion of hysteria over the Hilsner case in 1899.

The most powerful weapon of the *Neue Freie Presse,* according to Hitler, was a deadly silence; according to Zweig, the Viennese bourgeoisie was ready to see as inconsequential that which the *Neue Freie Presse* ignored. So Freud despaired at the thought that *The Interpretation of Dreams* would not get a review. So Karl Kraus was never again mentioned in the *Neue Freie Presse* when he abandoned it to start a paper of his own. So Theodor Herzl found himself on the point of a similar secession when Benedikt refused to report a word about the fledgling Zionist movement. And so the anti-Semitic agitation provoked by the Hilsner affair was passed over with minimal attention. One can almost sense the editors squirming with discomfort behind that peculiarly lighthearted No-vember tale of the insanely deluded embroiderer, an elliptical para-ble to sum up a season of explosive irrational hatred. When the Polna murder itself was referred to in an editorial heading, it was "The Fable of Ritual Murder" or else "Blood Fairy Tale"—*Blut-märchen*—a phrase of dismissal. The editors approached the whole phenomenon in a spirit of aloof reticence, silent and dismissive. This reticence did in fact constitute a journalistic "sacrifice," as Steed suggested, for it left an apparent lacuna in the reporting of the news of the day. However, something came along at just the right time to fill that space, a pair of sensational cases.

If one returns now to the editorial comment on the Hummel trial, one finds oneself wondering whether the issue of child abuse also served as a vessel for suppressed horror over the exactly contempo-rary ritual murder hysteria:

> All day long to have to listen to the details of a deed of unprecedented crudeness! But one's indignation is finally dulled, because one can't apply a human standard of measurement to such dreadful behavior . . . A complete explanation is not to be found. With painful surprise one says to oneself that in an age of civilization there can be such people only by an atavism.

This view of child abuse was also just how a nineteenth-century Viennese Jewish liberal would have articulated his view of anti-Semitic agitation over ritual murder: crude, immeasurably inhu-man, dreadful, inexplicable, painful, uncivilized, atavistic. There is a certain tragic irony to the perspective of the liberal on the thresh-old of the twentieth century, who could see irrational anti-Semi-tism and vicious child abuse as atavisms out of the primitive past— and not as harbingers of things to come. For how could a nineteenth-century liberal, who believed in the progress of civiliza-tion, suspect that the new century would bring anti-Semitism to unimaginable proportions and consequences, and would also see child abuse recognized as a terrifyingly common syndrome?

In *The Interpretation of Dreams,* when Freud analyzed the "dreamwork," he proposed a process of "displacement" which oper-ated in the formation of dreams. Where "censorship" prevented some psychologically disturbing element from entering the dream directly, there might take place a "transference and displacement of psychical intensities" which allowed some other element to substi-tute. The phrasing of the rhetorical response to the Hummel trial in the *Neue Freie Presse,* as quoted above, makes it possible to suppose that child abuse did indeed "displace" anti-Semitism, which was subjected to the editor's policy of self-censorship; the psychological intensity of rhetorical repugnance seems almost to have been transferred from one issue to the other. What is absolutely certain is that one issue substituted for the other in a more straightforwardly material manner: as printed matter filling the columns of the *Neue Freie Presse*. For there certainly was one subject that was strikingly passed over, while at the same time the paper introduced a new subject which had never been discussed before in the Viennese press.

Child abuse offered sufficient potential for sensationalism to serve as an effective substitute, even a distraction. And, furthermore, there was an implicit thematic connection which gave a certain point to the substitution: the undeniable reality of child murder to substitute for the "fable" of ritual murder. This was the sense in which the *Neue Freie Presse* appealed for attention to child abuse, rather than to the "eternal senseless vilification of the Jews." It is difficult to tell whether the editors made the connection consciously or half-consciously; they might have just been following their professional reflexes, for certainly the adoption of a substitute issue made excellent journalistic sense. The child abuse sensation of 1899 came at just the right time for the troubled spirit of Jewish liberal journalism—which is as much as to say that without the troubling anti-Semitic agitation, child abuse might not have become such a huge sensation at all. It was a remarkable coincidence that, in November 1899, two sets of parents came to trial in Vienna for murdering their children, but that alone did not determine that the leading newspaper of the city would make those trials into the great issue of the day. For child abuse was a subject so unpleasant that, throughout the nineteenth century, the public had rarely been willing to recognize its existence. In November 1899, however, there was another urgent subject of the day that was, for some Viennese at least, more unpleasant still.

## A BUTCHER'S KNIFE

For the Viennese who created and patronized the extraordinary culture of the fin de siècle, there seemed to exist, however briefly, some profound inner relation, perhaps neither fully conscious nor explicitly articulated, between the horrors of child abuse and those of the anti-Semitic blood libel. In November 1899, they were two specters, darkly presiding over the apocalyptic death of one century and the birth of the next. But the connection was neither uncertain nor vague, and the two horrors were, in fact, interlocking pieces of the same sociological puzzle. The crucial question was simply this: If Leopold Hilsner did not kill Agnes Hruza—and there was virtually no evidence that he murdered her, let alone ritually murdered her—then who did?

On October 11, two days before Hedwig Keplinger and her daughter were found dead in the woods, the *Neue Freie Presse* contained a brief notice that in Polna the police were questioning the mother and the brother of Agnes Hruza. Then on October 16, the day that Hedwig Keplinger and her daughter were buried together, there was another short notice that in Polna the police were searching the house of the murdered girl's mother. The very next day, a somewhat longer notice announced the results of the search: A knife had been found and confiscated by the police in the mother's house. It was a knife that was used for butchering pigs (obviously it could have nothing to do with Jewish ritual), but the police seemed to feel that it could also have been used (in the coy phrase of the newspaper) for "another less harmless purpose."

So then, supposing that Hilsner was innocent, who might have killed Agnes Hruza? In Prague the future president of Czechoslovakia, Thomas Masaryk, bravely played the part of Emile Zola in the Hilsner affair, and in 1900 Masaryk published his justification of Hilsner, *The Meaning of the Polna Crime for Ritual Superstitions*. Masaryk was largely concerned with exposing the flimsiness of the evidence against Hilsner, but at the same time, like Zola, Masaryk could also accuse. Above all he accused the superstitious anti-Semitic masses, and, in addition, he pointed a finger at certain suspicious individuals in the matter of the crime itself. Masaryk began by observing that the anti-Semitic agitation had established a vivid juxtaposition of images between the evil Jew and the loving family of the murdered girl. Since her father was dead, the family consisted of her mother and brother.

> In contrast to Hilsner, the warmest sympathy was called forth, unconsciously and consciously, for the Hruza family. Who could help being moved by the misfortune of the young victim and her old mother? It is only the sign of a healthy moral sense that people, shrinking back from the crime with dread, should think of their own families in relation to it.

Masaryk felt that people's fantasies and emotions were further influenced by the "romantic and unusual" nature of the crime: committed in the woods just before Easter. People "experienced it as a sort of theatrical tragedy." And the Catholic clerical forces behind the anti-Semitic agitation (such as Lueger and his Christian Socialist party in Vienna) helped make the girl into a "martyr," while "the surviving family members were presented, in contrast to the accused, almost as ideal beings."

Yet, in spite of "healthy moral sense," it was just these "ideal beings" whom Masaryk found most suspect when he analyzed their testimony in the case. The mother of Agnes Hruza took a suspiciously long time to become concerned about her missing daughter, and then, when she did take an interest, was immediately sure the girl had been murdered. (Others thought the missing girl had run away to Vienna to go into service—as Hedwig Keplinger had so fatefully done.) There was local evidence that the Hruza family was far from loving, was indeed so quarrelsome that local opinion suspected them of the crime—before a Jewish suspect was conveniently apprehended and accused. The mother showed herself both eager and contradictory in her attempts to implicate Hilsner, and Masaryk thought it would be well worth looking into the death of the girl's father seven years before, because he too was found dead in the woods. Finally, at the time of the murder of Agnes Hruza, it had been observed that the brother's hands were covered with scratches, while the mother had a mysterious bruise on her face—possibly the marks of some recent struggle. In short, Masaryk made it perfectly clear that, if everyone had not been so ready to believe that a Jew killed Agnes Hruza for the sake of her blood, the girl's mother and brother would have been the most prominent suspects. J'accuse.

Freud in 1899 appealed to his readers not to reject flatly as monstrous his proposal of Oedipal hostilities within the family. "Who could help being moved by the misfortune of the young victim and her old mother?" asked Masaryk, with ironic intent. How then could the most respectable newspaper of bourgeois Vienna dare to imply that this same old mother had slaughtered her daughter like a pig with a butcher's knife? Would respectable readers accept such a suggestion? But remember: The discovery of the knife was announced in Vienna on the day after Hedwig Keplinger's funeral, the day after she was buried together with the daughter she had shot in cold blood. Everyone in Vienna knew that Hedwig Keplinger had killed her daughter. A month later, as the anti-Semitic agitation intensified, everyone in Vienna knew that Juliane Hummel had killed her daughter Anna. If Anna Hummel was a little martyr, there was certainly no one who thought her surviving parents were "ideal beings." And there was yet another martyrdom still to come to trial, another case of child abuse and murder. The child abuse sensation of 1899 shattered, for a moment, the Victorian idealization of the family. It revealed, beyond any question, that parents could indeed butcher their children. The prosecutor at the Hummel trial found that "one could almost doubt the omnipotence of maternal love." In fact this doubt was but a momentary disruption of Victorian domestic sentimentality, and the issue of child abuse would soon be buried and repressed again. But at the moment of its unprecedented eruption in 1899, disturbing though it may have been, the child abuse sensation carried a valuable message to those who were horrified by the Polna case. Nasty murders could indeed take place within families: even mothers could murder their daughters.

No Freudian could fail to notice the potentially subliminal association of Anna Hummel and Agnes Hruza with their identical initials. But that is only a detail. Child abuse was no mere substitute for anti-Semitic agitation in the pages of the liberal press, no mere evasion of or distraction from a greater unpleasantness. The child abuse cases of November, following upon the case of Hedwig Keplinger in October, contained within them the "solution" to the murder mystery at Polna. They lent credibility to the most likely alternative explanation of who could have killed Agnes Hruza. The anti-Semitic masses of Austria-Hungary ranted about ritual murder; the civilized liberals of Vienna responded by discovering the phenomenon of child abuse. Both were unthinkably monstrous atavisms—but one was a superstition, a fable, a fairy tale, and the other was a matter of record and fact. It was thus that readers of the *Neue Freie Presse* weighed the issue of child abuse against the eternal senseless vilification of the Jews.

## "BRAVO"

"Were you fond of the child?" the judge asked Juliane Hummel, and when she said she was, the spectators laughed. For how could a mother have been fond of a child whom she had tortured to death? Later in the trial, after the catalog of her atrocities had been fully reviewed, the judge put his question again: "Do you still dare to say that you loved the child?" And this time Juliane Hummel said no, just that one word. There was no laughter in the courtroom now, but rather something almost as inappropriate: People clapped their hands in applause. Her retraction and reversal, her admission that she did not love her child, was so psychologically reassuring—and at the same time so dramatically satisfying—that the spectators

could not help revealing themselves as an audience—an appreciative dramatic audience in a city famous for its connoisseurship of
the theater. When the death sentence was announced for Joseph
and Juliane Hummel at the very end of the trial, there were cries of
bravo from that audience. The *Neue Freie Presse* recorded "an
acclamation the like of which we cannot remember ever before at a
condemnation to death." That clapping of hands, and especially
those cries of bravo, harkened back to the first heralding of the
Hummel trial by the invocation of Hauptmann's *Hannele*—and
further back to the juxtaposition of Hedwig Keplinger and Sarah
Bernhardt. Once again sociological ugliness was transformed and
contained by an obsessively theatrical vision.

The reception and appreciation of the issue of child abuse did not
take place only in the courtroom. Indeed, the courtroom was just a
stage within the larger stages of turn-of-the-century Vienna and the
declining Habsburg empire. If, within the courtroom, child abuse
was conceived according to contemporary values of dramatic form
and class comedy, outside the courtroom the issue was interwoven
with such larger preoccupations as the separate world of the urban
lower classes and the mass hysteria of superstitious anti-Semitism.
The press acted as intermediary between the inner stage and the
outer world, in fact opening up the audience so that spectators in
the courtroom could be joined in their horror and laughter and
applause by the Viennese public at large. The spectators and the
newspapers, part of the same culture, could help each other along;
the former cried bravo, and the latter invoked *Hannele*. Above all,
they seemed to have the same sorts of instincts when it came to
controlling and diminishing the implications of the trial—whether
it was a matter of refusing to face psychological complexity, or
laughing at parental platitudes in lower-class dialect. For if the issue
of child abuse could not be repressed in November 1899, if indeed
there was even reason to bring it out into the open at just that time,
there was also from the beginning an unmistakable determination to
neutralize the issue, limit its implications, and eventually make it
go away.

"In the moment when you cry bravo, you make everything into
theater again." This comment, so perfectly apt for the conclusion of the Hummel trial, was actually a line from Viennese drama,
from Schnitzler's one-act play *The Green Cockatoo*. The play was
set in Paris in 1789, at a theatrical club where aristocrats went to
see actors act the parts of violent criminals. The date, however, was
July 14, and the reality of violent revolution at the Bastille was
about to intrude upon the titillating theatrical violence of the club.

The play had its Viennese premiere in March 1899, and it was so obviously a play about Schnitzler's own time and place that the Austrian censorship was only temporarily taken in by the eigh-teenth-century French setting. Eventually the authorities caught on, and began to suspect that the play was insidiously revolutionary; it was said that the imperial archduchesses themselves, the daughters of Franz Joseph, had found the play offensive. *The Green Cockatoo* was removed from the autumn repertory of the Burgtheater, and the famous Viennese actor Joseph Kainz was then scheduled to perform instead as King Ahasuerus in Grillparzer's *Esther*. Were it not for the change in repertory, *The Green Cockatoo* might well have been performed at the time of the Hummel trial. There was, in fact, a convergence between the trial and the play—which illus-trated just the point that Schnitzler was making: "Reality enters into the play—the play into reality." Perceptions of child abuse were conditioned by the prevailing cultural values of fin-de-siècle Vienna—the very same values that the city's leading playwright explored in his play of that year. For the ugly sociological reality of child abuse was confronted no more seriously and honestly at the Hummel trial than Schnitzler's French aristocrats faced the reality of violence and revolution in *The Green Cockatoo*.

"In the moment when you cry bravo, you make everything into theater again—and the pleasant horror is gone." So spoke the cyni-cal poet, the leading part intended for Joseph Kainz. But an uneasy marquis replied: "I don't find the horror so pleasant. Let us applaud, my friend, so that we can free ourselves from this spell." They could have been spectators at the Hummel trial. The case of Hedwig Keplinger could be easily sentimentalized and aesthetically trans-formed; the Hummel case cast a more oppressive spell. And if the spectators at the Hummel trial, by cheering and laughing and ap-plauding, were able to master their horror and free themselves from the weighty implications of child abuse, there was yet another test before them. For the Hummel trial was followed two weeks later by another trial—at which the very same issues of child abuse and child murder were posed in a form that was still harder to confront and, at the same time, still harder to conjure away. Vienna was not yet free of that hypnotic spell cast by the grotesquely mutilated corpse of a battered child.

# CHAPTER THREE

## The Kutschera Case:
## Child Abuse and the Innocence
## of Childhood

*Sigmund Freud with his wife and daughter, Anna*

## "MOST PRECIOUS PARENTS"

THE Hummel trial of November 14 and the Kutschera trial, which ran through the last days of November, represented the two seismographic peaks of the child abuse sensation. Indeed without those two cases there would have been no sensation at all. During the two weeks that intervened between these trials, however, the press registered those lesser quakes and rumblings that reflected the new and exceptional consciousness of the moment. The strange, romantic suicides and murders, reported as minor items of newsworthy violence in the month before the Hummel trial, seemed to give way all at once to a new interest in violence against children and the possibility of parental abuse.

On November 17, three days after the Hummel trial, Stephanie Marscha, the thirteen-year-old daughter of a Viennese ironworker, attempted to commit suicide by jumping out of a fourth-floor window; she had been issued a reprimand in school, and was afraid of being punished at home. Just such an incident had occurred in October (the twelve-year-old Frieda W.), but in November it received far more attention. Stephanie's suicide letter to her parents was quoted in full.

> With trembling hands and weeping eyes, I write you this letter. In school I have been reprimanded for laziness, chatter, and laughter. I was given a letter of reprimand which you, best of parents, were to sign. And on that account, for fear of punishment, I am putting an end to my life itself. I also want to spare you, most precious parents, the grief and offense to which I condemn you with this letter from school. I well know, dear parents, that this deed I am going to commit will hurt you more than the letter of reprimand, but I think that this hurt will not last forever, at any rate not for Mother. For afterwards you will have one person less to cause you grief and offense. For all that I have done up till now, I beg you on my knees for forgiveness . . .

In spite of the expressions of devotion to the best, most precious, and dearest parents, on closer examination it was discovered that

119

Stephanie's mother—actually her stepmother—punished the girl harshly for the smallest offenses. The stepmother came from the middle class, and found it hard to adjust to being the wife of a worker. When the ironworker visited his daughter in the hospital and asked why she had behaved so "godlessly," she replied: "I wanted to be saved!"

It is possible that Stephanie Marscha's fear of punishment became suicidal terror precisely because everyone was talking about the details of the Hummel case, and it is probable that the Hummel case made Vienna more sensitive to this new incident. It is certain, however, that the Hummel case was directly behind the apprehension of a woman who was brutally abusing her seven-year-old retarded daughter; the police were notified by someone who had been following the Hummel trial, and therefore made a report. The child was taken away, and the mother was to be prosecuted. Meanwhile, a Viennese servant girl also faced prosecution for dropping the five-month-old infant of her employer; the baby's neck was broken. And a cleaning crew discovered in a Viennese roof gutter the corpse of an infant who must have been killed years before. Children were not the only victims of violence of course: On November 18, the mother of eight children killed herself, drowning herself in a well, because her husband was caught stealing two pairs of shoes. On November 19, a locksmith's assistant was tried for attempting to murder his wife with a hammer; they too had had eight children, of whom only three had survived. On that same day, Freud wrote to Fliess that little Anna had a cold, and the young poet Martin was not doing well in school. Freud wished he could visit Fliess in Berlin for a day: "I could tell you all sorts of funny things about Vienna."

On November 21, Victoria Kail was charged in court with the "negligent killing" of her two-year-old child. She had left the child in its crib for a few minutes without raising the bars, and there was a fatal fall. (Two-year-olds do not usually die when they fall out of their cribs, and nowadays such a story would be immediately suspect as concealing a possible case of abuse.) The child was a little girl named Anna. Neighbors testified to beatings with a cooking spoon, and the *Neue Freie Presse* gave the trial considerable attention, ready to determine whether this was "an Affaire Hummel small-scale." (This grandiose designation almost seemed to rank the Hummel case with the Affaire Dreyfus in Paris.) But Victoria Kail was judged to be no Juliane Hummel in the end, no cruel "raven mother," as the prosecution charged. She and her husband, a carpenter's assistant (they had married just recently and legitimized their two children born out of wedlock), testified that they beat their children just lightly, "as one usually does with a child." The mother mentioned particularly administering light beatings when Anna was "unclean." She had left Anna's room for a minute only, to get a glass of water for three-year-old Friedrich, who was apparently in the room at the time of the fatal fall. Victoria Kail was observed to be sickly and excitable, actually suffering convulsions in the courtroom as the charges were read. The prosecution insisted that the punishment of such a mother not be regarded as an infringement against domestic freedom, and argued that in England— "certainly a land of great freedom"—such a case would merit three years of hard labor. The judge, however, sentenced Victoria Kail to one month.

On the following day, November 22, the missing twelve-year-old Gustav Hohn was brought to the attention of the Viennese public. The son of a wholesaler, he had run away from home a week before when his stepmother punished him for tearing his pants; she pushed him through a window, and struck him on the head with a hammer. He told his sister that he'd rather drown himself than go home again to the punishments of his stepmother. Vienna was advised to look out for a blond boy with blue-gray eyes, dark blue pants (patches at the knees), black socks, mountain-climbing shoes, and a reddish-brown hat with a green band. That same day, Theodor Herzl wrote in his diary about the letter he was sending to the Russian czar, submitting "the Zionist plan for the final solution of the Jewish Question," and humbly requesting an audience in St. Petersburg. "The solution of this painful question," wrote Herzl to the czar, "would be a great and splendid act, worthy of our time, worthy of the most magnanimous sovereign."

On November 25, a team of Meiji Japanese legal observers studied Austrian justice at the trial of the butcher's assistant for the attempted murder of his beloved Leopoldine Zipperer. It is not easy to imagine what the Japanese made of the summation for the defense: "If the jury members saw such an incident in the theater, they would emotionally dry their eyes, and their wives and daughters would weep." On November 26, the *Neue Freie Presse* published its "Appeal to All Feeling People," calling for a splendid monument to shelter abused children. On November 27, Mahler conducted his new production of *Die Meistersinger,* bowing his head before the hissing of the anti-Semites. Then on November 28, the Kutschera trial opened, and, with that, the minor intervening cases of Stephanie Marscha, and Victoria Kail, and Gustav Hohn, were reduced to overshadowed insignificance, merely related incidents between the "Affaire Hummel" and the tremendous three-day Kutschera trial.

Together these two trials may constitute one of the most significant explorations of child abuse in history, until our own times, and the Kutschera case, partly because the Hummel case had already prepared the ground, exercised an even more compulsive fascination upon Vienna. For three days the courtroom was mobbed, and mounted police had to hold back the crowd outside when there was no more room inside. The newspapers of Vienna gave pages and pages of descriptions and transcriptions. One might have looked at the front page and supposed that Vienna was properly concerned with the doomed empire's fatal nationality problems, as well as the important foreign news of the distant Boer War. But one had only to open the newspaper to discover inside that Vienna was utterly obsessed with this excruciating case of child abuse and murder.

## "AN OBSCURE AND SOMBRE POEM"

"At this time the Moosbrugger case was attracting much public attention." So began the eighteenth chapter of Robert Musil's *The Man Without Qualities*. This gigantic novel, which recreated in profound analytical complexity the final years of Habsburg Austria, also examined what it meant, subjectively, for Vienna to be obsessed with a case of violent crime. Moosbrugger was one of the most important figures in the novel, a carpenter who had savagely stabbed to death a prostitute, for no comprehensible reason. His case became intertwined with the development of the novel, and he himself became an object of fascination to the other characters, as he was to the entire city. In 1899 the newspapers devoted pages and pages to the Hummel and Kutschera cases, while crowds mobbed the courtroom and were turned away at the gates—and Musil, many years later, wrote about what such an affair might have felt like for the people who lived through it, the subjective experience of public obsession.

> And there was, furthermore, the remarkable circumstance that, even when the facts had scarcely become publicly known, Moosbrugger's insane excesses had been felt to be "something interesting, for once" by thousands of people who deplored the sensationalism of the newspapers, by busy officials as by fourteen-year-old schoolboys and housewives wrapped in the haze of their domestic cares. Although indeed one sighed over such a monstrosity, one was inwardly more preoccupied with it than with one's own affairs. Indeed, it was quite likely to happen that some staid assistant under-secretary or bank-manager

would say to his sleepy wife as they were going to bed: "What would you do now if I were Moosbrugger?"

The child abuse cases, undoubtedly, possessed the same dual aspect as the Moosbrugger affair, both public sensation and private obsession. They even offered a similar pretext for illicit fantasies of violence.

Through the protagonist, Ulrich, the man without qualities, Musil explored in greater depth the compelling fascination of the fictional case of murder.

And by what qualities did Moosbrugger cause the excitement and the gooseflesh that for half of the two million people living in this city amounted to practically as much as a family quarrel or a broken-off engagement? Here the case stirred up personal emotions to an extraordinary extent, invading areas of the soul that at other times lay dormant . . . This horrible way that society had of toying with its victims preoccupied Ulrich. He felt the same thing going on in himself too. There was no impulse in him either to liberate Moosbrugger or to go to the aid of the law, and yet all his feelings stood up on end like the fur on a cat's back. Something beyond his understanding made Moosbrugger a closer concern of his than the leading of his own life; Moosbrugger held him spellbound like an obscure and sombre poem in which everything was faintly distorted and displaced, revealing a mutilated significance drifting in the depths of the mind.

Those who read in the newspapers about the Hummel case and the Kutschera case must have felt as Ulrich did: the gooseflesh, the cat's fur standing on end, the invasion of dormant parts of the soul. Some of this we can still feel ourselves when we read about these cases a century later. But Musil's image of Ulrich held "spellbound" by Moosbrugger chimed with Schnitzler's invocation of the "spell" that held the titillated audience of French aristocrats. At the same time, Ulrich's consciousness of something "distorted and displaced," of "a mutilated significance drifting in the depths of the mind," corresponded to Freud's analysis of "dreamwork" and "displacement." These phrases and ideas came from the same cultural milieu that shaped the presentation of the child abuse cases. And above all, it was Musil's likening of the Moosbrugger case to "an obscure and sombre poem" that conveyed the special character of preoccupation with violence in turn-of-the-century Vienna. In fact, as it turned out, one of those who was most articulately obsessed with the Kutschera case was none other than Felix Dörmann, that archetype of the fin-de-siècle poet who had taken such an interest in Hedwig Keplinger.

Juliane Hummel held the central place in the Hummel trial; her husband, Joseph, likewise charged and likewise executed, remained on the periphery of public attention. But Juliane Hummel was so timid, so quiet, so self-effacing in the courtroom that the spectators felt almost cheated of the monster they had hoped to find. In Marie Kutschera they found a personality to merit and justify such a public sensation, and she, much more than Juliane Hummel, exercised the kind of personal fascination that Musil attributed to Moosbrugger. Marie Kutschera was the stepmother of seven children, and all seven of them were so sadistically abused that she was said to have made their home into a torture chamber. The eleven-year-old girl, not a healthy child, succumbed to such treatment, and died on the night of December 10, 1898, almost a year before the trial. The girl's name was Anna—one more detail to link this case to the Hummel case, which it so gruesomely resembled. Marie Kutschera was being tried for her life, charged with the murder of her stepdaughter. So utterly central was Marie Kutschera in this case that her husband, Rudolf Kutschera, the father of the children, was being tried alongside his wife only on the lesser charge of aiding and abetting her in the murder. While she faced the gallows, he could be condemned to at most twenty years' imprisonment.

For the *Neue Freie Presse,* the Kutschera case began not as a poem, but like the story of Hedwig Keplinger, as a fairy tale. In fairy tales there were cruel stepmothers, and the newspaper cited the examples of Cinderella, whose stepmother made her sleep in ashes, and Snow White, whose stepmother commissioned the huntsman to bring back her internal organs as proof of her death. But just as *Hannele* was deemed not tragic enough to do justice to the Hummel case ("life does not follow poetry"), so the fairy tales were mere stepping-stones for approaching the full horror of the Kutschera case. The stepmothers of Cinderella and Snow White, compared to Marie Kutschera, were "gentle doves compared to the hawk who tears its victim to pieces with savagery." The image of the hawk suggested the power of the fascination that she exercised, far more powerful than that of Juliane Hummel, who was so disappointingly gentle in appearance.

The invocation of the fairy tale stepmothers emphasized the one aspect of the Kutschera case that could have made it less disturbing than the Hummel case: Juliane Hummel was a mother, while Marie Kutschera was only a stepmother. "Faith in the mother" did not have to be redeemed this time in quite the same way. There was, however, another factor of comparison that made the Kutschera case ultimately far more disturbing and far more difficult to deal with, especially for readers of the *Neue Freie Presse*. Rudolf Kutschera was not, like Joseph Hummel, a laundry laborer. Rudolf Kutschera was a post official, a civil servant, a respectable member of the middle class. While the *Neue Freie Presse* began its coverage by telling fairy tales about stepmothers, the *Arbeiter-Zeitung* began by virtually crowing over the fact that the accused parents belonged to "the so-called better circles." The lowliness of the Hummel parents had made it that much easier to dismiss them, even laugh at them, and keep the child abuse issue at a reassuring distance from bourgeois Vienna. Child abuse could not be so easily disposed of in the Kutschera case.

Juliane Hummel was socially so out of place in the courtroom that her attempts to defend herself were hopelessly, pathetically—even laughably—ineffective. She never stood a chance. Rudolf and Marie Kutschera, however, were far more presentable defendants, and far better able to mount a serious defense. It took only a one-day trial to arrive at a unanimous conviction and death sentence for Joseph and Juliane Hummel. The Kutschera trial lasted three full days, and the outcome was neither obvious nor unanimous. "I can only say, with a clear conscience, that I am not aware of having done anything wrong," announced Marie Kutschera to the court on the first day of the trial. The press reported that she responded to the prosecution with real energy and passion, that she defended herself like a lioness or a tigress. Such images, even more than the hawk, suggested the power of her "spell," in which repulsion could even mingle with a certain element of strange admiration.

That the defense in the Kutschera trial was long and strong was highly significant; it meant the most problematic issues of child abuse received a much fuller airing than at the previous trial. The line of defense was fundamentally the same, and Marie Kutschera assured the court: "I beat the children, but I didn't abuse them, only disciplined them." Whereas everything the Hummel parents said was lightly and dismissively passed over, the Kutschera parents virtually turned their own trial into a trial of the children. Marie Kutschera insisted that the children were not simply disobedient, but utterly depraved, deserving of the most cruel punishments; they had been disgustingly corrupted by the "housekeeper" who took care of them during the years between the death of their mother and their father's remarriage. This housekeeper was allegedly a prostitute, referred to by her last name as "the Felzmann." So it was because of the evil influence of "the Felzmann" that the oldest girl

Ludovica deserved to be stripped and whipped—for the girl was a slut. And her brother Gustav had to be tied down, hand and foot, for a week—because he was plotting to poison his parents. Eleven-year-old Anna, who finally died, was regularly beaten on her fingers, because she was always stealing the brandy—and was furthermore involved in precocious sexual practices.

The moral character of the children was extensively debated in the courtroom, but the medical condition of the children's bodies was a fact not subject to debate. Their wounds and injuries were described in excruciating detail, and the court doctor presented an autopsy report on Anna, which catalogued her injuries, in order to argue that the sum of the abuses was the cause of her death. One arm was broken; there were countless abrasions, lumps, and scabs; the lower extremities were covered with blue and brown spots; there were infected wounds on the fingers; and one fingernail was completely missing so that the bone was laid bare. The prosecutor, Kleeborn again, in his summation showed himself well aware that such a corpse could cast a spell of its own.

> Little Anna was a child full of innocence and charm. She touched the hearts of all who knew her—but no one had the power to save her from death. And she, who in life could not protest because the murderous hand of her stepmother held her mouth closed, in death she speaks to us. And just as in the old legend the wounds of the victim begin to bleed when the murderer approaches the bier, so before our inner eye the child has raised herself up, and with a mutilated hand indicating the stigmata of her wounds, her blood accusation cries out to heaven. And she will be heard.

This was a trial of spells and incantations, of legends and fairy tales, of stigmata and of cries to heaven. And the reason that the prosecutor had to call up from the dead the mutilated body of the child to address the jurymen and the spectators, was to counter the spell of that lioness, that tigress, that hawk, who held the compelling center of the trial and invaded the soul of Vienna.

What was the nature of the fascination that Marie Kutschera exercised over the anonymous men and women of the Viennese public, on the housewives and schoolboys and officials, on the staid assistant undersecretaries and bank managers? Would she have been for the man without qualities, as Moosbrugger was, "a closer concern of his than the leading of his own life"? As it happens, there were recorded two anonymous letters that Marie Kutschera received, hinting at the power of the impression that she made on the anonymous public. One was printed in the press at the time of the trial as representative of public opinion:

The complete contempt of humanity and all the tortures of hell are not sufficient punishment for an infamous woman like you, who has tormented to death a defenseless child. Any animal is better than such a woman.

The second anonymous letter, actually a telegram, was printed only after Marie Kutschera had been condemned to death, printed only "as a curiosity." The telegram was sent to Marie Kutschera by a number of women to express their sympathy for her and their faith in her innocence. The concluding words of the telegram were just this: "God help you!"

## "COMPLETELY DIFFERENT, COMPLETELY DIFFERENT"

Marie Kutschera was born in the town of Budweis, known today as Ceske Budejowice, for it is in Czechoslovakia. She came from the province of Bohemia, which in 1899 was the heart of Austria's poisonous nationalities problem, as well as the origin of the anti-Semitic ritual murder agitation. Budweis was a hundred miles from Vienna, but Bohemia was so distinctly a separate province that the press could report that Marie Kutschera came "from far away." At any rate, there was probably something reassuring about the fact that she—like Hedwig Keplinger and Juliane Hummel—was not truly Viennese. Her first husband was a prison official, and this was originally reported in the press in such a way as to make it sound as if she herself had been in prison; her lawyer had to write to correct this misleading impression and testify to her thoroughly respectable past. Marie Kutschera was a Catholic. She was a widow when she married Rudolf Kutschera and brought her own child to make a family with his seven. Anna Kutschera died within the year, on December 10, 1898, and her stepmother was arrested the following week.

Marie Kutschera gave her testimony on the first day of the trial, and, though she was frequently recalled to the stand on the subsequent days, though she was always the central figure no matter who was testifying, it was on that first day that she established and impressed herself upon the courtroom and in the public mind. She was thirty-nine years old, small in stature, and she appeared dressed in black. Dark blond hair was carefully put up behind. Her yellowish skin was wrinkled like parchment and oddly bloodless. Her features were hard, as if of stone, and there was something masculine about them, in the opinion of one reporter. The nose was large and flattened; the eyes were small, deeply set, and piercing. The *Arbeiter-Zeitung* found it to be the head of Megaera, one of the furies: "From the first glance one believes the woman capable of the deed she is accused of." The *Neue Freie Presse* noticed that she moved her lips, as if whispering to herself, and the paper speculated with more of an open mind: "If she is guilty, her punishment has already begun."

The latter organ, famous for its cultural and theatrical concerns, borrowed from the world of the stage to render for its readers the impression made by Marie Kutschera in the courtroom. "Her wrinkled, stiff, dismal face reminds one of Death as he was performed by the unforgettable actor Robert—except that she lacks his nobility." The *Neue Freie Presse* was so timely in its theatrical consciousness and so confident of the theatrical culture of its readers that the reference to the unforgettable actor—now long forgotten—could be casually taken for granted. The character of Death was presumably from Hofmannsthal's celebrated verse play of 1893, *The Fool and Death*, in which Claudio, the troubled aesthete, was confronted with and claimed by Death himself. This odd presentation of Marie Kutschera was marvelously characteristic of fin-de-siècle Vienna. In the comparison was the hinted suggestion that Marie Kutschera was somehow symbolically bringing down the curtain on the aesthetic nineties. At the same time, this vision of Marie Kutschera as performing a part belonged to the world of *The Green Cockatoo,* where acts of violence took place in some undefined realm between reality and theater. Yet while Juliane Hummel was presented as a figure from popular comic drama, the monstrosity of Marie Kutschera was dignified with an analogy to the highly serious poetic drama of the fin de siècle.

Certain personal characteristics clearly differentiated her conduct on the witness stand from that of Juliane Hummel. No one had failed to observe that Juliane Hummel was so surprisingly quiet, so hard to hear. Marie Kutschera, however, was characterized by the reverse formulation: everyone noticed that she was hard of hearing. While Juliane Hummel was constantly chided to speak up so that everyone could hear her replies, Marie Kutschera required everyone else to speak up so that she could hear their questions. The psychological balance was symbolically reversed, especially since her weak hearing gave her an air of imperviousness to what was being said around her and about her. Furthermore, whereas Juliane Hummel was so notably reticent, so hesitant to speak—very possibly because she felt so socially out of place—Marie Kutschera was described as "long-winded." She did not limit herself to hesitant little replies to the questions put to her. She spoke at length to defend herself, to tell her side of the story. In this respect, too, the psychological balance was quite different from that of the Hummel trial, and this was surely connected to the different social classes of the defendants, as well as their different personalities. With complete confidence Marie Kutschera replied to the judge's first routine question about whether she understood the charge and considered herself guilty: "Indeed I well understand the charge, but in no respect do I consider myself guilty. It will be shown that everything was completely different, completely different." In that final repetition her longwindedness appeared as an aspect of her confidence, and at the same time a consequence of her having a story of her own to tell.

In another revealing moment, early in her testimony, she was cool enough to turn the judge's question rhetorically back on him. He asked whether she starved the children, and, denying it indignantly, she also pointed out that a post official's salary was not much when it came to taking care of so many children. "Please, Herr Hofrath," she said, comfortable with his title, "you figure out what's left after you've deducted rent, clothing, shoes, and so on." If one thinks back to the Hummel trial, it is simply impossible to imagine Juliane Hummel turning a question back on that other judge, who hectored her so sarcastically. Marie Kutschera was much bolder, and the force of that injunction—"you figure it out"—was also felt by the jury, the spectators, the reporters, and the public.

The "longwinded" heart of her testimony was her account of what happened on the night of December 10, 1898, the night of Anna's death. The events of that night would be gone over again and again during the course of the trial, and Marie Kutschera's version was indeed, as she said, "completely different, completely different," but her version was the first to be presented from the witness stand. As a courtroom witness she may have been longwinded, but as a storyteller she showed herself to be not without a certain talent for dramatic narrative.

> Emil and I accompanied his father to the station, because that evening he [Rudolf Kutschera] had to go away. On the return I bought cheese and butter for the evening meal, and then we went home. There I found all the children still awake, Anna too, whom I had already sent to bed before going out. Anna was especially loud, dancing around the room and crying out. When I put her to bed she couldn't be calmed. Again and again she stood up and started to sing, so completely without sense: *Ja, ja!* I asked what was wrong with her, and Rudolf [the son] answered me: "She is drunk again." Several days before I was

missing some money, and the children must have bought schnapps with it.

"Do you mean to say that the children were drunk?" the judge interrupted, finally getting in a word. "Yes, certainly," said the witness. "Especially Anna always wanted schnapps. When I wanted anything out of her, she would beg for a mouthful of rum." This question of schnapps was very important throughout the trial. Marie Kutschera insisted that Anna was an eleven-year-old alcoholic, one of the grave moral defects that required constant punishment. She furthermore insisted that the terrible wounds and bruises on the corpse came either from Anna's fighting with her siblings, or from her stumbling and falling in a drunken stupor. The prosecution claimed that Marie Kutschera administered the alcohol to her stepchildren, and that she herself was the real alcoholic in the family.

Perhaps the most chilling thing about Marie Kutschera's account of the night of December 10, was her dramatic rendering of Anna's part. She didn't actually perform the child's "dance" in the courtroom, but she sang the child's song—*Ja, ja!*—in an altered voice of imitation. The newspapers described the tone as a lament. The monologue of Marie Kutschera continued with only brief interruptions from the judge.

> Anna could not be brought to rest, and jumped up out of bed maybe ten times, ran out into the kitchen and then back again into the room. She kept crying out and singing: *Ja, ja, ja!* I was feeling very bad, and I just kept thinking about how I could bring the child to rest . . . Around 10:00 the neighbors knocked on the wall and yelled. I called out, "The pig is drunk again. I'm suffering from it myself!" My headache had become worse, and I had to lie down in bed. So I said to Emil: "If she doesn't stop calling out, make her quiet." Around 10:30 I still heard her. When I looked into the children's room around midnight, Emil was holding her mouth shut. She had still kept calling out: *Ja! Ja! Ja!* She hadn't cried, always just: *Ja! Ja! Ja!* And I said: "She's not giving any peace?" And Emil said: "No!" But when I went over to the bed, I saw that she was lying wrong. I seized her, and her head fell down and kept wobbling back and forth . . . I shook her to make her come to, and I called: "Antschi! Antschi!" But the head just fell down. She was cold.

The tone and delivery of this testimony reminded at least one reporter of an unforgettable actor performing the part of Death.

As for the deathbed scene itself, there was no getting around the fact that here, as in the Hummel case, it would not be entirely straightforward work to prove an intentional action of legal murder. The judge was well aware of this, and as soon as she had finished her story, he confronted her with an overheard remark that could be construed as evidence of murderous intention and fear of apprehension.

> JUDGE: And a little while later didn't you make the remark: "Why did the slut die right now and not in the hospital!"
> MARIE KUTSCHERA: That is not so. I am being made to seem bad, and I don't know why! I said to a woman I know: "It's true it would have been better if Antschi had died in the hospital when she was so sick, instead of now in such a way."
> JUDGE: It all comes to the same thing, just that you express yourself today rather more tenderly than at that time.

But it was not the same thing, and she had handled the judge both coolly and skillfully, showing that her remark, whatever the precise wording, was by no means explicitly murderous. Furthermore, she took the opportunity to remind the courtroom that Anna had indeed recently been very sick in the hospital—and who was to say that she hadn't died of her recent illness? The other explanation of the death, already implied in the defendant's account of the crucial night, was that Anna was accidentally killed by her brother Emil, who was holding her mouth shut so the neighbors wouldn't hear her sing.

## IMMORAL ACTS AND SEXUAL INDECENCIES

It was not enough for the defense to show that abuse culminating in death was not exactly the same thing as first-degree murder. That ambiguous distinction had failed to save the Hummel parents only two weeks before. At the Kutschera trial the defense focused on another ambiguity, the fine line between abuse and discipline. The Hummel defense had touched on that point, but Juliane Hummel had lacked the confident self-possession, the dramatic presence, and the bold imagination of Marie Kutschera, when it came to explaining why the children were punished. "I approached the children with the greatest love and devotion," said Marie Kutschera, recalling her entry into the family, " and I must say they felt the same for me." At this point there was "ironic laughter" in the courtroom, but the Kutschera trial, though it contained some such moments, was not to be a comedy like its predecessor. The ironic laughter quickly died away as she went on. "I did not know that behind my back a web was being spun." With that ominous introduction, she went on to relate vividly how she had been doing the laundry one

day, when suddenly a woman appeared out of nowhere and attacked her. "Jesus!" cried out the terrified Marie Kutschera, but the
strange woman knocked her down and kicked her until blood came
out of her mouth. The spectators in the courtroom were not laughing now. The wicked female apparition, who could not be warded
off even with the name of the son of God, was none other than "the
Felzmann." Marie Kutschera claimed that it was thus, with this
brutal kicking, that she learned of the existence of this prostitute
who had lived with Rudolf Kutschera for a year and taken care of
his children. It was she who had made the children depraved, and
who now turned them against their stepmother; there was very
nearly the suggestion of witchcraft. "I came into that house as a
good and respectable woman," said Marie Kutschera, "and behind
me plots were forged." The children—at the instigation of the
Felzmann—disobeyed her, insulted her, stole from her, and ran
away from her. To a question about ten-year-old Richard, who was
whipped on his bare feet, she replied, "Oh, he was fine, I was the
martyr." There was laughter in the courtroom at that. She had been
too brazen or, more likely, too hysterical, but the moment passed
quickly, and no one laughed as she moved on to discuss the delicate
issue of sex.

For sex was at the bottom of her insistence that the children
deserved their punishments. Disobedience and rudeness, and even
stealing and drinking, after all, might merit the strongest discipli-
nary action, but one has only to consider the nineteenth-century
medical literature on masturbation to see that sex was punished
with torture. The recommended devices for the control of masturbation, with their leather straps and metal spikes, were indeed
instruments of torture, and if the press denounced Marie Kutschera
for turning her home into a torture chamber, sex was her best
justification. The French governess Celestine Doudet, after all,
ended up killing one of her charges in the course of preventing
masturbation, and she was imprisoned for three years. Vienna, with
its famous medical school, was earnestly concerned with this great
issue of the day. In 1885 the famous Dr. Hermann Nothnagel at the
University of Vienna published his classic *Handbook of Medicine,*
and did not fail to mention a useful little metal cage to help boys
control themselves. Around the turn of the century, another Austrian medical authority, Dr. Julius Söllner, designed a new and
improved version of that cage, to be sold with a pair of handcuffs
for extra security. The beatings and burnings and bindings of the
Kutschera children could be viewed rather differently, if they were
a concerned parental response to masturbation. Marie Kutschera

went even further, and suggested that, under the disgusting influence of the Felzmann, the children had gone beyond masturbation
and were already experimenting with all sorts of sexual indecencies.

At the center of the discussion of this issue was the eldest of the
Kutschera children, Ludovica; she was fourteen when her mother
died in 1895, seventeen when her father remarried in 1898. Apparently she felt close to the highly suspect Felzmann, and it was to her
that Ludovica went when she ran away from home to escape from
Marie Kutschera. Ludovica wrote to her father: "I am going to the
Felzmann. If she won't take me in, I'll drown myself—the wife
treats me worse than a dog." Indeed Ludovica was said to be
worked at home like a slave, with Marie Kutschera's own son,
Ignaz, standing over his stepsister with a whip. The family whip,
used on all the children, was described at the trial: a "Russian"
instrument with studded leather straps attached to a short handle.
Ludovica wrote to the Felzmann: "I want to flee to you, dear
mother, for that wife tortures us." Marie Kutschera claimed that
Ludovica was under the influence of the wicked Felzmann, that the
letters were all dictated to the girl, and, above all, that Ludovica's
intimacy with the Felzmann was evidence of the girl's moral ruin.
For according to Marie Kutschera, Ludovica was the key figure in
the Felzmann's "plot" to regain her place in the Kutschera house,
and drive the new stepmother away. The Felzmann supposedly
incited Ludovica to steal from her own house: money, jewelry, even
a rug and two fiddles. And, worst of all, the Felzmann made Ludovica into a whore.

Marie Kutschera testified that her own profound propriety was
deeply shocked when she discovered that Ludovica was meeting
men in hotels, and then that Ludovica was being treated for syphilis. There may have been some truth to this, for the prosecution did
not insist on Ludovica's purity, only that it was her stepmother
whose cruelty drove her to "shame." Ludovica, of course, was
seventeen years old, the age at which Hedwig Keplinger gave birth
to her fateful illegitimate daughter, the age at which the Baroness
Mary Vetsera became the lover of the Crown Prince Rudolf. Ludovica's "immorality" gave Marie Kutschera the opportunity to
emphasize her own middle-class respectability, the strongest point
in her favor. "I have lived in honor for forty years," she told the
court, after describing Ludovica's wickedness, "and I came to
Kutschera thus." She testified that Ludovica begged for forgiveness,
but that she herself could only firmly reply: "You have brought
shame and disgrace upon us, because you have sunk to the level of
the commonest slut." Other witnesses later testified that the step-

mother's reproaches were less self-possessed, though no less emphatic. They described Marie Kutschera dragging Ludovica out of the house by the hair, ripping the shirt off her back to show the lash marks to the boys on the street, and crying out: "Look how nicely colored she is! You can have her for a few coins!" When this story was told in court, Marie Kutschera commented only, "It's not easy for me to fight for my holy honor." One might have questioned the sanity, but surely not the sincerity, of her outrage at Ludovica.

Marie Kutschera, however, was being tried for the murder of Anna, not Ludovica, and the most significant aspect of the defendant's testimony, on this issue of sex, was the suggestion that the eleven-year-old Anna had also been sexually corrupted by the influence of her older sister and, of course, the Felzmann. It was the monstrous mistreatment of Anna that had to be justified. "The children committed immoral acts," said their stepmother, "especially Anna." And then, more specifically, when the prosecutor demanded to know why Anna was whipped: "I must confess, it happened ten days before her death, because she was instigating sexual indecencies with Richard and Max." Richard and Max were, at the time, aged nine and seven respectively. Anna was especially whipped on her fingers so perhaps her stepmother was sincerely obsessed with the possibility of masturbation. There were also witnesses who had heard her denounce the eleven-year-old as a slut. Presumably she believed in the girl's sexual depravity, and was not simply inventing it on the witness stand to fortify her defense. The judge took her charges of immorality seriously enough to clear the courtroom for forty-five minutes, and hold a closed session on the children's alleged sexual activity. For those forty-five minutes, an enigmatic caesura, the public and the press were excluded, and afterwards they were told only that Marie Kutschera had accused Anna and the boys of "an array of gross immoral acts." We have, however, seen enough evidence of her dramatic imagination and narration to suppose that she did not disappoint the judge with the details of her revelations.

Juliane Hummel, when she was asked if she was fond of her child, said simply yes, and the word was met with laughter. Marie Kutschera, asked a similar question about her stepchildren, replied, typically, at greater length and with more conviction: "Yes, and especially Annerl, she was my darling." This unexpected response was met, not with laughter, but with audible agitation in the courtroom, and the defendant was provoked to cry out again with emotional fervor: "Yes, she was my darling!" Then Marie Kutschera began to weep out loud. Looking back at that moment, one cannot help feeling that the great mystery of the trial was not what was said in the secret session about the children, but rather what was apparently never said at all about Marie Kutschera. For all her hysterical outbursts, her sexual obsessions, her paranoid fantasies of evil plots and conspiracies, nobody said anything about psycho- pathology. Although she was so much more dramatically unbal- anced than Juliane Hummel, still no one at this trial in Freud's Vienna was able to consider her psychologically. The whole issue of child abuse was so threatening that it was simply too much to consider what it could mean that Marie Kutschera had tortured to death her darling, her sexually depraved darling.

Could anyone in 1899 have fathomed the psychological complex- ities of such a case? As it happens, just the year before in 1898, a novella was published by one of the world's greatest living writers, a novella whose heroine strangely resembled Marie Kutschera in certain crucial respects. *The Turn of the Screw* by Henry James was the tale of an English governess who adored the two darling chil- dren entrusted to her care, but became convinced that they had been corrupted by a pair of evil, sexually suspect adults (including the former governess). Though the evil pair was now dead, the governess believed that the children continued to be haunted and corrupted by the ghosts. She was determined to make the children confess to their supposed depravity, and their reactions to this were ultimately so violent that the little girl suffered an emotional and physical collapse, while the little boy actually died in the gover- ness's passionate embrace. It was her obsession with the children's depravity that made James's governess an anticipation of Marie Kutschera—and also that each woman killed the child she claimed to love best. For three decades *The Turn of the Screw* was received as just a brilliant ghost story. Only in 1938 did the critic Edmund Wilson interpret the story as a psychopathological study of sexual repression and obsessional delusion: there were no ghosts, only a psychotic governess. Since then, it has also been suggested that James may have taken his heroine, to some extent, from the story of Miss Lucy R., an English governess in Vienna whose case was published in 1895 as one of the *Studies on Hysteria* by Josef Breuer and Sigmund Freud.

The psychopathology of Marie Kutschera in 1899, like that of James's governess in 1898, went unremarked. If she said the chil- dren were depraved, then the court simply had to decide whether they were so, or whether she was lying in her own defense. Thus, when it came time to sum up at the end of the trial, the prosecutor singled out, as the most disgusting thing about the case, Marie

Kutschera's gross hypocrisy, her "Tartüfferie." He reminded the jury of the affectionate nicknames she had used—Annerl, Antschi—and how she had imitated that song—*Ja, ja, ja!*—of the child on her deathbed. Precisely those details that might have been taken as the clues to her psychological problems were instead interpreted as unambiguous hypocrisy. In the end, the prosecutor got the conviction that he wanted, but that was on the third day of the trial. As it happens, certain comments later revealed that on that first day, when Marie Kutschera gave her testimony, the jury was still on her side. The men without qualities were by no means immune to the power of her presentation.

## "TORMENTED BY MY CHILDREN"

After the secret session on the immorality of the children, the crowd "stormed" back into the courtroom for the secondary attraction of that first day, the testimony of Rudolf Kutschera, the post official, the children's father. He was not at home on the night of December 10, when Anna died, and this made his relation to the murder charge that much more tenuous, in a case where proving intent to murder was already complicated enough. Thus he faced a lesser charge, aiding and abetting his wife, which was not subject to the death penalty, but at most twenty years in prison. This unequal culpability, no doubt, made the whole child abuse issue in this case less impossible to accept—for Marie Kutschera was only a stepmother, and, anyway, as in the Hummel case, public fury and fascination tended to focus on the woman who abused. If, however, the murder of Anna Kutschera was conceived as the sum of the abuse that she suffered—a legal point that was debated at the trial—then Rudolf Kutschera, like Joseph Hummel, certainly played his part. There were witnesses who told of his beating the wanton Ludovica until *he* was too exhausted to stand up. One account which made a great impression on the courtroom—though, typically, it was held against the stepmother most—described his beating the children, with her egging him on to strike again and again: *"Hau zu! Hau zu!"*

The *Arbeiter-Zeitung*, despite its satisfaction at discovering child abuse among the middle classes, "the so-called better circles," hesitated to go further than the prosecution in this respect, and proclaimed the post official only "morally responsible."

> It is completely out of the question that Rudolf Kutschera was unaware of the persecutions that his child Anna endured from the ac-

cused Marie Kutschera. It was his responsibility, as father and legal representative of his children, to prevent the mistreatment of them and especially of his daughter Anna . . . Under the circumstances, he must have recognized that the continuation of these tortures would lead to the death of his child. And this father stood at the center point of the mistreatment without saying a word in defense of his tortured child, without moving a finger to shield her.

Everyone was much more interested in the woman referred to as "the post official's wife." And at the end of the trial, at the last minute, the prosecution withdrew all charges against Rudolf Kutschera, "left him to his conscience," a free man—while his wife was condemned to death.

Rudolf Kutschera was born in the town of Blindenmarkt, which lies between Linz and Vienna. His father was a railway foreman, who raised himself up to become a railway official and made sacrifices so that his son might become a civil servant. When this elder Kutschera saw the miserable transformation in his grandchildren after their father's remarriage, he reproached his son for not feeding them enough. To this Rudolf Kutschera replied: "The children shouldn't eat so much, or they'll become dumb and won't learn anything." By 1899 the elder Kutschera was retired and remarried. His wife was apparently not greatly loved by her stepson, and one witness recalled Rudolf Kutschera saying about his own step-mother: "If only the old slut were dead, I'd make a glass out of her ass." She herself appeared in court, but refused to testify against her stepson.

Rudolf Kutschera was forty years old in 1899. His appearance was described as "elegant" and "modern," with a dark "Assyrian" beard and a twirling mustache. He wore spectacles, and there was general agreement on the "intelligence" of his expression and manner. There was something stiff about the way he carried himself, but his testimony, in contrast to that of his wife, was completely calm. His tone of voice was described as "honorable," and a military testimonial from his past service described him as a man who loved honor, and as a positive influence on his subordinates. If Joseph Hummel in appearance was "typical," the "Viennese from the bottom," then the elegant Rudolf Kutschera, the urban gentleman with his twirling mustache, also appeared as an unlikely prototype to face such a terrible charge. However, though neither man may have looked like a monster, an educated, honorable middle-class "type" like Rudolf Kutschera was far better prepared to deal with the charge in court. "I must declare myself absolutely not guilty," said Rudolf Kutschera, taking the stand. "For I know that I did everything I could to make my children into useful members of human society." From his very first words, he showed himself to be in diction and sentiment, as well as in appearance, an educated member of the middle class, and there was no ironic laughter in the courtroom.

To such an honorable tone, the judge responded in kind, asking Rudolf Kutschera relatively unaggressive questions, encouraging him to tell the hard story of his life. This the defendant did, quite sympathetically, beginning with the death of his first wife in 1895, which left him alone to care for seven children between the ages of four and fourteen. In fact, an eighth child had just been born and died, and his wife's death followed quickly upon the loss of the child. Colleagues had offered to help him out by adopting the children, but he was determined to keep them and raise them properly himself. The older boys were receiving a Catholic parochial education, and one of the boys was receiving special training for a Vienna boys' choir. A post official's salary was inadequate for such a large family, and Rudolf Kutschera told the court how his colleagues used to tease him about how frugal he was, because he had to save every penny to support his family. His family ate horse meat, he testified, insisting with dignity that if it was prepared well, it tasted very good.

In 1896 the Felzmann came to live with them. She was officially the housekeeper, but it was made quite clear to the court that she "lived with him in a common household"—that she was his mistress. She also took care of the children. Rudolf Kutschera testified that he had no idea, at the time, that she was a prostitute; it was his second wife who finally figured that out, and opened his eyes. Meanwhile, the Felzmann seemed to take care of the children properly, and the only problem in the household was that she wanted to marry him. Honorably he told her: "My heart is too wounded—I loved my wife too much to be able to marry again yet." Then the Felzmann began to make scenes, and in 1897 he dismissed her. His new housekeeper was the widow Marie Matucha, who eventually, in 1898 when his heart was less wounded, became his second wife. It was she who discovered that the Felzmann had been a prostitute, and furthermore learned, supposedly from the children, that the Felzmann entertained men in the house when he was at work. In "discovering" all this, the new housekeeper and future wife was also, of course, securing her own position, for the Felzmann, though dismissed, was furiously determined to regain her place in the Kutschera house. She attacked her successor, violently kicking, and sent threatening letters, so that Rudolf Kutschera finally had to ask the police to intervene.

Just as his wife did, though far more calmly, Rudolf Kutschera turned the accusation against him into an accusation against the children. This he did with complete composure, and even the astonishing opening sentence failed to rouse ironic indignation in the courtroom.

> During my second marriage I was tormented by my children, who now, probably under the influence of the Felzmann, caused me heavy grief. It hurts me to have to speak ill about my children, but even if it breaks my heart I must say it here. They were suddenly showing very bad tendencies. They stole from me when they could, and they ran away often. Always to the Felzmann. From there they always sent me letters, and I had to go pick them up. Once Ludovica fled, and in the evening I received a telegram from the Felzmann saying my daughter was with her. I went there with a detective . . .

Like his wife, Rudolf Kutschera was allowed to go on and on, in uninterrupted monologue. Occasionally the judge would urge him to be more concise. The opening sentences were most revealing: At a trial in which the children's mutilated bodies had already been graphically described as evidence to the jury, Rudolf Kutschera now testified that the children "tormented" *him,* that they caused him grief. It was he who had been abused by them.

Never did Rudolf Kutschera stoop to Joseph Hummel's futile trick of putting all the blame on his wife, though in the end the elegant post official achieved precisely the outcome that the laundry laborer had clumsily and unsuccessfully pursued. There was a sort of dreadful gallantry in the way Rudolf Kutschera backed up the testimony of his wife, supporting her grotesque denunciations of his children's "bad tendencies." He too testified that Anna stole money to buy schnapps and get drunk. He insisted that he never mistreated his children, but only beat them when it was necessary for their "moral education." Like his wife, he was arguing, fundamentally, that their atrocious conduct merited their atrocious punishment. That he was able to present this argument calmly, without any of the hysterical elements of her testimony, demonstrated the plausibility of his perspective in the context of conventional nineteenth-century attitudes toward raising children. Rudolf Kutschera did not look like a monster; he looked like a typical middle-class official. And in his honorable tone he presented himself as a typical middle-class father, punishing his children for their "bad tendencies," beating them in the interest of their "moral education."

So straightforward was the father's exposition that the prosecutor, cross-examining him, only tied himself up into knots trying to
get the witness to admit that he was aware that his wife was
abusing the children.

> PROSECUTOR: At the time when you were living with the Felzmann
> and had a much lower salary, the children looked passable. Then
> when you had a much better income . . . and without anything else
> changing in your situation except having a new wife, the children
> quite suddenly began to degenerate. How do you explain that?
> RUDOLF KUTSCHERA: I don't know how to explain that. The Felzmann
> allowed the children all sorts of freedoms.          ·
> PROSECUTOR: Yes, but they had been, according to witnesses, fine chil-
> dren, and were praised in school. Suddenly, all at once, when the
> new mother came . . . your daughter went out on the streets, your
> sons ran away and became thieves. How did that happen? How is it
> possible?
> RUDOLF KUTSCHERA: The Felzmann let the children have their own
> way, and already under her care they drank beer and schnapps.

Rudolf Kutschera seemed to feel that cruel punishment was the
proper antidote to the permissiveness of the Felzmann. The prosecutor was quite ready to accept that the children were bad, but
hoped to show that they were bad as a consequence of being
abused—thus robbing the parents of their justification. What was
most remarkable, however, about this cross-examination of Rudolf
Kutschera, was that the prosecution was obviously not interested
in prosecuting him, only in pressuring him to testify against his
wife. The most that he was being asked to admit to was that he was
aware of what she was doing.

That he denied. "All your children, with the exception of her
child, were mistreated," said the prosecutor. "Didn't you see anything of that?" But Rudolf Kutschera just said no, he didn't. He
mentioned in fact that he gave his daughter Anna a bath before
going away on the night of her death, and he didn't notice any signs
of mistreatment. Either he was lying, or he was blind, or he regarded a body covered with bruises as perfectly appropriate for a
child who stole money to buy schnapps. At the time that he mentioned that bath on the first day of the trial, no one realized that it
was going to turn out to be, legally, the key to the whole case.

## THE FELZMANN IN COURT

At the beginning of the second day in court, it was no longer quite
clear who was on trial: the parents for abuse and murder, the

children for their "bad tendencies," or, finally, the mysterious Felz-mann for corrupting the children. The lawyers for the defense were determined to show that, because of the influence of the Felzmann, the children were so very bad that no punishment could be consid-ered too extreme. The plausibility of such a defense, in the social context of the turn of the century, was demonstrated by the fact that the prosecution accepted the fundamental premises of the de-fense. Far from insisting that the children's moral qualities were irrelevant, were no possible justification for torture and murder, the prosecution preferred to try to argue that the children were not so bad as all that, and that their badness was the consequence, not the cause, of their abuse.

First to testify about Anna's moral character were two nuns and a countess, and the presence of these representatives of the clergy and aristocracy emphasized the difference in social tone between the trial of the post official and his wife, and that of the laundry laborer and his. Anna had spent a long time sick in the hospital, probably with tuberculosis, and Sister Ottilie and Sister Klotilde had cared for her there. Countess Fritzi Marschall, in a spirit of charitable aristocratic condescension, sometimes hosted convales-cent children after they left the hospital, and one of her guests was Anna Kutschera. The two nuns, of the Order of the Heart of Jesus, were chaperoned in the courtroom by an older nun, who stood beside them as they testified. They told the court that Anna was an intelligent child, but moody and disobedient. In fact, the healthier she became, the more she was disobedient, and sometimes she had to be forbidden to leave her bed until she obeyed. Curiously, there was a request from the jury that Marie Kutschera perform for the nuns her imitation of the voice of the dead child, supposedly so that they might say whether it sounded familiar. Such an odd request seemed to come from some compulsion to reenact the most mesmer-izing moment of the previous day. Marie Kutschera obliged them with her mimicry: "Ja, ja, I'll do it soon." Sister Ottilie, however, could only say that she really didn't remember whether Anna sounded like that.

Countess Fritzi Marschall found herself indisposed on that sec-ond day of the trial, and could not appear personally in the court-room, but she had written out her testimony to be read. According to the countess, Anna Kutschera, during her convalescence, showed herself to be "intellectually gifted but with few good quali-ties of character." The child seemed to want to be good, but still she was inclined to tell lies, and once she "appropriated" a breakfast roll to satisfy her sweet tooth. According to the pedagogical formula of the countess, "Strictness was of no use, but with mildness the child was easy to manage." Apparently, just as the bourgeoisie felt entitled to lecture to the lower classes on child rearing, so the aristocracy might condescend to offer its own precepts to the middle class. It turned out that Anna had been not only cared for by a countess, but also invited by a baroness to convalesce at a Baltic resort. This latter opportunity she had ungratefully declined, and Marie Kutschera explained that it was because Anna didn't want to be "trained." Anna supposedly told her stepmother that "at the Countess Marschall's there was also a baroness who was always training her." The child's reluctance to be patronized by her social superiors was thus presented as further evidence of her impossibly bad character.

There was one particular point to which the countess did not address herself in her written testimony, but she could not avoid it when she eventually appeared in person on the third day of the trial. She began with a repetition of the story of the sweet tooth and the breakfast roll, and then, asked specifically, she said she had never noticed any problem with schnapps. Finally, she was asked about the influence of the Felzmann, and whether Anna understood the "abominations" of her older sister Ludovica. The countess testified that Anna claimed to have learned "unspeakable abominations" from the Felzmann. "The ten-year-old child was also instructed about things, and often used expressions, that seemed unbelievable." She was "knowledgeable far beyond her age." Thus from the Austrian aristocracy itself came a word of confirmation for whatever tales Marie Kutschera may have told in the secret session on the first day. This was a crucial point, for sexual precociousness, like child abuse, was considered unspeakable and abominable. The defense was aware from the beginning that if anything could justify torturing a child, this was the way to the parental heart of a Victorian jury and a Victorian public.

One of the most interesting and mystifying aspects of the testimony of the countess was her emphatic insistence that Anna Kutschera loved her stepmother. "She spoke in rapturous expressions about her mother," said the countess. "She really raved." To this the judge replied with a certain disbelief by asking which mother Anna was referring to. The countess, however, was quite certain: "The stepmother, Frau Kutschera. The child always distinguished among the first, second, and third mothers." According to the countess, Anna "jumped for joy" when her father and stepmother came to visit her during her convalescence. Perhaps the countess rearranged her memories—especially with the confusion of the three mothers—but the references to Anna's raptures and ravings suggested that the girl herself might have entertained some fantastic conception of her stepmother. Marie Kutschera, after all, had exclaimed about her "darling," and the psychopathology of the relationship could have gone both ways—with twisted, ambivalent delusions on both parts. In fact, just when the countess spoke of Anna's raving about her stepmother, Marie Kutschera jumped up from her seat in the courtroom, probably the only person there who was capable of registering the entangled psychological message. When the judge saw her jump up, all he could say was, "Look how well you hear!" This sarcastic reference to her deafness clearly indicated his own imperviousness to the psychological intensity and complexity of the moment. The countess also remembered a letter that Anna received from her stepmother, and quoted it from memory: "My dear good Antschi! Just don't shame me, you the only one from whom I still hope to have joy!" This sort of testimony was problematic for everyone, even for the defense: for if Marie Kutschera really thought Anna was so dear and good, then what explanation—or justification—could there be for abusing the child?

If the parents' defense consisted of accusations against the children, the prosecution undertook to defend them. The earnestness of the case against the children was demonstrated by the fact that their school report cards were produced as evidence of their character. Ludovica, Emil, Anna, and Richard had all attended a school which gave a special grade for "moral conduct," and they had all received top grades. Anna, in addition, also received the top grade in religion. One of Anna's teachers was then called to the stand to describe her as "a blooming, fresh, happy child, and very good," as well as "a model of cleanliness." This teacher had taught Anna for three years without noticing any pernicious character traits, and only once catching the child in a lie. The judge wanted to hear about that lie. The teacher told how once Anna had begged for some food from other children, saying she hadn't brought anything from home, but then it turned out that she had eaten her bread on the way to school. The teacher did receive a visit at school from Marie Kutschera, who said that Anna was a liar, and that one had to be very strict with her. The teacher obligingly promised to punish Anna if she told lies in school. Even more interesting was a visit to school by Rudolf Kutschera, to speak to one of the teachers of Anna's younger brother Richard. Richard admitted to his teacher that he had sold his schoolbooks to buy sweets, and so his father was summoned to the school for a conference. There the furious father insisted that he could do nothing to reform Richard, and the boy would have to be put in an institute of correction. As proof that he had tried his best to discipline his son, Rudolf Kutschera showed the teacher Richard's bare back covered with brownish wounds from ferocious beatings. Nothing could better illustrate the undefined, unrecognized nature of child abuse in the nineteenth century than this vignette of the father who displayed the evidence of abuse in order to prove that he had done his paternal best.

Anna Kutschera was accused of disobedience, dishonesty, alcoholism, theft, and sexual depravity. Anna's brother Gustav, however, was actually accused of attempted murder, when it came time to explain why he was abused. It was an instance of abuse that made a great impression on the court, for Gustav had been tied down hand and foot for an entire week, exposed to the hot sun at the window, unable to shoo away the flies on his face. Rudolf Kutschera had already explained to the court, on the first day of the trial, that some of the children did have to be tied up sometimes, because otherwise they would run away from home—which they frequently did. In this, as in so many other respects, they were bad children who required the strictest treatment. On the second day of the trial, it came out that Marie Kutschera had given a much stronger reason for keeping Gustav bound. A neighbor in the same building told the story.

> At that time the rumor spread about in the house, and we all went and demanded to be let in to see for ourselves. Frau Kutschera let us in. My husband told her to untie the boy. She said: "I am the mother, I can do what I want." The people shouted: "You're no mother, you don't have the right!" At that, she told us that the boy had brought home poison from school, to put in the coffee and poison his parents.

Another neighbor testified that Marie Kutschera actually demanded of the bound boy: "Won't you admit that you wanted to poison us?" And Gustav replied: "Yes, I wanted to poison you."

This witnessed confession of intended murder could only be met by the prosecution with the assertion that Marie Kutschera extracted forced confessions from her victims. On the one hand, in the light of her vivid conviction of wicked conspiracies all around her, it would have been quite in character for Marie Kutschera to have believed in a poisoning plot among the children. On the other hand, the children might well have wanted to poison such a stepmother, whether or not they actually plotted to do it. The court, as usual, was apparently oblivious to the psychological complexities of the story. First, the judge announced that inquiries had been made, and there was no evidence of the children having stolen poison from the school. And then, after thus showing how seriously the court had taken the poisoning accusation, the judge made it into a joke: "As for 'poisoned coffee,' we have all at some time had bad coffee to drink." This witticism was greeted with "merriment" among the spectators. For the court, there was no middle way in between the most earnest and literal inquiry into missing poisons, on the one hand, and the most frivolous dismissal of the whole thing as a joke, on the other. The story, however, was of telling significance for an appreciation of the case as a whole. In general, the Kutschera parents, who abused their children, defended themselves by arguing that it was their children who made them suffer: "I was the martyr," and "I was tormented by my children." Nothing could have been more symbolically fitting than that the parents, specifically charged with murder, should also have turned that accusation around, and alleged that the children had sought to murder them. Thus child abuse could be presented not only as a moral obligation ("to make my children into useful members of human society"), but even as an act of self-defense.

The prosecution, defending the children, insisted that if they were bad, it was only because they were so badly treated. The parents' defense, however, holding that mistreatment followed misbehavior and not vice versa, did not go so far as to ask the jury to believe that the children were naturally evil and depraved. That would have been too much to ask of those nineteenth-century gentlemen—as Freud would discover some years later when he published his ideas about childhood sexuality. The Victorians were sentimental about childhood, as well as about motherhood, and so the case for the defense, while omitting nothing in compiling the crimes of the children, carefully attributed their wickedness to the corrupting influence of the Felzmann. This solution could spare both parents and children the ultimate responsibility for the family tragedy, and would least disrupt the sentimental family values of the nineteenth century. The appearance of the Felzmann herself in the witness stand, on the second day, was one of the high points of the trial, and the impression she made was judicially important for the final weighing of the misdeeds of the parents against those of the children.

Before she herself testified, the court heard the testimony of a certain Dr. David Weinstock, who had taken the Felzmann as his housekeeper after she was dismissed by Rudolf Kutschera. One day there appeared in the doctor's medical consulting office a woman, veiled and dressed in black. It was Marie Kutschera and she carried a letter, an insulting and threatening letter written to her by the Felzmann. Dr. Weinstock also received a note from Rudolf Kutschera requesting, as a matter of honor, that he not allow a respectable woman to be harassed in this fashion. The doctor there-fore dismissed the Felzmann, and she promptly reacted by taking mercuric chloride from his office for an unsuccessful attempt to poison herself. Dr. Weinstock characterized the Felzmann, for the court, as "hysterical," and since he was a doctor, he must have used the word with a certain awareness of its clinical, psychopathologi-cal meaning. This testimony, following upon the allegations of Rudolf and Marie Kutschera, could not have left the courtroom favorably disposed to receive the testimony of the Felzmann in person. The jury was furthermore forewarned that she had served a six-month jail sentence for the threatening letters she sent, and they should bear in mind this prison record when evaluating her credibil-ity as a witness.

On the witness stand, for the first time, she was allowed the dignity of a full name: Josephine Felzmann. She was small, thin, pretty—dressed all in black. She said she was thirty-eight and a widow. Her German showed a Hungarian accent, pointing to an origin in the alien other half of the Habsburg monarchy. The judge questioned her about her past, and she admitted that when she was young she once tried to shoot a lover who abandoned her. How-ever, when it came to discussing her recent six months in prison, she absolutely denied that she had ever sent any threatening letters. In fact, when she was convicted, the letters were never produced as evidence. Now, in court again, she declared that the whole business of the letters was fabricated by Marie and Rudolf Kutschera to get her out of the way. The fact that the letters had not been actually produced and examined before made such a strong impression now that the judge virtually apologized to the witness. "The court at that time," he told her, "had no reason not to believe the Kutschera testimony." It was the measure of their respectability that their word alone had been enough to send her to prison for six months, and that same respectability, even under siege, was the chief asset of the post official and his wife at their own trial.

When it came to the heart of the matter, the accusation that she had corrupted the children, the Felzmann defended herself with a calm simplicity that, according to the reporters, made an unexpect-edly favorable impression.

JUDGE: It has been said, especially about Ludovica who also tells dreadful lies, that you led her astray and introduced her to immoral relations.

JOSEPHINE FELZMANN: That's a lie. Please, I cared for the seven children like a mother.

JUDGE: Did you drink schnapps?

JOSEPHINE FELZMANN: At most, if I worked all day, I allowed myself a mug of beer.

JUDGE: No one reproaches you for that. But you are also said to have given the children schnapps to drink.

JOSEPHINE FELZMANN: That is absolutely untrue.

The dramatic testimony of Marie Kutschera had prepared the courtroom to find in "the Felzmann" nothing less than an evil witch. When she turned out to be only an ordinary little woman with a Hungarian accent, who simply protested her innocence, the unexpected incongruity must have provoked at least a tentative reconsideration of the stepmother's bewitching performance the day before. If the impressions made by the two women were compared at this point, some of those present might even have begun to wonder which was the witch. For if Josephine Felzmann was not evil, and did not corrupt the children, then why were the children so corrupt as to require such chastisement? When the judge dismissed her from the witness stand, she insisted on making one last statement to the court: "Please, I must still remark that I was never a prostitute." The judge replied with irritation: "That's not relevant. Your examination is over." But it was relevant, for if the Felzmann was not a wicked woman and an immoral influence, then Vienna had no alternative but to face the fact that the horrors of the Kutschera case were strictly between the parents and the children.

## "COMPLETELY SELF-EVIDENT"

While the direct responsibility of the Felzmann for the Kutschera tragedy seemed less plausible after she testified on the second day, on that same day another issue of indirect responsibility came to light. One of the witnesses who testified that day was the police commissioner who was involved in returning the children to their parents when they ran away from home. It also turned out that he had received accusations of cruelty against the Kutschera parents, presumably from neighbors, and even accusations from the parents themselves directed against the children for theft. All in all, the police commissioner had had to deal with the problems of the Kutschera family twenty-three times during 1898, and so it was certainly not true that the matter came to the attention of the authorities only after Anna's death in December. As in the Hummel case, there was here again every reason and opportunity to become aware of what was happening, and to intervene—except that this sort of awareness hardly existed in the nineteenth century, and police intervention in such family matters was still considered a public infringement upon the domain of private life.

The police commissioner, in fact, seemed quite sure of himself and his conduct when he gave his account on the witness stand. There was only one thing to be done with runaway children.

JUDGE: How did you respond in such cases?
COMMISSIONER: I summoned the parents to come fetch the children.
JUDGE: Did the parents refuse to take the children?
COMMISSIONER: No, I took it as completely self-evident (*selbstverständlich*) that the children should be taken by their parents. Except once Frau Kutschera didn't want to take one of the boys.

At this point, Marie Kutschera spoke up, and interrupted the examination to give her own account:

That was Gustl. I said I would take him when my husband came home. The boy had threatened violence against me and against his siblings . . . The commissioner said: "You must take the child." I said: "I'll take him and tie him up."

Gustl, of course, was the affectionate diminutive for Gustav, the boy she suspected of trying to poison her. When we read the exchange between the judge and the police commissioner, it may disturb us that the police failed so completely to protect the children from their abusive parents. Such a reaction, however, very much reflects our own contemporary perspective, and in 1899 these moments from the trial were susceptible to a quite different interpretation. For the police commissioner himself, his course of action was "self-evident." That strikes us as unenlightened, but it is at least somewhat comprehensible. Much more difficult for us to fathom is what Marie Kutschera was driving at in her interruption, and how the defense viewed the testimony of the police commissioner. One must bear in mind the reversal of roles on that second day, when the children were being accused, and then it becomes clear that Marie Kutschera herself was accusing the police of a failure of duty. That duty was not to protect the children from her, but, in this case, to protect her from the children by keeping Gustav in custody until her husband came home to protect her. Here again she made the point that she had no choice but to punish them, to tie them up, to abuse them. It is twists such as this one that allow us to appreciate the determined nonrecognition of child abuse in the nineteenth century.

To the police commissioner, it was self-evident that the children should go back to their parents—which suggested that the great "Appeal," for the establishment of a monumental asylum for abused children, was with all its inadequacies still a controversial conception. The police commissioner considered this matter self-evident, however, not simply because he was too naively sentimental to imagine that parents could mistreat their children. When he was asked about reports to the police of whippings in the Kutschera family, he told the judge frankly that the reports had not alarmed him. That the children were whipped seemed obvious and natural to him, indeed—he seemed to like the word—"self-evident." That was how he expressed himself in court. How the police responded at the station, at the time the reports were made, came out in the testimony of the neighbor who reported the binding of Gustav: "He told me I should leave him in peace." The *Arbeiter-Zeitung* seized upon this sarcastically with the heading "The Police Commissioner Needs Peace"—but his response to the report was a perfectly natural one, in view of the other axioms that he regarded as self-evident. His perspective was neither eccentric nor particularly callous—and that was precisely the dilemma of trying to define and prosecute child abuse as something distinct from the generally accepted conception of nineteenth-century parent-child relations.

Indeed only the socialist *Arbeiter-Zeitung* took up the issue of the police, and of how they had handled the Kutschera case. From the very first day of the trial, it was that, along with the social class of the defendants, which gave the case its great interest from the socialist perspective: "The three-day jury trial will unroll a dismal picture of the moral condition of the married couple who belong to the so-called better circles, and at the same time also a picture of the activity of our police." The failure of the police to respond to reports of abuse in the Kutschera family was attributed in the *Arbeiter-Zeitung* to "a deficiency of intelligence, education, energy, and good will." Not until the character of the police was improved would it be possible to guarantee "that a blood sacrifice need not occur before the surviving children are liberated from the claws of their parental tormentors." The image of Anna Kutschera as the "blood sacrifice" suggested again that implicit juxtaposition with Agnes Hruza at Polna, but the image was also meaningful in itself. It was quite true that if Anna Hummel and Anna Kutschera had not actually died, there would have been no child abuse sensation at all in 1899. The *Arbeiter-Zeitung*, however, in its eagerness to denounce the police, ended up taking a rather narrow view of the problem of child abuse. Reforming the police was not a meaningful

solution, when the police simply reflected the self-evident perspectives of society in general.

The sharp socialist attack on the police stood in contrast to the
virtually apologist remarks of the prosecutor in his summation to
the jury at the end of the trial. He wanted only to convict Marie
Kutschera, and was ready to make excuses for the police. In his
readiness to extend those excuses to society at large, however, he
showed himself, in his fashion, very nearly aware of the full implications of the case, even as he attempted to defuse them.

> I, and all of us, are conscious of an oversight; we all followed the form,
> and didn't pay enough attention to the matter. We didn't do what we
> should have done. But we all have an excuse: there are some things
> that are simply unbelievable.

Child abuse was the thing that was simply unbelievable in 1899,
and in excusing himself, and "all of us," the prosecutor posed, and
dismissed, the issue of general responsibility. Indeed, just as the
summation at the Hummel trial demanded the conviction of Juliane
Hummel in order to vindicate "faith in the mother," so here the
conviction of Marie Kutschera was to absolve "all of us." Another
blood sacrifice was necessary. The *Arbeiter-Zeitung*, typically,
picked up on the prosecutor's comment on following "the form"—
but interpreted it strictly as police routine: "The form! That's it!
The authorities must make war upon the form. The evil has been
exposed." But the forms in this case were not just police proce-
dures, and were not subject to the force of even the most intelligent
and energetic authorities. The forms were the deeply set mental
structures of the nineteenth century. Those were the forms that
determined what was self-evident, and what was simply unbelievable.


## "LIKE A GYPSY CAMP"

To the police commissioner who handled the runaway children, the
Kutschera family did not seem so unusual as to warrant special
investigation. The neighbors, however, especially the people who
lived in the same building, were aware that the Kutschera family
was different from other unhappy families. There were neighbors
who made reports to the police, and, as we have seen, there were
neighbors who demanded that Marie Kutschera unbind her stepson. At the trial, these neighbors seemed to vie with each other in
recounting the grisly details of the savage treatment of the
Kutschera children. By that time, however, Anna Kutschera was

dead, the parents were charged with murder, and the family was notoriously and sensationally set apart from other families. The neighbors found themselves with small parts to play at a trial that attracted crowds and filled the newspapers. There is, therefore, reason to doubt whether their testimony in 1899 really reflected the nature of their awareness in 1898.

Perhaps the most dramatic segment of the neighbors' testimony came from the husband and wife whose apartment was on the other side of the wall, and who could therefore report a sort of soundtrack of the night Anna died. The wife heard Marie Kutschera screaming at Anna, "Beast, slut, if there is a God, he must deliver me from this beast!" That certainly sounded like Marie Kutschera, the woman who believed herself to have been the martyr in the case. The husband, however, from the same listening point as his wife, testified to hearing more explicitly murderous exclamations:

> The children were playing first, and then suddenly one heard Anna crying and moaning, and then a muffled blow. Frau Kutschera said, "Now they've dropped a pot." Then immediately there was quiet. Later the whimpering began again, and one heard the voice of the defendant: "Isn't the slut dead yet? She must die before her father comes home!" She also said: "If there is a God, we'll be delivered from the beast." And: "Hold shut the slut's muzzle, so the neighbors can sleep!" We didn't sleep much that night.

Since husband and wife were together on the other side of the wall, the discrepancies in what they remembered overhearing were suspect, especially since his testimony—"she must die"—seemed so precisely tailored to the case of the prosecution. There may well have been revisions of memory, for the wife claimed that, just at midnight, she had been struck by a sudden, mysterious certainty that Anna was dead.

The dramatic points in their testimony, touching on the issue of murder, may have been unreliable, but the most utterly commonplace aspect of the situation they described was far more revealing than they could have realized. It was so commonplace that nobody seemed to notice it at the trial: the Kutschera family was the kind of family who kept their neighbors awake at night, the worst sort of family to have on the other side of the wall. Marie Kutschera was obviously aware of the grievance—"Hold shut the slut's muzzle, so the neighbors can sleep!"—and the righteous indignation of their sensational testimony could not be separated from the unsensational conclusion: "We didn't sleep much that night." That night in 1898 the neighbors couldn't get any sleep, and this conditioned their indignation over the abuse of the Kutschera children. Thus, from the testimony at the trial in 1899, we can try to recover something of the neighbors' consciousness of 1898, and to analyze to what extent child abuse was then recognized and identified as the problem that made the Kutschera parents unpopular in their building.

At the trial, the neighbors claimed that they were on the point of lynching Rudolf and Marie Kutschera, and, in view of the attitude of the police, that might have been the most effective form of intervention available. The righteous declarations of the neighbors in 1899, however, could not conceal the concerns of 1898. One neighbor testified: "The tenants wanted to whip the parents, if they didn't move out." In other words, the neighbors were not intent on saving the children, but rather on getting rid of the whole family. There was never a lynching, but the one action that was taken before Anna's death was that the building superintendent gave notice to Rudolf Kutschera that he would have to move out of the building.

The testimony of the superintendent, who bore the Wagnerian name of Johann Tannhäuser, revealed the real reasons for which the family was given notice in 1898. It was not precisely because they abused their children, but rather because they could not main-tain the appearance of respectable tenants.

JUDGE: How did the Felzmann take care of the children?
SUPERINTENDENT: Very well. The children were very well behaved and always nicely dressed.
JUDGE: Did the Felzmann drink?
SUPERINTENDENT: Only beer.
JUDGE: And how was it when the new housekeeper, the future Frau Kutschera, moved into the house?
SUPERINTENDENT: One noticed an instantaneous change. The children were ragged and starved; they were out in the street more than at home . . . They ran around without shoes and begged for bits of bread from other children in the street . . . The family was finally given notice, and I didn't dare show the apartment to prospective tenants, because of what it looked like inside. Outside there was a plaque: k.k. post official. But inside it looked like a Gypsy camp.

This testimony revealed all too clearly that the problem in the building was not that the children were suffering and starving, but rather that they were barefoot and begging. They did not look like proper middle-class children; they looked like Gypsy children. In 1898 Tannhäuser feared prospective tenants would see the rooms not as a torture chamber—that was an image of 1899—but rather as a Gypsy camp. In fact, the concerns of the superintendent—peace and quiet and a respectable appearance—fit perfectly with those of his other tenants, who were being kept awake at night.

The Tannhäuser testimony strongly suggested that, before the death of Anna Kutschera and the arrest of her parents, the superintendent and the neighbors did not clearly identify child abuse as the problem with the Kutschera family. That was because child abuse was not readily identifiable to the Victorian eye. Instead child abuse was perceived as part of a general, mingled impropriety and indecency—for those categories were readily perceptible to the Victorians. The solution was not to remove the children from their parents, but rather to remove the whole family from the building. One witness, questioned on the inexhaustible issue of schnapps in the family, mentioned that there was a rumor among the neighbors that the children were given schnapps to get them drunk, so that the Kutschera parents "could have sexual relations with each other unembarrassed in front of the children." There was something fitting about the fact that Marie Kutschera, with her obsessive sexual accusations against the children, should herself have acquired a reputation for sexual depravity. The rumor was most significant, however, inasmuch as it demonstrated how every kind of impropriety was mingled in the Victorian imagination. Those mingled improprieties acted as a sort of camouflage for the unrecognized phenomenon of child abuse.

Such impropriety would have been only to be expected from the Hummel parents, the laundry laborer and his wife. The thing that made the Kutschera case so much more disturbing—and so much more compelling—was the incongruity between their social position and their domestic behavior. "Outside there was a plaque: k.k. post official," Tannhäuser testified. "But inside it looked like a Gypsy camp." The cryptic double "k" was the symbolic monogram of the Habsburg empire. Since the Austro-Hungarian compromise of 1867, the powers of Franz Joseph had been clearly delineated according to his dual character as Emperor (*Kaiser*) of Austria and King (*König*) of Hungary. His domain was thus both *kaiserlich* and *königlich*, imperial and royal, and the double "k" acquired an almost mystical significance as the formal designation of the Habsburg state. Musil had these initials in mind in *The Man Without Qualities*, when he named the country with the excremental pun "Kakania." Karl Kraus was deeply conscious of the fact that he had the same initials as the country he hated. To him Austria-Hungary was "the other K.K." and "the shadow of my true name." He celebrated in verse the collapse of the empire, after World War I, as a personal liberation from that shadow.

And so the charges against Rudolf Kutschera, the k.k. post offi-cial, did not simply cast a cloud over the post office. The double "k" designated him as the servant of the Austrian state, the Habsburg dynasty, the Emperor Franz Joseph—and the plaque outside his apartment implicated them all in his disgrace. Rudolf Kutschera was a man whose position in society was, on the outside, clearly defined: a respectable man of the middle class, a man in the service of the Emperor. Inside, however, in his family life, he lived like a Gypsy, an ethnic outcast, a man of no defined social position at all. Furthermore, since a father of his social position was expected to behave in a way that was not only defined, but fully "self-evident," his unarticulated deviation from the norm—from the "form"—was all the more alarming. For us the designation of "Gypsy" sounds grotesquely and offensively wrong, since Rudolf Kutschera might have been far more appropriately called a monster. The superin-tendent Tannhäuser, however, was not trying to express his out-raged humanity—for child abuse was an unrecognized outrage— but rather to express an incongruity between social position and private life. In the Habsburg empire, then in the process of being torn apart by its antagonistic nationalities, that outrage found ex-pression in terms of ethnicity. Gypsies were the worst thing Tannhäuser could imagine inhabiting his apartment building.

In 1913 the Habsburg empire was spiritually devastated by the revelation that Colonel Alfred Redl, a leading intelligence officer, had been betraying military secrets to the Russians. Stefan Zweig, who had known Redl slightly, later recalled that, at the revelation, "terror clutched at my throat." What was most shocking about the affair was the disparity between external appearances and the truth underneath. On the outside, Redl wore the uniform of the imperial army and was known to be working closely with the heir apparent, the Archduke Franz Ferdinand. Secretly he was a traitor, and pri-vately a homosexual, and both of these revelations together created a shocking insecurity about what might be found inside an Austrian military uniform. Thus the Redl affair was a demoralizing blow to the army—an army that was one of the few remaining pillars of an empire on the verge of destruction.

In its moral ramifications for the Habsburg state, the case of Rudolf Kutschera (who had himself been an army officer before entering the civil service) was comparable to that of Alfred Redl. The post official, like the intelligence officer, was revealed as a monster, and those revelations were menacing to the faith of Austrians in their doomed dynasty. Coincidentally, both Redl and Kutschera were the sons of railway officials; Redl rose higher and achieved a more lasting notoriety. The Kutschera case in 1899 ushered in the twentieth century in Vienna on a note of horror, while the Redl affair in 1913 was the evil omen of the coming war which was destined to destroy the Habsburg empire. Both men were deeply disturbing to their contemporaries, because of the incongruity revealed between public form and inner deformity—and in neither case could that incongruity be accepted and resolved. Alfred Redl was presented with a pistol to shoot himself, so he never faced trial. Rudolf Kutschera was tried, but at the last minute all charges against him were withdrawn, so he never faced judgment.

## THE TESTIMONY OF THE CHILDREN

On the third and final day of the trial, the children themselves were called to the witness stand. Through the first and second days, the judge had remained undecided about whether the children should appear in court. His own feeling was that their testimony would be unreliable, and furthermore they were legally entitled to refuse to testify against their parents. It was the jury that finally insisted that the children be summoned. The children had to be seen and judged so that the court might decide whether they really seemed so depraved as to deserve the abuse they had received. Thus the appearance of the children was momentous indeed, and the *Neue Freie Presse* found the third day of the trial to be "rich in exciting and important scenes" of a "highly dramatic nature." The tone here was more that of a theater review than a courtroom account. Like the Hummel trial, the Kutschera trial could be appreciated as theater, but its "rich" dramatic qualities went far beyond the merriment of popular comedy.

The children were preceded on the stand by the man who had been appointed their legal guardian. He assured the court that the children were good, honorable, and obedient. He had tested their honesty by entrusting them with small sums of money, and he had probed the veracity of their accounts of abuse by questioning them over and over again, to make sure the details were always the same. He never caught them in a lie. Under such guardianship the children could hardly help becoming aware that they too were on trial.

This excellent character reference for the children, as an introduction to their testimony, seemed to suggest that the trial might now turn decisively against the parents. In fact the guardian did narrate new details of abuse that the children had described to him, but there was also a whole new twist to the way this was presented, a change of emphasis. The guardian testified that Marie Kutschera had thrown a pair of scissors at thirteen-year-old Emil, so hard that they stuck in his forehead. Another time she burned him on the forehead with a hot clothes iron. The first time, she told Emil to tell his father he had fallen by the sewing machine on the scissors. The second time, he was to tell his father he had gotten the burns from stumbling into the oven. Evidently, the testimony of the children was now to be used to show that they had been abused exclusively by their stepmother, while their father had been kept completely ignorant of what was going on. Until the second day of the trial, it had seemed that the reciprocal accusations against parents and children might be resolved by shifting responsibility onto the Felzmann. After she had testified personally, however, that seemed like a much less likely way out, and therefore either the parents or the children would have to be found monstrously guilty. The testimony of the guardian, however, at the beginning of the third day, pointed to another possible evasion of that stark either-or opposition. Rudolf Kutschera already stood accused of a lesser crime than his wife, although they were being tried together in the courtroom and the public eye. The guardian now vouched for the testimony of the children, while, at the same time, promising that their testimony would absolve their father. This opened the way to the ultimate solution of the complicated sentimental tangles of the case: the children redeemed, the father absolved, the stepmother executed.

The guardian furthermore reported that the children overheard their father telling their stepmother of his distress over the condition of the children. If he had a revolver, he reportedly said, he would shoot himself. As in the case of Hedwig Keplinger, a parent who committed suicide could even be forgiven by the public for taking along a child as well. And as in the Redl affair, shooting oneself was the correct response for a Habsburg official on the point of disgraceful exposure. This testimony to the post official's readiness to kill himself made a favorable impression on the court.

The jurors could not fail to pick up on the guardian's implications, and one of them even asked him directly whether the children spoke of being mistreated by their father. The guardian assured the jury that the children only spoke of mistreatment from their stepmother. The father's lawyer took this one step further by asking how the children spoke of their father. The guardian replied unhesitatingly: "They say, 'We are fond of our father.' " That should have been no less ironically humorous than the assertion of Juliane Hummel that she was fond of her daughter—but in this case nobody laughed. Someone else even testified that ten-year-old Richard, after his father's arrest, had run away from his foster parents, saying that he was going to look for his father. On hearing this, Rudolf Kutschera began to weep in the courtroom. Richard was the boy whose lacerated back was shown to his schoolteacher, as evidence that his father was sincerely trying to make him a useful member of society.

Marie Kutschera was given an opportunity to reply to the testimony of the guardian, and she was fully aware of the new change of emphasis that shifted responsibility to her alone.

> I have nothing to say about that. It is all sad enough. I don't wish to incriminate my husband, for he is just as innocent as I am. There is not a word of truth in the whole thing.

Her comment, that he was as innocent as she, was a neat formulation of the claim that she was as innocent as he. As one might expect, however, from her previous volubility, it was not true that she had nothing to say in reply. She agreed, for instance, that her husband had been on the point of suicide, but interpreted his motives rather differently. With her usual dramatic flair, she recreated the scene, complete with quoted dialogue.

> I said to my husband: "I am going to leave you. Because of the children, I can't remain here any longer." And he said to that: "Marie, if you go away, I will put an end to my life."

Thus in her version, he wanted to commit suicide because the children were so bad to her, not because she was so bad to the children. Once again the accusation was perfectly reversed. Her boldest response, however, was to the matter of the scissors that allegedly stuck in Emil's forehead. At the very beginning of the trial she had dared to turn a question back on the judge when asked about her finances: "you figure it out." Now she turned on the jury: "Really, I ask you, gentlemen, you try to throw a pair of scissors so that they stick like that. Really!" Reporters remarked on the irony in her tone, remembering perhaps that at the Hummel trial irony had been the exclusive prerogative of the court to use against the defendant.

There was only one question that Marie Kutschera failed to answer satisfactorily. The guardian, recounting the night of Anna's death as the children had recounted it to him, mentioned that Anna had been put in a washtub of cold water. The judge remembered that Rudolf Kutschera had said that he gave Anna a bath before going away that evening—and didn't notice any marks of abuse on her body. Now the judge asked Marie Kutschera: "Why did you put Anna in the washtub when she had already been bathed?" It was a question that would come back to haunt her before the end of the day.

Three children testified—Max, Richard, and Emil—and their accounts bore out the implications of their guardian's testimony, condemning their stepmother, absolving their father. The guardian had, after all, as he himself related, gone over the story with them again and again—to test their veracity—so naturally their accounts fit with his. All that rehearsal must have long ago worn away the edge of spontaneous honesty, and the full year that had elapsed since their parents' arrest could easily have confused the memories of the children. At any rate, they rallied to their father at the trial. If everyone else in Vienna needed to believe that Rudolf Kutschera did not torture his children, how much more so must the children themselves have felt that need. As for their own defense, no one asked the children on the witness stand whether they stole, or drank, or masturbated. Their appearance in itself was their defense. If Josephine Felzmann with her questionable past and Hungarian accent could nevertheless, by her general impression, persuade the court that she was no witch, the appearance of eight-year-old Max Kutschera was far more immediately disarming. To the reporters he was "an especially lovely boy" in a sailor suit.

> His pants are in between short and long. One doesn't know if they're short pants that are too long, or long pants that are too short.

That was the *Arbeiter-Zeitung*, exploring the Marxist dialectic. The pants were short enough to show the boy's knees trembling as he spoke. He did not seem depraved.

What he said was not surprising. But hearing it from the mouth of the child, while watching him in his sailor suit, made child abuse seem less abstract. It also exploded the whole idea of merited punishment.

> JUDGE: Did your mother beat Annerl on the fingers?
> MAX: Yes, me too.
> JUDGE: Were you allowed to cry when you were beaten?
> MAX: If we cried we were beaten still more.
> JUDGE: Now tell us, were you fond of this mother.
> MAX: No, because she beat me so much.

The court already knew that at the time of his sister's death Max was found with his back and buttocks covered with yellowish green marks, and with irregular abrasions all over his fingers and on the back of his hands.

Ten-year-old Richard was asked directly, on the stand, wasn't it true that he was beaten so bloodily that his body stuck to the floor? "Yes, the blood stuck to the floor," he replied. That had been a year ago. Now he appeared in a nice gray suit, and testified in a soft voice that the press found "dispassionate." The judge had greater reservations about the child's disinterestedness, and began the examination accordingly.

> JUDGE: If you want, you can testify. If you don't want to, you can leave now. You don't have to say anything.
> RICHARD: Testify.
> JUDGE: Did anyone tell you to?
> RICHARD: No!
> JUDGE: It's a painful situation, letting children testify against their parents. When you testify you must tell the pure truth. You must not lie. So if you don't want to testify, you can go home. What do you want to do?
> RICHARD: I want to testify!
> JUDGE: I am innocent of all this!

Earlier, of course, there had been no problem with allowing the parents to testify against the children, and the complicated pattern of accusations and counteraccusations here culminated fittingly with the judge himself, Pontius Pilate, feeling the need to declare himself "innocent."

The judge, however, did not dispense with his reservations, as he elicited from the boy an account of the all-important night of Anna's death.

> JUDGE: Anna was forced to drink all the brandy?
> RICHARD: Yes, Mother held open her mouth and poured in the whole flask.
> JUDGE: Did Annerl cry out?
> RICHARD: Yes, but it was no use.
> JUDGE: And then she was bathed in cold water. Did Anna like the bath?
> RICHARD: She said, that's good.
> JUDGE: What then?
> RICHARD: Then Mother put Annerl in bed, and Emil had to sit down with her.
> JUDGE: Did your mother say anything to Emil?
> RICHARD: Yes, she said: Hold her mouth shut!

JUDGE: Why?
RICHARD: So she would die.
JUDGE: How did you come up with this idea?
RICHARD: She said to Emil: Hold her mouth shut so the slut will die
. . . She said to Anna: Slut, aren't you dead yet?
JUDGE: Is this all true? If you are lying, you are committing a great sin.
RICHARD: It was all just as I have said.

The judge's uncertainty about the reliability of the children as witnesses was all that remained of the previous days' accusations that the children were depraved. The tide was turning, and the judge was cautious precisely because Richard's testimony did not just accuse his stepmother of child abuse. By quoting her exclamations, he dramatically supported the charge of murder.

Richard's testimony, however, was altogether favorable to his father. He said his father beat him only when his stepmother said he had done bad things. He said his father didn't know how much she beat the children, because they were forbidden to tell him. He retold from the witness stand the story of running away from his foster home in order to find his father. The climactic moment of his testimony came when a juror interrupted the examination to put the question which, in one form or another, had already played such an important role in both the Hummel and Kutschera trials. "Were you fond of your father and mother?" asked the juror. "Yes," replied Richard, "but not of my stepmother!" At that reply there were cries of bravo in the courtroom. Here again, child abuse became theater, and this was one of those "exciting and important scenes" of a "highly dramatic nature." The boy's formulation had neatly solved the dilemma of the trial. He was a good child; he loved his father and mother. But Marie Kutschera was not his mother. She was his stepmother, and she was to bear the responsibility for what had happened. When the spectators cried bravo, they were cheering for the sentimental solution of a very nasty case.

The judge finally dismissed Richard from the stand with the comment that it was "a martyrdom for the child to be interrogated this way." Originally the judge had feared that the child's testimony would be bad for the case, but he too had been affected, and now he feared that it would be bad for the child. That he dubbed Richard a martyr was also telling, since, from the first day of the trial, the court had been wrestling with the claim of Marie Kutschera that she was the martyr. Richard left the stand with a little bow to the judge and jury. Passing the bench of witnesses, he found the woman who had given him foster care after his parents were arrested, and he paused gallantly to kiss her hand.

Thirteen-year-old Emil bowed deeply to the courtroom before taking the stand. He told how his stepmother had attacked him with the scissors and with the clothes iron. He insisted that his father had known nothing of the abuse of the children, that they were only mistreated when he was away. He told how he had been forced to hold shut Anna's mouth on the night of her death. It was while he gave his account of that night that the defense attorney began to suspect he was narrating things he could not have personally witnessed. Under cross-examination Emil admitted that he had actually read about some of these things in the newspapers. For the court the point was, or should have been, extremely problematic. Indeed the defense lawyer for Marie Kutschera immediately insisted that the testimony of the children was utterly vitiated by this discovery that they were integrating the news into their own witnessed experiences. To be sure, it did seem to make their accounts suspiciously unreliable, and it should have rendered equally dubious both their testimony in favor of their father and their testimony against their stepmother. Sentiment in the courtroom at this point, however, had turned so emphatically in favor of the children—with their charming bows and lovely little suits—that the prosecutor was able to override the objections of the defense with a legally empty but emotionally impassioned declaration of his faith in the children's testimony. The courtroom rewarded him with applause and more cries of bravo, again a response to the "highly dramatic nature" of the proceedings. Those cries of bravo did not mark just the transformation of the trial into theater, but also the sentimental transformation that had taken place over the course of the trial. On the first day, a secret session had examined the alleged sexual immorality of the children. Now, on the last day, the children were vindicated, not so much by anything that they said as by the sympathetic impression they made in the courtroom. There could be no legal objection to the spell cast by pants too long to be shorts and too short to be trousers.

The one child who could not testify, of course, was the one who was most central to the case, Anna herself. The prosecutor, however, actually conjured her out of the grave in his final summation, on that last day of the trial, and this rhetorical device served as the ultimate flourish after the testimony of Anna's living brothers.

> In death she speaks to us . . . Before our inner eye, the child has raised herself up, and with a mutilated hand, indicating the stigmata of her wounds, her blood accusation cries out to heaven . . .

The prosecution appreciated that the appearance of the children was the key to their vindication, and so Anna too was made to appear as a bloody ghost—for she had to be vindicated too, if the murder charge was to hold. When the prosecutor proclaimed her "a child full of innocence and charm," he was not being meaninglessly trite. For Anna's innocence had been hotly debated in secret session and in open court. Upon the issue of her innocence depended that of the guilt of her stepmother, and the vindication of one meant the conviction of the other. Thus, in the Kutschera case, a Victorian public weighed its sentimental ideal of motherhood against its sentimental ideal of childhood—and the children finally carried the day.


## ANNA'S BATH

The cries of bravo for the children showed that the emotional balance of the trial had shifted with their appearance on the third day. What followed, during the rest of that day's testimony, was almost anticlimactic, as the court attempted to arrive at a legal rationalization of the emotional resolution. Two doctors testified that Anna Kutschera died as a consequence of the sum of the abuses that she suffered. One of them compared the case to that of a soldier made to run the military gantlet past three hundred comrades with clubs; it could be the equivalent of a death sentence. A juror put a statistical question:

> JUROR: Could you, on your accountability, declare that there is at least a sixty percent probability that the abuses were the cause of death?
> DOCTOR: I declare it in full consciousness of my accountability.

The other doctor was willing to go further and declare Anna's death to have been absolutely certainly a violent one. She could not have died only from her past illnesses, and, in his words, "a ten-year-old child doesn't just die like a fly on the wall."

The problem with these declarations of probability was that, even if the sum of the abuses was definitely the cause of death, that did not prove an intention to murder. The reported exclamations of intent were never reliably exact—"Isn't the slut dead yet?"—and even if they were accurate, the immediate medical cause of death was stated as "nerve shock." How could Marie Kutschera have gone about murdering her stepdaughter by nerve shock?

That was how it came back to the bath. Anna Kutschera had already been bathed by her father earlier in the day. If she was already clean, then wasn't there something suspect about that second cold bath administered by her stepmother? A member of the jury questioned the doctor on the stand:

It isn't clear to us what was going through the mind of the defendant when she did that. Could she have read that one could kill someone in that way? . . . We jury members would never have dreamed that one could induce nerve shock that way and kill someone. And she is an uneducated woman. I make no secret of the fact that, until this evening, we have been on the side of the defendant.

This admission that the jury had been on her side showed how hard it was to believe in 1899 that a woman could do the things Marie Kutschera was accused of doing; it showed how very seriously the jury had considered her defense of counteraccusations. Now they began to take seriously the issue of the bath. The appearance of the children had swayed them earlier in the day, and it was the bath that became the pretext for accepting the murder charge. Marie Kutschera, they supposed, could have given her stepdaughter that second superfluous cold bath with the intention of inducing nerve shock, and thus committing murder. The doctors' arguments for death as the consequence of cumulative abuse were put aside, for, as one juror reasoned, "All the other children were also whipped, but none of them died." Only Anna was given an extra bath. After a lengthy discussion of the bath, the doctors testified that, when Anna left the hospital after her illness, her stepmother might well have been warned to be careful about cold baths. With that assur-ance, the jurors were ready to condemn Marie Kutschera to death. It was ironic, to be sure, that after hearing all the evidence about how she had tortured the children, the jury finally condemned Marie Kutschera for giving Anna a bath. In this case, however, the legal ambiguities of child abuse could be resolved only after the resolution of the sentimental ambivalencies.

Before summing up the case for the jury, the prosecutor an-nounced that, on the strength of the children's testimony, the charges against Rudolf Kutschera were being withdrawn, and he would be left to his conscience. This announcment was greeted with applause. The post official walked out of the courtroom with-out looking at his wife, who was about to be condemned to death. Outside he fainted, and when he regained consciousness, according to the reporters, he asked to see his children.

Meanwhile Kleeborn was delivering a potent summation. He had been, as it happened, also the prosecutor of the Hummel trial two weeks before, but that had been an easy prosecution compared to this one. This time, as he conceded himself, he was asking the jury to believe in a charge that was "simply unbelievable": that a re-spectable father and stepmother had tortured their daughter to death. Six years before, far away in Massachusetts, a jury had refused to accept a reciprocally unbelievable charge: that a respect-able daughter could take an ax to her father and stepmother. And so Lizzie Borden, in spite of strong evidence against her, had been acquitted. The Viennese prosecutor's summation had to be power-ful if Marie Kutschera was not to escape justice. He asserted the innocence of childhood, called upon the mutilated corpse of the dead child to cry out its "blood accusation," and denounced Marie Kutschera for her disgusting "Tartüfferie" in pretending to have cared for Anna. He demanded the death penalty: "Here mercy? No! Here mildness? No!" The courtroom, whipped up to an emotional frenzy, responded to him with "intoxicated applause." To no avail the defense lawyer countered with a lengthy legal argument for "accidental homicide," not murder; in vain he protested that the prosecutor was creating a "mood trial," based on emotion instead of proof. The *Arbeiter-Zeitung* commented, not quite approvingly, that in parts of the summation the prosecutor spoke as a poet.

Marie Kutschera, like Musil's Moosbrugger, held Vienna "spell-bound like an obscure and sombre poem in which everything was faintly distorted and displaced, revealing a mutilated significance drifting in the depths of the mind." The prosecutor vanquished her and obtained her conviction by becoming a poet himself, by casting spells and manipulating distortions and displacements. The conse-quence of such a trial was that the mutilated significance of the central issue, that is, the significance of child abuse, never rose from the depths to the surface in fully comprehensible clarity. But per-haps Vienna preferred to leave the issue like that, distorted and submerged, an obscure and uninterpreted poem. The prosecutor, however, was not the last poet to sum up the case. Three days after the conclusion of the trial, the Kutschera case was given its final and definitive formulation in the city's leading newspaper, the *Neue Freie Presse*. There Felix Dörmann, that fin-de-siècle poet turned journalist, who had artistically reconceived the story of Hedwig Keplinger, now turned his attention to child abuse in a long and prominent piece, entitled "The Kutschera Case." The piece began with a literary flourish, with an ellipsis, *in medias res,* as if in the middle of a fairy tale.

### The Kutschera Case (Part I)

. . . and a short time after she bore him the seventh child, the wife of the k.k. post official died . . .

The salary of the former junior officer and later post official had happily reached the extent of eighty florins. They had to live on that: that means, one had to pay the rent, one had to buy clothing, and finally one had to eat—a man, a woman, and seven children.

And now the woman had died . . .

The man had his work, and it wasn't easy, but hard, long, and exhausting. And when such a man has made it through his office hours, there is usually not much left of his humanity; his work has devoured it. Such a man, when he is freed from work after many hard hours, then he scarcely senses anything except as reaction phenomena. He has scarcely any other desires except to be free as quickly as possible from the impressions of his work and his excessive burdens. All life functions, all personal desires and needs, that have been suppressed for hours and banished to beneath the threshold of consciousness, strive upwards and demand satisfaction. The beast of burden wants to become a human being: he too wants to have something of life. Yes, if he didn't have to twist around every penny, then it would go better, then one could already have something—but like this! And finally this drive towards life and pleasure and goods, this drive that is also the spur of all development and all striving, this drive always finds its end in a woman. A woman is the cheapest thing, the most comfortable thing—so it appears at least to the shortsighted man who can't take a larger view of events and their connections.

And suddenly the wife of the post official died. It was not just a personal blow—by all appearances he was fond of her. It was not only a deprivation of physical satisfaction, which was evidently necessary to his temperament. For along with his wife there also died the mother and educator, or at least the keeper, of his children.

For all that a substitute had to be provided.

The man needed a woman, and the children too.

Thus the Felzmann came into the house.

She was a good mother to the children. That may appear astonishing to some people who consider the spotted past life of this woman. But they know nothing of the spiritual life of these poor creatures, and they know least of all about the Viennese kind. They are all good-natured and softhearted, and when it comes to children, they can sacrifice themselves. They all dream of becoming respectable, and if someone comes and says something to them about marriage, he can do with them what he wants. They all have an inclination towards respectability and bourgeois life, which has both a touching and tragicomic effect.

The Felzmann was a true and good mother to Kutschera's seven children. She gave to the children from her own savings when the monthly income proved again to be too small. She managed the household, cared for the man whom she already regarded as hers. In short, conditions seemed to have become bearable. She did all that she could, for she was fond of the children, and *he* wanted to marry her.

But it turned out differently.

It could have been that the intimate cohabitation of the couple was not so delightful as he had hoped. It could have been that he calculated on improving himself financially by marrying someone else. In short, the Felzmann had to leave the house. He even called upon the force of the police to help. And another woman moved in—and with her came doom.

She was the widow of a prison commissioner . . .

## POOR CREATURES AND BEASTS OF BURDEN

Thus Dörmann began, once again, to interpret the tragedy of the day—and to recreate it as literature. The minor aesthetic poet of Young Vienna, in whose verse Schnitzler had once noted "brutalities and tastelessness, lyric falseness and sloppiness," was again chosen by the *Neue Freie Presse* to give the story its definitive form for the cultured bourgeoisie. It was an important commission, for the readers of the *Neue Freie Presse* would have to register this phenomenon of child abuse if it was not to be forgotten. And it was a delicate commission, for those readers could not but feel threatened by such a nasty case on the edge of their own social world, "the so-called better circles."

Dörmann's opening was stylistically reassuring, for his readers found themselves in the middle of a fairy tale: ". . . and a short time after she bore him the seventh child, the wife of the k.k. post official died . . ." It was to be a Habsburg fairy tale, marked with the mystical, unmistakable double "k"—a bold beginning, which drew attention to precisely the most delicate feature of the case. Dörmann, however, could afford to be direct about the fact that his protagonist was a Habsburg civil servant. After all, from the tone of that very first sentence, it would have been clear to every reader that the k.k. post official, whatever he might have been accused of in court, was to be the sympathetic hero of Dörmann's literary recreation. In court, three days before, the charges against Rudolf Kutschera had been withdrawn, and he was left to his conscience. There were some who applauded at that time, but for anyone in Vienna who still felt uncomfortable about that convenient last-minute withdrawal of charges, Dörmann provided a thinking man's vindication.

First of all, Dörmann, the son of a businessman, depicted the existence of a post official as something economically and spiritually oppressive in the extreme—the poet never attempted to conceive of the life of a laundry laborer. It was furthermore difficult to reconcile the poet's picture of Rudolf Kutschera as a "beast of burden" with the courtroom descriptions of the man with the elegant twirling mustache and the "Assyrian" beard. Dörmann analyzed the oppressive lot of his hero in terms that were heavy with philosophical and psychological pretension. While Hedwig Keplinger's sufferings were narrated from within, and presented as endearingly shallow ("Another disillusionment. Is all this really worth the effort?"), Rudolf Kutschera's condition of oppression was analyzed from without, in far weightier phrases. His was a case of reaction phenomena (Reactions-Erscheinungen), life functions (Lebensfunctionen), suppressed needs, the threshold of consciousness, the drive toward life, sexuality and temperament, events and connections, the spur of all striving, and the drive that always finds its end in a woman. It was a sort of intellectual potpourri, with scraps of Schopenhauer and Nietzsche, those two staple philosophers for contemporary Viennese thinkers. But there were also awkward foreshadowings of Freud, and even Kafka, in Dörmann's interpretation of the suppressed oppressed condition of a civil servant—for Dörmann was obviously very much attuned to what was intellectually in the air. His sympathetic analysis of Rudolf Kutschera consisted basically of a glib economic determinism enhanced by the trappings of philosophical pessimism, combined to depict the unhappy fate of modern man. Still, the characteristic Dörmann touch of heavyhanded sentimentality was clearly in evidence: The wife of the k.k. post official dies three times in the course of the opening paragraphs.

The apex of sentimentality, however, was Dörmann's interpretation of the Felzmann. The court had clearly decided, after examining her, that she was not the evil figure she had been made out to be. Dörmann, however, went much further than that in his tender portrayal of her soft heart, her self-sacrifice, and her loving care of the children. She would probably not have been very happy with this public presentation of herself, however sympathetic, for the one thing she was most eager to deny in court—that she was a prostitute—Dörmann took completely for granted. In fact, it was essential to his sympathetically sentimental characterization: the Felzmann was the proverbial whore with the heart of gold. With her dreams of respectability, this version of the Felzmann could have been Dörmann's Hedwig Keplinger fifteen years down the line. For Hedwig Keplinger, as Dörmann presented her, committed suicide when her last chance at a respectable marriage collapsed, when her only alternative to death was a life of prostitution. And Dörmann's Hedwig Keplinger also passionately loved her child—the child she killed—just as the Felzmann was presented as self-lessly loving of children. Dörmann further described the Felzmann with civic pride as the typical "Viennese kind" of prostitute. In this persona she could have emerged from Schnitzler's literary world of seducers and conquests—though Schnitzler would not have drawn the character so tritely, so sentimentally. Indeed, there was a distinct note of falseness in Dörmann's conception of her as the truly Viennese prostitute. For not only did she deny being a prostitute at all, but everyone in court could tell from her accent that she was Hungarian.

In leaving out her Hungarian accent, just as in leaving out the twirled mustache and Assyrian beard of the post official, Dörmann allowed himself a certain liberty of detail in creating characters who again straddled the borderline between fiction and journalism. His account of the oppressive lot of a post official was the work of a poet imagining the life of a civil servant. Of prostitution, perhaps, Dörmann had more direct experience. There was an air of boastful connoisseurship in his explanation to those who "know nothing" of these "poor creatures." He, who knew so much, now told the world that they were all softhearted, they all dreamed of becoming respectable, they were all both touching and tragicomic. Dörmann at least tried to address himself, in his literary reconstruction of the case, to the psychology and sociology of civil service and prostitution. He did not yet have anything to say about the psychology and sociology of child abuse, because the whole point of his interpretation was that Rudolf Kutschera and the Felzmann had nothing to do with abusing or corrupting the children. In his hands, their vindication was poetically conceived, intellectually elaborated, and sentimentally proclaimed to the cultured bourgeoisie of Vienna. Dörmann had nothing to say about child abuse until it came time to introduce the next character in the piece.

## The Kutschera Case (Part II)

She was the widow of a prison commissioner, and for years she had lived in the atmosphere of the Karthaus prison, and her brain was saturated with images of criminals and of crimes, of punishments

and chastisements. She was also hard of hearing, and this circumstance seems important to me. No physical infirmity reacts so characteristically upon the soul as deafness. No other infirmity is so
capable as this one of awakening mistrust and spitefulness. The deaf
person always has the feeling of being mocked, always has the
feeling of seeming comic and laughable. That person interprets
falsely every movement of other people, takes them personally—
and all this awakens a perpetual feeling of vindictiveness and irritation. It must be proved to the others: I am not so helpless as you
believe me to be, I can take care of myself, and I will prove it to you.
The children called the previous housekeeper Felzmann "Mother,"
and they were attached to her. The new mother had a difficult
position. Earlier, before she married her first husband, she belonged
to the serving class [dem dienenden Stande]. From a subordinate
who was commanded and scolded, all at once she became an independent person. This change tends to have a very characteristic
effect on limited natures. It awakens in them something like a
perverse feeling of power [ein perverses Machtgefühl]. A servant,
who suddenly acquires authority, enters into the atmosphere of a
prison where insubordinate criminals are ruled with an iron fist,
where a brutal feeling of power [ein brutales Machtgefühl] celebrates its orgies in the hearts of subordinate people. Servant natures
are supposed to play the parts of masters over "delinquents." And
from this environment the deaf, mistrustful person, with the brutal
and aberrant instincts, came into the house of the former junior
officer and king of recruits, into a house full of children who were
just the way that children are.

The woman obviously had the feeling: I am living among open
enemies whom I must conquer . . .


## "A PERVERSE FEELING OF POWER"

Dörmann was doing something that no one else had done: He was
considering Marie Kutschera as a psychological case study, and
trying to explain why she treated the children as she did—that is,
why she abused them. In this respect, Dörmann's effort, for all its
amateur limitations, may well be a landmark in the history of psychology, one of the very earliest attempts to analyze the psychology
of an abusive parent. And there were admirable insights in his
portrait: He seized upon two details that had been incidental in the
trial—her deafness and her first marriage to a prison commissioner—and considered their possible psychological significance.

This was a psychological conception conditioned by physiological and environmental factors, and also by one other all-important issue, the heart and soul of Dörmann's analysis—the problem of social class.

> The new mother had a difficult position. Earlier, before she married her first husband, she belonged to the serving class. From a subordinate who was commanded and scolded, all at once she became an independent person. This change tends to have a very characteristic effect on limited natures. It awakens in them something like a perverse feeling of power.

Dörmann looked back beyond Marie Kutschera's second marriage to the post official, back beyond her first marriage to the prison official, and discovered the fundamental factor at the root of her fully flowered monstrosity: Once upon a time, she belonged to the serving class.

It was a brilliant stroke, which perfectly resolved the disconcerting problem of child abuse for bourgeois Vienna. Victorian family sentiment made it impossible to accept the fact of parents torturing their children, and at the trial it was the stepmother who was made to bear full responsibility, while the father was absolved. However, from the very beginning, the Kutschera case was also impossibly disturbing to bourgeois class sentiment in Vienna; that is what made the case of the post official and his wife so much more problematic than that of the laundry laborer and his wife. Now, with the post official himself absolved of all responsibility in court, Dörmann provided the final crucially reassuring detail: By origin, Marie Kutschera did not belong to the bourgeoisie. The monster, destined for execution, condemned to sole responsibility, was neither a true mother nor a true member of the middle class. With this last fact established by Dörmann, the whole problem of child abuse could be consigned with relief, by the readers of the *Neue Freie Presse,* to that separate other world of the lower classes, to the same "low level of civilization" where the Hummel case occurred.

Dörmann's personal experience of "the serving class" was probably similar in nature to his personal experience of prostitution: He knew those servants who had served him. That he considered himself something of an expert on the serving class was already apparent in his confident treatment of the theme, six weeks before, in "Hedwig Keplinger: A Servant Girl's Fate." There he had showed that he could be deeply sympathetic to a servant girl who was seduced and abandoned—even if she ended up killing her child. The obvious social difference between Hedwig Keplinger and

Marie Kutschera was that the latter succeeded twice, where the former failed altogether; Marie Kutschera made a respectable marriage to a middle-class man, and then a respectable second marriage after she was widowed. And it was precisely that difference, the successful elevation from a "subordinate" to an "independent person," that made Marie Kutschera into a monster. According to Dörmann, the change of class had the "characteristic effect" of bringing out the "perverse feeling of power."

Dörmann's suggestion seemed to be that social mobility was the root of all evil, including child abuse. This was a profoundly conservative message coming from a classically liberal newspaper. Liberalism, after all, had been, historically, the ideology of bourgeois individualism; it had been virtually founded on the idea of social mobility, and against the static but crumbling feudal social order. Yet Dörmann, in 1899 in the Neue Freie Presse, found himself concerned about too abrupt changes of social status, afraid of a situation in which a born servant "suddenly acquires authority" and, with it, a perverse and brutal feeling of power. The rhetoric of "power" and "authority" point us toward a deeper reading of Dörmann's text. It was not simply a social sermon: it was a work of political metaphor. Dörmann was not set against the serving class bettering itself socially, but, rather, he was profoundly anxious about how that class might exercise power politically. Dörmann's concern was about "servant natures" who may "play the part of masters," and this political treatment of Marie Kutschera fit perfectly with the preoccupations of European, and especially Austrian, liberalism at the turn of the century.

The keystone of Carl Schorske's analysis of fin-de-siècle Vienna was the idea that the city's extraordinary cultural explosion was a consequence of the political and ideological collapse of Austrian liberalism; for the bourgeoisie, art became "an escape, a refuge from the unpleasant world of increasingly threatening political reality." After the economic crash of 1873, the Austrian bourgeois liberals lost their brief hold on political power, and could only watch in frustration as the conservative Emperor ruled with conservative aristocratic ministers. In the 1880s, however, there were already ominous warning signs of a new and different kind of threat to political liberalism, a rumbling from below, and by the 1890s there was no mistaking the growing power and significance of new political parties that sought to mobilize the masses. Liberalism, even in opposition to the imperial government, found its political values and political power under attack from Georg von Schönerer's ferociously nationalist Pan-Germans, from Karl Lueger's clerical Christian Socialists, from Viktor Adler's Marxist Social Democrats, and from the ever more strident national movements of the Austrian Slavs, especially the Czechs in Bohemia. The mass appeal of such movements as these left the Austrian liberals helplessly surrounded on a constantly shrinking political domain. At the same time, the call for universal suffrage became more and more forceful, and the object would finally be achieved in 1907. Considering the kinds of arguments that nineteenth-century liberals raised against the demo-cratic extension of suffrage—notably, the alleged danger of giving the vote to those who were not ready to exercise it responsibly—there was an unmistakable parallel to Dörmann's concern about putting power in the hands of "servant natures."

This was the political background that sent the bourgeois aes-thetes to take refuge in the world of art. Stefan Zweig, looking back to his student years, remembered the period thus:

> The city was aroused at the elections, and we went to the libraries.
> The masses rose, and we wrote and discussed poetry. We did not see
> the fiery signs on the wall . . .

Even looking back after half a century had passed, Zweig could not seem to help writing about the emergence of mass politics—"the masses rose"—in terms of mystifying abstraction and generaliza-tion:

> The masses, which had silently and obediently permitted the liberal
> middle classes to retain the leadership for decades, suddenly became
> restless, organized themselves, and demanded their rights.

This was hardly a process that could have occurred "suddenly," as Zweig remembered it, and yet there were, no doubt, moments of sudden revelation, when even the most dedicated poets and aes-thetes could not help realizing what was happening in the political world. In Schnitzler's *The Green Cockatoo* of 1899, the aristocrats at their theatrical club in 1789 were about to discover that, outside, the masses were storming the Bastille. In turn-of-the-century Vienna, one such year of revelation, when the ugliness of politics was particularly hard to overlook, was 1897—the year of the con-troversy over the Badeni language laws for Bohemia. And by 1899 even Felix Dörmann, a paragon of poetic aestheticism back in the early nineties, was seriously alarmed by the nature of contemporary politics.

The year 1897 witnessed one shock after another to the liberal vision of politics in Austria. It began with the national elections in March, which were the first to test Badeni's franchise reform.

Count Casimir Badeni, a Polish aristocrat noted for a certain physical resemblance to Bismarck, had devised an extension of the franchise which, in the Emperor's view, should have settled forever the
whole issue of universal suffrage. In fact, under Badeni's plan, virtually all men would vote—but the five million newly enfranchised
voters would elect only 72 representatives to a parliament of 425.
The remaining 353 representatives would still be elected by the
previously enfranchised two million voters, who met the property
qualifications. This system thus added a fifth "curia," based on
universal suffrage, to the already existing four classes of qualified
voters. The Emperor and his minister might regard this as the final
solution of the suffrage question, but more prescient contemporaries
could recognize that it offered only a taste of what was to come in
an age of mass politics, which would eventually triumph through
true universal suffrage.

The Austrian liberals were particularly distressed by the election
results of March 1897. German nationalist sentiment had undermined the wings of the party so that the traditional liberal organiza-
tion of Ignaz von Plener and his son Ernst von Plener won only
fourteen seats in the Reichsrat. Even the Social Democrats won
fifteen. Furthermore, Karl Lueger's Christian Socialists did so well
under the new franchise—electing twenty-eight representatives—
that the liberals, still reeling from the national elections in March,
suffered an even more painful blow in Viennese municipal politics
in April. Since the revolution of 1848, Vienna's municipal government had been liberal. In 1895 the Christian Socialists had won the
city elections, but the Emperor had refused to confirm Lueger in the
office of mayor—and the liberal Sigmund Freud had smoked a cigar
in celebration. Now, after the national elections of 1897, the Emperor felt he could no longer continue to resist the will of the
Viennese electorate. Lueger became mayor, closing the book on a
half century of municipal liberalism, and the editors and readers of
the *Neue Freie Presse* had to face the fact that the city no longer
belonged to them.

While the national elections with the new franchise in March,
and the confirmation of Lueger as mayor in April, constituted specific painful defeats for Austrian liberalism, the crisis over the Badeni language laws created an ongoing trauma which shattered the
whole liberal conception of political life. That trauma became more
and more intense from the moment the laws were proposed in
April, until Badeni's resignation in November, and the crisis continued for two more years until the laws were withdrawn in Octo-

ber 1899. The point of the language laws was to make the Czech language as important as German in the administration of Bohemia, and the nationalist passions that the controversy roused virtually demolished the political life of the Habsburg empire. For Georg von Schönerer, it was the opportunity of a lifetime to mobilize violent German nationalist sentiment in Austria. The Reichsrat, the shrine of liberalism, succumbed to furious obstruction, and parliamentary politics collapsed as the representatives hurled their inkstands at each other. The Emperor could govern only by extra-parliamentary emergency measures. Meanwhile, the streets of Vienna became the scene of demonstrations and riots, to an extent unprecedented since the revolution of 1848. In fact, in 1897 there were those who felt that Austria was on the brink of some sort of revolution. Badeni fought a duel with one of Schönerer's parliamentary deputies, and the Emperor wrote to his mistress, "I think that Count Badeni has done Representative Wolf too much honor in fighting with him, for nothing but a caning is really due such people." But Austrian politics had passed the point where the masses and their representatives could be caned into subordination, according to the feudal vision; and neither could they be simply electorally excluded and politically ignored, according to the liberal vision.

On November 28, 1897 (exactly two years, to the day, before the opening of the Kutschera trial), thousands on the Ringstrasse screamed for Badeni's resignation, and Badeni resigned. Stefan Zweig, who at the time preferred to think about poetry, looked back on the moment of Badeni's resignation with a liberal appreciation of its fatefulness.

> The invasion of brutality into politics thus chalked up its first success. All of the underground cracks and crevices between classes and races, which the age of conciliation had so laboriously patched up, broke open once again and widened into abysses and chasms. In reality it was during the last decade preceding the new century that the war of all against all had already begun in Austria.

Zweig, like Dörmann, was a minor poet of Young Vienna in the nineties. Dörmann had lived through the same political watershed in 1897, just at the time of the demolition of the Cafe Griensteidl, and in 1899 he warned readers of the *Neue Freie Presse* that "a brutal feeling of power celebrates its orgies in the hearts of subordinate people." The origin of this evil, in family life as in political life, Dörmann traced to "servant natures"—like Marie Kutschera—playing the part of "masters." The danger came from making "all at once" an "independent person" (an enfranchised voter, perhaps) out of "a subordinate who was commanded and scolded." And caned, Dörmann might have added.

That Dörmann's psychology of child abuse should have been framed in political metaphors was altogether characteristic of fin-de-siècle Vienna, and historians have already noted other such connections between politics and psychology. Schorske's path-breaking 1961 article was entitled "Politics and the Psyche," and argued that the discovery of "psychological man" in fin-de-siècle Vienna emerged from "the dissolution of the classical liberal view of man in the crucible of Austria's modern politics." In 1973, in an article entitled "Politics and Patricide in Freud's *Interpretation of Dreams,*" Schorske analyzed the political contents and implications of some of Freud's dreams; he concluded that in the Oedipus complex, "Freud gave his fellow liberals an a-historical theory of man and society that could make bearable a political world spun out of orbit and beyond control." William McGrath published in 1986 a book entitled *Freud's Discovery of Psychoanalysis: The Politics of Hysteria.* McGrath argued that Freud's intellectual development in the 1890s was "closely interwoven with the violent political history of his time"—and that the crisis over the Badeni language laws was especially significant in this respect. In fact, such classic psychoanalytical concepts as "censorship" and "repression" may have had their origins in the contemporary political context. Dörmann, of course, was just an amateur psychologist, no genius like Freud, but the very crudeness of the poet's case study of Marie Kutschera revealed all the more clearly the integration of psychological and political concerns. Dörmann, like Freud, was confronting a new sort of problem, a psychological frontier, and his formulation was built upon the more familiar, though no less disturbing ground of contemporary politics. In fact, the anxieties generated by the Kutschera case seemed to feed upon liberal political anxieties, confirming, reinforcing, and explaining each other. And in the *Neue Freie Presse,* Dörmann could be sure of finding precisely that audience which was most receptive to his interpretation.

This mingling of anxieties fit neatly with another aspect of the child abuse sensation. Child abuse could be construed as a response to charges of Jewish ritual murder—a refutation that pointed to the possibility of violence within the family—just as child abuse could be presented as a warning about how the lower classes would exercise political power. Anti-Semitic agitation and the mobilization of mass political parties were overlapping preoccupations for liberal Vienna, overlapping horrors, and the child abuse sensation, a new horror, could serve to neutralize, criticize, and stigmatize the others. On the one hand, there was something opportunistic about this far from dispassionate approach to child abuse—for child abuse was not being seriously considered for its own sake, on its own terms. And on the other hand, there was something impressively creative in seizing upon such a new phenomenon as child abuse and  making it serve such imaginative purposes. When Schorske wrote about pioneers of mass politics in fin-de-siècle Vienna, the men who created a "politics in a new key," he emphasized the turning from a liberal "politics of reason" to a new "politics of fantasy." According to Schorske:

> Schönerer, Lueger, and Herzl all began their careers as political liberals and then apostasized to organize masses neglected or rejected by liberalism in ascendancy. All possessed the peculiar gift of answering the social and spiritual needs of their followers by composing ideological collages . . .

In Dörmann's piece "The Kutschera Case," in the *Neue Freie Presse,* Austrian liberalism responded in kind to the new political forces, responded in the "new key." Rational political argument alone was inadequate to the challenge of mass movements and parties, and so Dörmann and the *Neue Freie Presse* experimented with the formulation of fantasy and the creation of collage. By metaphor, by association, by poetic and literary and journalistic craft, the Hummel trial and the Kutschera trial could become either a refutation of the ritual murder charge or a liberal political prophecy. Dörmann suggested that Marie Kutschera abused her stepchildren because she came from the serving class, and was raised up to exercise her perverse and brutal feeling of power. By implication, if readers of the *Neue Freie Presse* wondered what it might mean for a mass party to achieve power in Austria, they had only to consider the fate of the Kutschera children. Stefan Zweig, writing in exile during World War II, a Jewish intellectual refugee from Hitler's Europe, might have considered that Dörmann's prophecy had come true.

These were the urgent and complex motives behind Dörmann's emphasis on the fact that Marie Kutschera, once upon a time, "belonged to the serving class"—but, as it happens, she had never belonged to the serving class at all. During the trial, the *Neue Freie Presse* did not go into the question of her origins, but the *Arbeiter-Zeitung,* especially interested in this case of abuse among "the so-called better circles," had ascertained the relevant details. On the very first day of the trial, these were explicitly set forth:

> Rudolf Kutschera is a state official, and Marie Kutschera came from that same milieu which she has never stepped out of in her life. As the

daughter of an official of Prince Auersperg, she became the wife of an economic official in the Karthaus prison, and then, after his death, the housekeeper and then the wife of the post official Kutschera.

There was no question about it: she was the daughter of an official, before becoming the wife of two others. If she was ever "commanded and scolded" in the distant past, it was not as a servant, but only as a child. And there was a special irony in the fact that her father was connected to the administration of a Prince Auersperg. For there were two princes of that family who were both prominent in Austrian politics in the previous generation, Prince Carlos Auersperg and Prince Adolf Auersperg—and both princes headed liberal ministries during the brief heyday of Austrian liberalism. In short, Marie Kutschera was not just the daughter of a middle-class official, but even from a family especially affiliated with the liberal world. For Schorske, the creators of Viennese fin-de-siècle culture were the "children" of Austrian liberalism—and Marie Kutschera was also literally just such a child. It was a detail that Felix Dörmann, another such child, suppressed.

Dörmann's treatment of Hedwig Keplinger, narrating her inner monologue, amounted to a work of fictionalization. Also in his handling of the Kutschera case, the details of the post official's elegant mustache and beard, of the Felzmann's Hungarian accent, could be left to one side if they clashed with the literary characterization. How then should one interpret Dörmann's explicit falsification of the social background of Marie Kutschera? It is, of course, possible that Dörmann shamelessly fabricated the crucial detail, in order to suit the sensibilities of his readers. Those sensibilities, however, were so pervasive and compelling that Dörmann probably just assumed he was right, knew nothing to the contrary, and took advantage of poetic license to put the finishing touch on his story. Then the characterization was complete: his exploration of child abuse by political metaphor, his analysis of how the lower classes use—and abuse—power.

His story, with its crucial falsification, was published in the *Neue Freie Presse,* and thus became the definitive version of the Kutschera case. None of its liberal readers would have been likely to check that falsehood—which seemed so plausible and appropriate—against the details published a week before in the sectarian socialist *Arbeiter-Zeitung.* Dörmann's poetic falsehood was enshrined as public truth. Thus he explained to Vienna the circumstances in the background of Marie Kutschera that conditioned her monstrosity: her deafness, her marriage to the prison official, and above all her origin in the serving class. Dörmann, however, had

not hesitated to describe Hedwig Keplinger at the climactic moment of murder and suicide. So, now, he boldly concluded his piece
on the Kutschera case by analyzing the psychology of the stepmother when she was actually abusing the children.

## The Kutschera Case (Part III)

The woman obviously had the feeling: I am living among open
enemies whom I must conquer. But they were also enemies who
gnawed at the meager bread of the family, for the house was a house
of misery. The widow had brought a son along with her, and he
was the eighth child in the house. So ten people were supposed to
exist on about eighty florins. Sometimes hunger must have reigned.
And as hunger demoralizes, the wildest and most brutal instincts
are freed, and men are made into beasts. This will be understood
only by someone who has himself starved, not for sport or curiosity,
but in cold and despair. There must have been more than a few days
when there was neither bread nor firewood to be found in the
Kutschera house. I would like to sum up the situation once more.
Misery, a house of children with hungry stomachs, a vexed woman,
hard of hearing, full of mistrust, a man worn out by his work who
wants to have peace, or at most diversion, when he comes home—
but really when does he come home?

And she, the pseudo-mother, alone with the children—the children swarm about—begging, starving, they seek after that which
they do not find at home: bread, warmth, and love. Each swarming
has punishment as its consequence. Perhaps the woman at first still
wants to have an educating effect, as she understands it. Probably
from her own youth she also still has the old whipping instinct, and
believes that is the only possible method. In any case, later there
comes into play all the emotions resulting from her prison past and
her deafness. And also something else: in the train of a megalomani-
acal feeling of power, cruelty is almost always lurking. To be able to
punish, to have to punish, becomes a pleasure. Blood and wounds,
cries of pain, convulsive limbs, begin to become pleasant and agreeable images. The secret histories of the monasteries and prisons
could tell us something of this. The word torture-joy [*Folterfreude*]
is not a new one, no more so than the famous words of a French
poet: *Ici, l'on torture.* And it went so far that Frau Kutschera
tortured her children. Her type stands roughly in between the professional foster-parent killer, the angel-maker, who slowly liberates,
in a murderous way, the women of the lower classes from the social

burden of their children, and the type of that institutional headmis-
tress who has her pupils disciplined for the slightest transgression
with rod and knout, in order to have the pleasure of her complete
power and cruelty.

## "EVERYTHING STRANGE AND SICK"

Dörmann first added to his case study of the family the conditioning
factor of miserable poverty, dramatically evoked—as no one ever
bothered to do on behalf of the Hummel family, who were genu-
inely poor. In Dörmann's version one could almost forget that this
was the family of a middle-class official—which was just what
bourgeois Vienna would have liked to forget. This account was
perhaps closer to one of Hitler's explorations of the social question,
his parables of life in the social depths of the urban world. Here too
one must suppose that Dörmann allowed himself a certain poetic
license, making the Kutschera situation seem less disturbingly relevant to the bourgeois readers of the newspaper. Dörmann reassured
them that human beings did not abuse their children, unless they
had been transformed by hunger into "beasts." Dörmann even reminded his readers that they could not imagine the demoralization
of hunger, since they had never truly experienced it—unless perhaps "for sport or curiosity." In evoking starvation for them, of
course, he meant to appeal to precisely that prurient curiosity, and
there was something pompous and false about his implication that
he, the poet, really understood hunger from experience. On the
other hand, Dörmann's psychological elaborations on Marie
Kutschera involved states of mind that any respectable citizen, or
any poet, could conceivably know from experience—even if Dörmann managed to suggest that they were consequences of humble
birth. Marie Kutschera was subject to paranoia, seeing the children
as her enemies, and, above all, she was a sadist who took pleasure in
torture.

The concluding emphasis on sadism again showed Dörmann
thinking more psychologically than anyone had at the trial. And
yet, while sadism was certainly not irrelevant to the case, neither
was it a particularly illuminating approach to the specific problem
of child abuse. It was, however, profoundly illuminating for what it
told about Dörmann himself. His treatment of the issue of sadism
offered an important clue to what he found so compelling about
child abuse. "To be able to punish, to have to punish, becomes a
pleasure. Blood and wounds, cries of pain, convulsive limbs, begin
to become pleasant and agreeable images." It was an important

moment in the piece, for it was the moment where Dörmann came closest to writing interior monologue for Marie Kutschera, the same technique of fictionalization that he had employed in the story of Hedwig Keplinger. The catalog of "images" could almost have been within the subject's consciousness, and at the same time it was in these images that Dörmann came closest to bringing his poetic art into play.

Blood and wounds, cries of pain, convulsive limbs: these were also the images that filled Dörmann's poems in the early nineties. Such were the invocations of the "decadent" poet of the fin de siècle. If someone were to undertake the inane task of compiling a concordance to such a minor body of verse, there would be much exotic floral vocabulary—but "blood" and "wounds" and "pain" would be outnumbered only by the recurrences of the word "torments." There were, for instance, these lines from Dörmann's fragment of a verse play, "Tubal and Lilith."

> For torments thirsts the flaming soul,
> For torments that no one has known until now,
> For torments that no one has put into words,
> For those highest, ultimate, deepest torments . . .

> (Nach Qualen durstet die entflammte Seele,
> Nach Qualen, die kein Mensch bis heute trug,
> Nach Qualen, die kein Mensch in Worte zwang,
> Nach jenen höchsten, letzten, tiefsten Qualen . . .)

These were Dörmann's poetic values, and they conditioned his conception of the Kutschera case: a case of torments of an unprecedented nature. Even more important, in this respect, was a poem that Dörmann wrote as a sort of credo and manifesto, "What I Love," in the collection *Sensations*, published in 1892. It was one of his most famous poems in the nineties, and Karl Kraus singled it out for special contempt when he satirized the poets of the Cafe Griensteidl. The first verse and the last verse seemed to foreshadow Dörmann's later interest in Hedwig Keplinger and Marie Kutschera.

> I love the hectic, slender
> Narcissus with blood-red mouth;
> I love thoughts of torment,
> Hearts pierced and wounded . . .

> (Ich liebe die hektischen, schlanken
> Narzissen mit blutrothem Mund;

Ich liebe die Qualengedanken,
Die Herzen zerstochen und wund . . .)

I love what no one would choose,
What could be loved by no one:
My own most inner essence
And everything strange and sick.

(Ich liebe was niemand erlesen,
Was keinem zu lieben gelang:
Mein eigenes, urinnerstes Wesen
Und alles, was seltsam und krank.)

Karl Kraus mocked Dörmann's proclaimed predilection for "everything strange and sick," and there was indeed something pompous
and affected about this self-consciously perverse and decadent manifesto. The poet, whose "tastelessness" was noted even by his
friends, could not resist the cliché, even in his expressions of perver-
sion and decadence.

However, the formulas of "What I Love" in 1892—the blood-
red mouth, the thoughts of torment, the hearts pierced and
wounded, and everything strange and sick—could be set alongside
the "pleasant and agreeable images" he attributed to Marie
Kutschera in 1899: "blood and wounds, cries of pain, convulsive
limbs." Felix Dörmann in 1899, ready to move on from the poetic
and aesthetic decadence of the early nineties, seeking a more meaningful relation to social reality in journalism, discovered in the
Kutschera case precisely those clichés of decadence that he had left
behind. The critic Arthur Moeller van den Bruck, a literary herald
of the Third Reich, censured Dörmann's poetry for its "flirtation
with horrors"—and it was an ongoing flirtation, easily adapted
from poetry to journalism. Indeed, Dörmann had only to move from
the poetry of Sensations to sensational journalism.

It was his poetic fascination with "everything strange and sick"
and "hearts pierced and wounded" that drew him to the cases of
Hedwig Keplinger and Marie Kutschera, to child murder and child
abuse. This was the element of cultural continuity between his
vocation as a decadent poet in the early nineties and his new calling
as Vienna's interpreter of child murder and child abuse in 1899.
And that continuity was part of the intellectual history of the decade. It was ironic that Dörmann, seeking for himself a meaningful
movement from poetic aestheticism toward social realism, should
have ended up creating, for the Viennese public, a version of reality
hopelessly colored by those same aesthetic values, from which he

could never free himself. Dörmann, more than anyone, responded to the Kutschera case as a poet, was held spellbound, and helped to make it into "an obscure and sombre poem in which everything was faintly distorted and displaced." And it was Dörmann's conception of the case that revealed, behind those distortions and displacements, the cherished cultural values of the fin de siècle.


## ELEKTRA

Dörmann provided an explicit cultural connection between Young Vienna and the child abuse sensation of 1899. It was not Dörmann, however, but Hofmannsthal who was the true poet of Young Vienna, the boy whose genius overshadowed Dörmann's talent from the very beginning of both their careers. Hugo von Hofmannsthal was only twentyfive in 1899, regarded as perhaps the greatest living poet in the German language, and on the verge of a personal and artistic crisis that ended in the renunciation of lyric poetry. Hofmannsthal always, even as an adolescent prodigy, had been a poet whose exquisite aesthetic genius was tempered by his consciousness of the treacherousness of aestheticism. In *The Death of Titian* and *The Fool and Death,* aestheticism was poetically analyzed, but never embraced. Even so, by the end of the decade, Hofmannsthal found himself in search of what he called "connection with life" (*Verknüpfung mit dem Leben*); he experienced an agonizing loss of faith in language and literature, which he later recorded in 1902 as an Elizabethan epistolary confession by a fictional Lord Chandos writing to Francis Bacon. Lord Chandos wrote, "I have lost completely the ability to speak or to think of anything coherently." Hofmannsthal's personal crisis found a certain resolution in marriage in 1901, followed by the birth of children in 1902 and 1903. The artistic crisis was surmounted only by putting aside lyric poetry and turning to drama.

In his longing for that "connection with life," and in his determined adoption of a new literary genre, the greatest of the Young Vienna poets demonstrated a trajectory not so unlike that of the less gifted Felix Dörmann. Both men were putting findesiècle poetry behind them, and seeking in a change of genre to achieve something more socially meaningful in the new century. For Dörmann the Kutschera case became a part of this transformation, an opportunity at the very end of the decade to address serious social and psychological issues in the leading newspaper of the city. Hofmannsthal, on the other hand, left no written evidence that he took any notice of the Hummel and Kutschera trials. He could not have been unaware of them, however, for the child abuse sensation filled the newspapers, and Hofmannsthal was in Vienna during the month of November 1899.

On November 10, a few days before the Hummel trial, he wrote from Vienna to a friend.

> Indeed when one works, one is not lonely. For on the deepest level, one burrows about among one's deepest memories, and touches on everything one has ever experienced and seen and sympathized with. And one connects oneself through work, often more deeply than through intercourse or reflection, with other human beings.

On November 17, a few days after the Hummel trial, Hofmannsthal was no longer so reclusively absorbed by his work, and sent a note to Schnitzler suggesting that they meet. Thus we know that both men were in Vienna at the time.

> I'm not free Sunday, but tomorrow Saturday night. Please—I hope we can get together—decide on a rendezvous and send me a pneumatic dispatch . . .

On December 8, a week after the end of the Kutschera trial, Hof-mannsthal wrote from Vienna to a friend about that important writer's issue of unfinished literary projects.

> I believe the only things to do is this: as seldom as possible to give up something one has started, as seldom as possible to surrender to outer or inner resistance, as seldom as possible to renounce one's early work and seek new foundations.

This last letter showed that the poet remained in Vienna through both child abuse trials. It was also significant in view of the fact that Hofmannsthal was about to renounce his genius for lyric poetry and establish a completely new literary "foundation." At the same time, there was another less obvious significance, connected to Hofmannsthal's literary activities in 1899. For in that year, he did the thing he claimed to do as seldom as possible: He started a new project, and then gave it up.

Hofmannsthal's collected work contains the synopsis for a comic drama, sketched out in 1899, but never written. The title was "Mother and Daughter." It concerned a countess and her adolescent daughter in Oedipal rivalry, both in love with the same unworthy, social-climbing musician. The plot culminated in the banishment of the musician, and the revelation that the faithful old family servant was actually the girl's natural father. Hofmannsthal imagined Eleanora Duse in the part of the countess, but he never

finished writing the play. He was, in fact, on the edge of his traumatic crisis of artistic expression.

Those final months of 1899 could not have been encouraging for
the completion of a comedy about mothers and daughters. The
news of the day concerned Hedwig Keplinger and her daughter,
Juliane Hummel and her daughter, Marie Kutschera and her daughter. Could this have been one reason why Hofmannsthal abandoned the play? But perhaps he did not abandon it entirely, for
when he turned to his next important work in 1901, his crisis
behind him, it was his German version of the Sophocles *Electra*. It is
perhaps the single play in the entire history of drama which could
most appropriately bear the title "Mother and Daughter." And it
was definitely not a comedy. In fact, the central relationship between mother and daughter, between Clytemnestra and Electra,
was one of murderous hatred. Whether or not Hofmannsthal was
consciously or unconsciously influenced by the child abuse sensation, this much can be said with certainty: in 1899 he was planning
a comic drama about mothers and daughters, but he gave it up, and
instead his next major project, his first of the twentieth century,
was a terrible tragedy of mothers and daughters. His conception of
the theme had certainly undergone a complete transformation.

Hofmannsthal did not invent the Electra story, of course, any
more than Freud invented the Oedipus story which he wrote about
in *The Interpretation of Dreams*. Indeed, Hofmannsthal's imagination was even more strictly disciplined than Freud's in this respect,
for the poet was working from Sophocles, even if the German version was a "free" one. But Hofmannsthal *chose* the Electra story,
just as Freud chose Oedipus. Freud's choice was a scientific one, for
the Oedipus myth illustrated certain observations he had made
about the nature of family relations, as expressed in dreams. By the
same token, Hofmannsthal's choice of Electra could not have been a
random one; he too wanted to write about hatred within the family—and at the same time that he himself was marrying and starting
a family of his own. Both geniuses, by their respective choices,
demonstrated visions that could see beyond the general Victorian
domestic sentimentality, which conditioned the public reception of
the Viennese child abuse sensation in 1899. Freud, the scientist,
came by his vision from analyzing his dreams and his patients.
Hofmannsthal, the artist, must have come to his vision as described
in the letter of November 1899: "For on the deepest level, one
burrows about among one's deepest memories, and touches on
everything one has ever experienced and seen and sympathized
with." Hofmannsthal chose the subject of Electra in 1901. In that

same year, Gustav Mahler chose certain poems of Friedrich Rückert to set to music as "Die Kindertotenlieder"—"Songs of the Deaths of Children." Mahler too was in Vienna, conducting *Die Meister-singer,* on the night before the opening of the Kutschera trial. Hofmannsthal's *Elektra* is best known today in the form of the magnificent opera that Richard Strauss composed, with the play as his libretto. It was an important episode in the history of opera, for *Elektra* led to the great Strauss-Hofmannsthal collaboration, which over the next twenty years created *Der Rosenkavalier, Ariadne auf Naxos, Die Frau Ohne Schatten,* and *Arabella.* Before the premiere of the opera *Elektra* in 1909, however, Hofmannsthal's *Elektra* had a life of its own as a play, beginning with the Max Reinhardt staging in 1903. The critics were overwhelmed by its emotional violence and psychopathological intensity. Alfred Kerr judged it a work of "blood revelry," but more than mere "decadence horror." Regarding the climactic murder of Klytemnestra, Kerr wrote: "In Sophocles the murder of the guilty satisfies the morality of a whole people, but in Hofmannsthal it is more the private thirst for ven-geance of an epileptic." For Maximilian Harden, Elektra's illness was not epilepsy, but hysteria—"She is Agamemnon's hysterical daughter." If Hofmannsthal was indeed writing about hysteria, he was in the excellent company of his good friend Schnitzler—and also two little-known doctors, Josef Breuer and Sigmund Freud. In short, Hofmannsthal's depiction of mother and daughter suggested all the psychopathological complexity that was absent from the trials of the mothers who murdered their daughters in Vienna a few years before.

Hermann Bahr, once the high priest of Young Vienna, the man who "discovered" Hofmannsthal as a high school student, reacted to Elektra, as performed by the actress Gertrud Eysoldt, as the embodiment of hatred.

> Eating hate. Drinking hate. Spitting hate. Wounded with hate, volup-tuous with hate, mad with hate. No longer a being who hates, but hatred itself . . . Terrible, say the people, shuddering together. Terri-ble. But Greek in just that . . . For that is Greek: to find beauty in the terrible.

Greek, and also Viennese. Everyone knows that the object of Electra's colossal hatred is her mother Clytemnestra, and the mo-tive is revenge for the murder of her father Agamemnon. There is also, however, another less well recognized dimension to that ha-tred, which is present in Sophocles, and even more present in Hof-mannsthal. It became explicit in the central scene of recognition, when Electra encountered the stranger who was actually her brother Orestes. Before he declared himself, he questioned her about her terribly changed appearance and about her life in the house of her mother and her mother's lover. Although Electra was no longer a child at the time of Orestes' return, the story that came out was unmistakably a story of abuse. Sophocles presented it in these lines:

> ELECTRA: My father's murder—and I the murderers' slave—
> ORESTES: By whose compulsion?
> ELECTRA: A mother's—in name, but nothing else, a mother.
> ORESTES: What are her weapons? Force, privation?
> ELECTRA: Both. Force and privation, and malice of every kind.

The passage from Sophocles was short, but clear. In Hofmannsthal's "free" version, it became more graphic, and more intense:

> ORESTES: So did they let you starve—or did they beat you?
> ELEKTRA: Who are you with your many questions?
> ORESTES: Tell me! Tell me! Tell!
> ELEKTRA: Both! Both! Both! Queens do not thrive when one fodders them with rejected vegetables. Priestesses are not made to jump to the whip . . .

Starving, beating, whipping: here was a daughter abused by her mother, not in the room of a laundry laborer, not in the apartment of a post official, but in the palace of a king. With all those exclamation points Hofmannsthal emphasized violently what Sophocles presented with such classical restraint.

Hermann Bahr noted that at the performance, during the scene of confrontation between Elektra and Klytemnestra, the audience became particularly "agitated, shaking itself like a horse who snorts with impatience." Certainly it was far more agitating than anything else the Viennese could have seen on the stage about mothers and daughters—and a far cry from the comedy Hofmannsthal had planned to give to Vienna in 1899. Indeed, before the premiere of *Elektra* in 1903, the one recent opportunity for the public to observe a mother such as Klytemnestra might have been in 1899, at the trials of Juliane Hummel and Marie Kutschera. Hofmannsthal's choice of theme and subject, whether or not he was influenced by the trials, was at least a remarkable instance of cultural convergence. He, like Dörmann, like Freud, was ready to take an interest in certain unthinkable aspects of family life. In 1899, when Juliane Hummel was sentenced, there were cries of bravo in the courtroom, "an acclamation the like of which we cannot remember ever before at a condemnation to death." In 1903, when Hofmannsthal's

*Elektra* was performed, Elektra danced a dance of exultation after her mother had been killed, and then the curtain fell so that the audience could applaud and acclaim an unforgettable performance of a horrifying drama.

## THE GODDESS OF JUSTICE

That it was Felix Dörmann who presented Vienna with the definitive formulation of the Kutschera case, in the pages of the *Neue Freie Presse,* made the child abuse sensation of 1899 more than just an episode in the social and judicial history of the city. The conjunction of Felix Dörmann and the *Neue Freie Presse,* the prototypical poet of Young Vienna and the journalistic pillar of Austrian liberalism, established these child abuse cases in their cultural and political context. Was there also a connection to Hofmannsthal, to "Mother and Daughter" and *Elektra?* Was there any significance in the thematic association with Mahler's *Kindertotenlieder?* These may have been no more than interesting instances of cultural convergence, but there was at least one unquestionable case of intellectual cognizance, for one of the towering geniuses of the city did remark upon the child abuse trials—and not obscurely either, but prominently in public. Karl Kraus wrote about the Hummel and Kutschera cases on the front page of *Die Fackel,* in the very first issue of the twentieth century.

Kraus's treatment of the cases in *Die Fackel* was radically different in perspective from that of Dörmann in the *Neue Freie Presse*— for Kraus despised the aesthetic poet and detested the liberal newspaper. In "Literature Demolished" in 1897, Kraus had treated Dörmann with mockery, laughing at his "withered nerves," his ecstasies and mannerisms, and of course his passion for "everything strange and sick." When Dörmann's modest talents received some public recognition, Kraus couldn't keep from remarking in *Die Fackel* that he was ashamed to be living in "a world in which Herr Felix Dörmann can receive a poetry prize." Kraus's contempt for Dörmann was only a minor diversion for the great satirist, but his hatred for the *Neue Freie Presse* was one of the governing passions of his life. "There are two fine things in the world: to be part of the *Neue Freie Presse* or to despise it. I did not hesitate for one moment as to what my choice had to be." Actually, 1899 was the year that Kraus made that choice, declining Benedikt's offer of an important editorial position in January, and then founding *Die Fackel* in April. Whether or not Kraus's hatred of Benedikt was properly "Oedipal," as suggested at the Vienna Psychoanalytic Society, he certainly developed a sort of mythology of his own to express that hatred. Benedikt was "the king of the hyenas," while the *Neue Freie Presse* was simply "an old whore." For Kraus, the appearance of Dörmann in the *Neue Freie Presse* was a fitting conjunction for both the poet and the paper. He was amused to think of the old whore going in for "new literature" by publishing Dörmann: the worst of the old and the worst of the new. Naturally, Kraus in *Die Fackel* saw the child abuse cases rather differently from Dörmann in the *Neue Freie Presse*.

"Year out, year in," Kraus began—an appropriate opening for the lead article in the first issue of the new year, the new century. The court and the press had disposed of the child abuse cases just in time to mark the end of the century, just in time to face the twentieth century with a clean slate. Dörmann's final summation of the Kutschera case appeared on December 3, 1899. Kraus, by giving the cases one last public presentation in January 1900—"year out, year in"—seemed to insist that the issue could not be consigned to the old century, closed forever with a few executions and a few words from Felix Dörmann. But Kraus did not succeed in keeping the issue alive, only in having the last word. Karl Kraus, after all, was one lone genius, and *Die Fackel* was written for his intellectual devotees. Still, it was true that his savage satirical campaigns could sometimes keep alive issues that the Viennese public preferred to forget.

The heroine—or, rather, the villainess—of the opening sentences was neither Juliane Hummel, nor Marie Kutschera, but instead the mythological Themis, daughter of Uranus, the goddess of justice.

> Year out, year in, the eyes of our Themis are covered. But when evils that everyone has long recognized finally cry out, then terrified she tears the blindfold away and throws up her hands in astonishment: "One wouldn't have thought it possible!" And then she is excessive in punishment. In all the years that we have been able to follow this rule of justice, which time and again fires upon scapegoats, no one has dared to speak out in censure. But the most recent deed of our punitive justice makes an accomplice of anyone who watches any longer in silence.

It was a brilliant satirical opening, with frank mockery masking a more subtle irony, the kind of brilliance that justified Kraus's famous insistence that his pieces always be read twice. ("My request is a modest one—after all, I do not ask that they be read once.") The image of Themis, as a Victorian lady of hypocritically shockable sensibilities, offered easy, outrageous humor, but embedded in the phrases that Kraus constructed with such legendary scrupulous' ness, there could be read a design of subtle but sweeping satirical reversal. "In all the years . . . no one has dared to speak out . . . " And the deed "makes an accomplice of anyone who watches any longer in silence." Kraus adopted precisely the portentous phrases which characterized public indignation over child abuse and turned those same phrases against "our Themis," against Austrian justice. It was not the abuse of the child that forced Kraus to "speak out" or else become an accomplice; it was the abuse of justice.

As part of this ironic reversal of indignation, Kraus presented Themis, not Juliane Hummel or Marie Kutschera, as she who had committed the terrible "punitive" deed, who had been, in fact, "excessive in punishment." With Kraus the choice of words was never accidental. What then did he make of those other excessively punitive characters, the parents who were tried in court? It was typical of Kraus that he boldly took his stand not on Marie Kutschera, whose legal defense was so prolonged and so nearly effective, but rather on Juliane Hummel, whose death sentence was always a foregone conclusion, whose utterances of self-justification were laughed out of court. Kraus was ready to reconsider and reformulate her case.

> Juliane Hummel and her spouse mistreated their sickly child. Neigh' bors repeatedly reported them. The authorities remained inactive, but finally pulled themselves together, and bestowed upon the inhuman parents a reprimand. But the child remained in their hands, and be' cause on its account they had suffered the shame of a reprimand, they began to hate it. And so the mistreatment became more frequent and more crude. The weak body and broken life'energy did not hold out; the little one died.

While Dörmann presented the Kutschera case in three painstaking character portraits—the post official, the prostitute, the step' mother—Kraus's telling of the Hummel story was so stark and impersonal that there was almost no characterization at all. The parents were simply "inhuman"—and perhaps for that reason be' neath further personal consideration; their social and occupational level was not even mentioned, neither as explanation, nor in exten' uation. Kraus, who would later be outspoken in his contempt for psychoanalysis ("psychoanalysis is that mental illness for which it regards itself as therapy"), here seemed consciously to eschew all psychological and sociological factors, in order to lay bare the essen' tial significance of the case. And child abuse was not exactly the issue that he was getting at.

If he did not try to explain child abuse, it was partly because he seemed to take it for granted. The prosecutor of the Kutschera case received "intoxicated applause" after he declared that all Vienna was absolved of responsibility, since the case was "simply unbelievable." Kraus's reply to that was his caricature of Themis, shrieking with indignation, "One wouldn't have thought it possible!" For Kraus, child abuse was an evil that "everyone has long recognized," though no one had ever spoken about it. When he flatly stated "Juliane Hummel and her spouse mistreated their sickly child," he didn't feel that it required any explanation at all. Indeed, in Kraus's version, they did not yet even hate their child at that point; hatred came only after "the shame of the reprimand." *Die Fackel,* like the *Arbeiter-Zeitung,* was quite ready to hold the "authorities" responsible for the child's death—but for Kraus that too was a subsidiary point; his real intentions lay elsewhere. When Kraus glibly linked the judicial reprimand to parental hatred, he only revealed again his utter lack of interest in the deeper psychological ramifications of the case. For Kraus, generally so articulate in his hatred, there were certain kinds of monstrosity about which one could say nothing. Decades later, in 1933, he was to arouse the greatest controversy with the public admission: "I cannot think of anything to say about Hitler."

What he did say, however, he said with great care, and there were crucial semantic ramifications in his narration of Anna Hummel's death. "The weak body and broken life-energy did not hold out; the little one died." Kraus was obsessed with the importance of linguistic connotations, and here he demonstrated that acquitting the Hummel parents of killing their daughter was simply a matter of subject and object, of active and passive verbs. If Anna Hummel simply "did not hold out," then they did not kill her. For him this was no idle semantic game; Kraus deeply believed that all serious issues, fundamentally, were linguistic issues. In the 1920s he remarked: "Opinions, trends, *Weltanschauungen*—what matters first and last is only the sentence." In the 1930s he responded to the rise of fascism by organizing language seminars. When challenged for analyzing punctuation problems while the Japanese were bombarding Shanghai in 1932, he replied that if all the commas were in the right places, Shanghai would not be burning. And thus the Hummel case too, in 1899, could be analyzed as a problem of active and passive, subject and object. For if the grammatical revision was sufficient to absolve the accused parents, then how could they be legitimately condemned to death?

In this case, absolute grammatical precision was the counterpart and guarantor of absolute legal precision—and the latter was a matter of life and death, since murder was a capital crime. That Anna Hummel was abused, there was no doubt. "But for no individual act of mistreatment, not even the last one, was there proof of the intention to bring about death." Kraus admitted, as did the defense at the trial, that the parents might be guilty of manslaughter, or of inflicting "serious bodily injury resulting in death," but he insisted that they did not murder the child. Indeed, it was virtually an issue of linguistic unclarity, of the undefined nature of *Misshandlung*—mistreatment, abuse. It was, on the one hand, distinct from discipline; on the other hand, neither was it murder. Only by grappling honestly with the question of what child abuse really was—a task that Kraus himself was not ready to take on— could one have fairly reacted and responded to it.

"Word and essence," wrote Kraus, elsewhere, "that is the only connection I have ever striven for in my life." In *Wittgenstein's Vienna,* a philosophical and historical study by Allan Janik and Stephen Toulmin, Kraus emerges as highly relevant to Wittgenstein's analysis of language and its limits. For Janik and Toulmin, it was a fundamental characteristic of fin-de-siècle Vienna to "attempt to evade the social and political problems of Austria by the debasement of language." Correspondingly, they viewed Kraus's linguistic preoccupation as a reflection of his "moral hatred" of "slovenliness in thought and expression." Writing about the Hummel case, Kraus declared that a jurist must be "like a surgeon who must have a clear head and calm hand amidst the most painful excitement over human suffering, so that he can handle the knife with artistic skill." Kraus anticipated here not only the linguistic rigorousness of the Viennese philosopher Ludwig Wittgenstein, but also the "pure theory of law" of the important Viennese jurist Hans Kelsen. For Kraus, all these issues were implicit in the child abuse cases of 1899, for the cases created a miasma of linguistic, legal, and sociological ambiguities. What we can see, in historical retrospect, is that these ambiguities were inherent in the impossible dilemma of how to define clearly, and thus prosecute justly, a crime that was legally and sociologically unprecedented.

## "THE END OF THE WORLD BY BLACK MAGIC"

For Kraus, once the murder charge had been falsely formulated, there was no hope of an honest prosecution or a logical verdict from the men of the jury.

> Part class justice, part sentimental justice [*Gefühlsjustiz*]. And the second is often even worse than the first. The hearts of these men who are fathers overflow with disgust, and he who himself now and then

has taken hold of his child roughly, he wants to distinguish all the more sharply between the love that disciplines and the hatred that torments. Sentiment [Gefühl] overcomes logic. The extent of the confusion in their heads was shown soon after at the trial of the Kutschera couple, for the jurors left the question of intent to kill for the doctor to decide—who could not testify as an expert about that—and the jury foreman anxiously asked about sixty percent probability. The speech of the state prosecutor stirred up excitement; that excellent jurist muzzled his hairsplitting differentiating logic, and poured out his sentiment [Gefühl] in powerful words.

Just as in Dörmann's piece, the reiterated word "power" (Macht) betrayed the political subtext, so in Kraus's piece it was the word "sentiment" (Gefühl) that pointed to the implicit vein of broad cultural criticism. Schorske attributed to fin-de-siècle Vienna "an amoral Gefühlskultur"—a culture based on sensitivity to and cultivation of sentiment, emotion, and the psyche. To Schorske, the intellectual historian, it appeared as an indispensable condition of the city's unique cultural brilliance. To Kraus, the contemporary critic, it was the root of the city's moral and cultural corruption. Dishonest and slovenly sentiment—stirring up excitement, exploiting confusion, overcoming logic—brought about the unjust death sentence. Since Kraus was the enemy of sentiment, there could only be an unbridgeable opposition between his interpretation of the cases and that of Felix Dörmann. For Dörmann was the perfect product of and spokesman for Gefühlskultur, the culture of sentiment.

It was entirely in keeping with Kraus's perspective that he should have devoted more thought to the psychology of the jurors who perpetrated the abuse of justice, than to the parents who abused their children. In so doing, he formulated an insight that applied not only to the men of the jury, but to the men and women of the public at large. Again, for Kraus, the problem was fundamentally a matter of heart and sentiment.

> The hearts of these men who are fathers overflow with disgust, and he who himself now and then has taken hold of his child roughly, he wants to distinguish all the more sharply between the love that disciplines and the hatred that torments. Sentiment overcomes logic.

Both the Hummel parents and the Kutschera parents defended themselves in court by arguing that they were as innocent as any parent administering discipline. It took Karl Kraus, a man who hated Vienna and the Viennese, to reverse that formulation, and suggest that every parent could be implicated in the guilt of the defendants. In this respect Kraus's piece contained the kernel of the most provocatively radical of all possible interpretations of the child abuse trials: The particular monstrosities of the Hummel and Kutschera cases were presented as only excessive variations on the accepted patterns of nineteenth-century parental discipline. While the prosecutor might absolve the public for failing to see something "simply unbelievable," Kraus accused the Viennese of closing their eyes because it was all too familiar. The sharp distinction between love and hatred was made, not to clarify, but to evade and escape from the issue. If parental hearts were overflowing with disgust, then the flow had to be channeled toward the Hummel and Kutschera parents, lest the tide turn inward. Kraus's psychological depiction of the fathers of the jury suggested that his hypocritically astonished Themis—"One wouldn't have thought it possible!"— was not only the goddess of justice, but at the same time a Viennese mother.

In depicting the dishonestly disgusted father, "who himself now and then has taken hold of his child roughly," Kraus was approaching a theme that was to become fundamental in his cultural criticism. Three years later in 1902, he published an essay entitled "Morality and Criminality"—"Sittlichkeit und Kriminalität"— which in 1908 became the book title of a thematic collection of pieces. Kraus's satirical point was the hypocrisy of public morality and of its judicial formulation under Austrian law. Most often, the particular object of his satire was the prosecution of prostitution, which, to his mind, revealed Austrian public morality and justice at their most hypocritically ludicrous. Just as men who beat their own children were the ones who condemned Juliane Hummel and Marie Kutschera, so the same men who gave prostitutes their business were the pillars of public indignation and legal prosecution. "Morality is a venereal disease," commented Kraus. "Its primary stage is called virtue; its secondary stage, boredom; its tertiary stage, syphilis." From his comment on the Hummel and Kutschera jurors, he could have also developed a parallel aphorism in which child abuse became the tertiary form of a different kind of moral righteousness.

"Eros and Themis" was the title of another piece in the collection, and the same shockable Themis now exclaimed in outraged astonishment over sexual crime—prostitution, homosexuality— "One wouldn't have thought it possible!" Eros, to Kraus, was a private god, a matter of private morality which did not belong in the law or the courts. This points us toward the reason why the child abuse issue, though it enabled Kraus to think through and anticipate the moral and legal themes that would soon become central to his satire, was not in itself an issue that he could confront and pursue. For serious consideration of child abuse could only suggest the need for the further encroachment of public law on the ambiguously private sphere of family life—while Kraus was moving, generally, in the opposite direction. The manifest symptom of this inherent contradiction was that Kraus's mockery of Themis in 1899 brought him to the verge of a peculiar defense of Juliane Hummel and Marie Kutschera. Clearly, child abuse, thus presented, was not a moral and legal issue that Kraus could relentlessly follow through to its ultimate implications. For it was one thing to favor Eros against Themis, but quite something else to champion Medusa or Megaera.

Kraus hated Austrian justice, but nothing could rival his hatred of the Viennese press. He saw it as a force of satanic evil, corrupting and debasing everything it touched; in a famous apocalyptic title he prophesied "The End of the World by Black Magic'"—black newsprint. But just as the child abuse issue put Kraus in the potentially uncomfortable position of denouncing Themis on behalf of Juliane Hummel, so the sensation over the trials put him in an uncharacteristically ambivalent position with respect to his obsessive hatred of the press and its black magic.

When the verdict fell, I was the only one who publicly dared to state his misgivings. The organs of public opinion—I represent only my own opinion—enthusiastically agreed with the guilty verdict. The horrible depictions of the sufferings of the child, which they published, were not the least of the reasons why the verdict fell as it did. I saw also, at the most serious occasion, the delight in sensationalism [Sensationslust] of the reporter at work. I was disgusted at the sight of the intoxicated humanitarians, but this time I felt all too sharply that I did not want to prosecute them. For today, when the publicity of a trial is not in the admission of a hundred spectators, but rather in the publication of the newspapers, the nature of deterrence—which is the purpose of justice—has been altered. It is not so much the punishment finally inflicted which has the deterrent effect, but much more that the facts of the case become well-known as the trial unfolds. And it deters not so much those who are capable of the same crime, but much more those others who, better constituted, are nevertheless sometimes in danger of overstepping the limit beyond which crime begins. Some mothers who read of the sufferings of Anna Hummel may have, in those days, jerked back the hand that was already raised to strike against a soiled child. Some chastisements may have turned out milder than otherwise.

Thus, when Kraus looked at the child abuse cases, he not only felt his characteristic contempt for Austrian justice, but also that same abhorrence of the press—"I was disgusted"—which was the hallmark of his career. And yet he had to qualify and contain his hatred: "I was disgusted at the sight of the intoxicated humanitarians, but this time I felt all too sharply that I did not want to prosecute them." That qualifying "but" marked such a rare moment in the history of *Die Fackel* that all alone it would be enough to tell us that child abuse was a problematic issue for Karl Kraus. For Kraus, in January 1900, had an inkling of what we can see clearly today. Though the Viennese press may have been shameless in its sensationalism, though it may have employed the most grotesque devices to evade and manipulate and distort the central issues, nevertheless, in exposing to the public the submerged problem of child abuse, the newspapers achieved something momentous.

Years later, Kraus wrote an operetta song to be sung by an evil "Black Printer"—who was surely supposed to be Moritz Benedikt. In the first verse, the Black Printer presented himself as nothing less than divinely omnipotent, but by the last verse he was revealed as hopelessly satanic.

> Before we started printing
> there was no heaven or earth.
> For these are of our minting,
> to us they owe their birth.
> They issued from our vapor
> —God saw, and took the hint—
> and so the world as paper
> we print . . .
>
> So printing, hinting, minting,
> we make life what we will.
> True worth endures no tinting,
> delusion brings the thrill.
> Black as the regions hellish
> and yellow as sulphur's glint,
> the devil's imps embellish
> newsprint!

The measure of Kraus's hatred of the press was his appreciation of its power. There was nothing so insidious as the magical power to recreate "the world as paper," to "make life what we will." No one would have appreciated better than Kraus, if he had caught the lie, the way Felix Dörmann and Moritz Benedikt made Marie Kutschera into a member of the serving class. However, by virtue of the same power, were it not for Moritz Benedikt and Felix Dörmann, the child abuse issue would not have existed at all for the cultured Viennese bourgeoisie. "Before we started printing there was no heaven and earth"—and no child abuse either.

Ulrich, considering the Moosbrugger case in *The Man Without Qualities,* could not be certain: "Was that a fragment of the trial at which Ulrich had been present—or only something out of the re-ports he had read?" And if the Viennese of 1899 depended on their newspapers for that brief moment of consciousness, when child abuse was recognized, the historian today is even more utterly dependent on those same newspapers for the rediscovery and recon-struction of that moment. The "world as paper" of 1899 has be-come a world of yellowed and crumbling paper—but it is all we have. Kraus grudgingly recognized in 1899 that, with respect to the particular issue of child abuse, it was better than nothing.

Kraus read the *Neue Freie Presse* faithfully and obsessively, and he could hardly have reacted to Dörmann's presentation of the Kutschera case with anything less than cultural nausea. His denun-ciation of the "Sensationslust" of the reporter fitted Dörmann per-fectly, the poet of *Sensations.* Certainly Kraus and Dörmann ap-proached child abuse in radically different ways. And yet, there was something in common, something that linked these two inter-pretations by the two most important Viennese cultural figures who responded to the child abuse sensation. For both men, when they considered the child abuse cases, did not really focus on child abuse. They saw in those cases so many other things: what they found most hateful, most disturbing, or most fascinating about Vi-enna, their city. Dörmann saw the wonderful warmheartedness of Viennese prostitutes, the frightening prospect of the lower classes aspiring to political power, and the evocative poetic imagery of tormented fin-de-siècle decadence. Kraus saw the slovenliness and hypocrisy of Austrian justice and the disgusting sensationalism of the Viennese press.

Each man brought to the subject of child abuse his own social and cultural preoccupations, and those were reflected back again in each man's interpretation. It was as if child abuse was indeed "an obscure and sombre poem." It could be interpreted, but not hon-estly understood, or even directly confronted. In its depths it was too obscure, too horrible, too unbelievable. But just as Kraus was forced to see some good in the newspaper accounts, so there was a certain valor in the efforts of both Kraus and Dörmann to write about the subject at all. For there was, by contrast, not one word of observation or recognition of the Hummel and Kutschera cases from the one Viennese cultural figure to whom they seem to cry out for comment. It is as if Sigmund Freud were not in Vienna at all during November 1899. But he was there. And his weighty, even semiotic, silence is as historically fascinating as the public utterances of Felix Dörmann and Karl Kraus.

## "TRULY A NEGLECTED CORNER OF PSYCHIC LIFE"

When Hedwig Keplinger murdered her daughter in October, Freud had just returned to Vienna from his summer vacation at Berchtesgaden, and he was anxiously awaiting the publication of *The Interpretation of Dreams*. At the time of the story of those two bodies in the woods, Freud was writing to Fliess some thoughts about masturbation and homosexuality. When Joseph and Juliane Hummel were being tried in November for the murder of their daughter Anna, Freud was—still anxiously—waiting and hoping for reviews of his book. He feared the worst, for he knew his book contained "too much that is new and unbelievable," and that "we are, after all, terribly far ahead of our time." The week before the Hummel trial, he wrote to Fliess about the frightening illnesses of his children, including the four-year-old Anna Freud; the week after the trial, he wrote about his own migraines and depression. As for Freud and the Kutschera trial, there was nothing in the Fliess correspondence to indicate Freud's awareness or interest.

Two days before the opening of the Kutschera trial, on November 26, Freud was expressing relief that Fliess's daughter Pauline was recovering from a grave illness, possibly cholera. "Stemming from good blood, she too will grow and thrive," wrote Freud. "I look forward to seeing her some time in the now-enlarged children's room." In the same letter, Freud noted that "the dream book has not yet occasioned any outcries." On December 9, a week after Dörmann summed up the Kutschera case in the *Neue Freie Presse*, Freud noted an interesting coincidence in two cases he was treating:

> Two of my patients have almost simultaneously come up with [self] reproaches following the nursing and death of their parents, and have shown me that my dreams about this were typical. The reproach is in every instance bound to attach itself to revenge, spiteful glee, taking satisfaction in the ill person's excretory difficulties (urines and stools). Truly a neglected corner of psychic life.

Freud did not note the larger coincidence: that both these patients brought up this spiteful, vengeful hatred of their dying parents at precisely the same time that Vienna was obsessed with two cases of hateful parents and was applauding their condemnation to death. The child abuse sensation peaked and subsided without leaving a trace in Freud's intimate correspondence with Fliess. Neither was it destined to enter into his monumental corpus of books and articles in the years to come.

This silence is surprising and disappointing, because Freud was, arguably, the most daring, the most brilliant, and the most important analyst of family relations who ever lived. The glories of his genius were those devastating explorations of the subtleties, ambivalences, and hostilities between parents and children. For Kraus, parents and children were an intellectual sideline; for Freud they were at the heart of his life's work. And in November 1899, the same month of both the Hummel and Kutschera trials, *The Interpretation of Dreams* was published, including the first public formulation of the Oedipus complex, the revolutionary proposition that the parent-child relation was one of sexual desire and mortal hatred. This notion challenged the long and deeply cherished family ideal of sentimental benevolence. Freud could hardly be expected to foresee that his Oedipus complex would one day become the triumphant banner of psychoanalysis, the most famous association with his famous name, eventually almost as much of a fashionable cliché as the sentimental ideal it demolished. In 1899, in *The Interpretation of Dreams,* Freud could only implore his readers not to dismiss the Oedipus complex as "monstrous," not to be blinded by "cultural standards of filial piety." Freud's plea, published at the beginning of November 1899, could almost have been an anticipation of the child abuse cases of that month; like Freud's Oedipus complex, they too pointed to a "monstrous" reality that invalidated the prevailing cultural pieties. When Freud wrote to Fliess in December that the book contained "too much that is new and unbelievable," he might have been echoing the summary for the prosecution in the Kutschera case: "simply unbelievable." When Freud referred his readers to "everyday observation," he might reasonably have noted the Hummel and Kutschera cases as evidence that his ideas, if monstrous, were certainly not fantastic.

In Kraus's treatment of the cases, the issues of child abuse seemed, at first, to fit remarkably well with his personal preoccupations: social hypocrisy, the dishonesty of Austrian criminal justice, and the shameless sensationalism of the Viennese press. On closer examination, however, it was evident that child abuse led Kraus into potentially uncomfortable and uncharacteristic qualifications. But if Kraus seemed to avoid the most essential issues of the child abuse cases, Freud avoided the cases altogether. And just as for Kraus, so also for Freud: Though at first glance the cases seemed ideally suited to feed his particular genius and stimulate his psychological concerns, child abuse was, in fact, deeply problematic for his intellectual development at that time. Freud's silence must be explored as a matter of intellectual history, and it suggests once again the unexpected ways that the child abuse sensation fit and combined with the many other combustible cultural elements of fin-de-siècle Vienna. If one considers, first, the precise formulation of the Oedipus complex, and then, looking back, Freud's controversial renunciation of his "seduction theory," one can better appreciate the problematic place of child abuse in the development of psychoanalysis.

## OEDIPUS

The Oedipus complex was presented in a section entitled "Dreams of the Death of Persons of Whom the Dreamer Is Fond"—which was in itself a subsection under the less wordy and more general heading "Typical Dreams." The crucial subtitle, which marked such an important place in intellectual history, seemed to echo the fundamental question in the examination of Juliane Hummel. "Were you fond of the child?" asked the judge, and the spectators laughed when she said she was. When he put the question again, later in the trial, and she admitted she was not, then the audience applauded the resolution of the contradiction. For how could she have been fond of the child she killed? Freud was writing for the same Viennese audience of 1899, and he presented that audience with a very similar dilemma. For Freud had already, in an earlier chapter of his book, established his central principle for the interpretation of dreams: "A dream is the fulfillment of a wish." And if that principle was to be consistently applied, even to "Dreams of the Death of Persons of Whom the Dreamer Is Fond," then there was no getting around the syllogistically logical conclusion.

> The meaning of such dreams, as their content indicates, is a wish that the person in question may die. And since I must expect that the feelings of my readers, and any others who have experienced similar dreams, will rebel against my assertion, I must try to base my evidence for it on the broadest possible foundation.

Of course they would rebel; or they might even, like the spectators at the Hummel trial, simply laugh. For Freud's premise was precisely that which seemed so incomprehensible in the child abuse cases: that people may hate and harm family members whom they also love and care for.

The rebellious audience that Freud envisioned—"my readers and any others who have experienced similar dreams"—was not so far from Kraus's conception of the jurors at the Hummel trial—"he who himself now and then has taken hold of his child roughly." Like Kraus, Freud implicated everyone; the dream was a "typical" one. But Freud was also prepared to modify those implications, to reassure his readers to a certain extent. He formulated the problem as one of "evidence," as if he himself were the judge, as if his readers were on trial for a family murder.

> If anyone dreams, with every sign of pain, that this father or mother or brother or sister has died, I should never use the dream as evidence that he wishes for that person's death *at the present time*. The theory of dreams does not require as much as that; it is satisfied with the inference that this death has been wished for at some time or other during the dreamer's childhood. I fear, however, that this reservation will not appease the objectors; they will deny the possibility of their ever having had such a thought, with just as much energy as they insist that they harbour no such wishes now. I must therefore reconstruct a portion of the vanished mental life of children . . .

Thus Freud paved the way for the exposition of the Oedipus complex, by assuring his readers that these dreams of death reflected only childhood wishes, that their dreams could not be used as "evidence" against them as adults. By reassuringly consigning the murderous wish to childhood, however, Freud quietly, implicitly, ruled out of consideration the direction of such wishes against children themselves. For children could not yet have children, and if the murderous wish originated in childhood, then it could not be directed against one's child. Freud did in fact explicitly—though without drawing attention to it—limit his field of inquiry: "If anyone dreams that his father or mother or brother or sister has died . . ." Sons and daughters, it seemed, were not most typically the objects of such dreams.

The omission was not incidental. Subtly but unmistakably, it marked the entire formulation of the Oedipus complex, which was conceived entirely as a problem of the child.

> How are we to explain his death-wishes against his parents, who surround him with love and fulfill his needs . . .
>
> A solution of this difficulty is afforded by the observation that dreams of the death of parents apply with preponderant frequency to the parent who is of the same sex as the dreamer: that men, that is, dream mostly of their fathers' death, and women of their mothers' . . .

> It is as though—to put it bluntly—a sexual preference were making itself felt at an early age: as though boys regarded their fathers and girls their mothers as their rivals in love, whose elimination could not fail to be to their advantage.
>
> Before this idea is rejected as a monstrous one . . .

And thus Freud explained the hostility that "lies concealed in the relation between parents and children." But that hostility was not, properly speaking, *between* parents and children, for at its origin, as described by Freud, it was not reciprocal in nature. It was the hostility of children *against* their parents, indeed of a child against "parents who surround him with love and fulfill his needs."

Clearly such loving and caring parents were not exactly the issue in the Hummel and Kutschera cases. And whereas at first glance those cases might have seemed to offer the evidence of "everyday observation" that could demonstrate the plausibility of his Oedipus hypothesis, Freud's phrases and nuances suggested something quite different. The evidence of the child abuse cases of 1899 could actually have served to undermine the Oedipus complex, as specifically formulated in *The Interpretation of Dreams*. Freud illustrated the initial theoretical exposition with the imaginary case of a prototypical child permitted to sleep beside his mother when his father was away. "He may easily begin to form a wish that his father should *always* be away, so that he himself could keep his place beside his dear, lovely Mummy." Stylistically, Freud was on the verge of lapsing into the artificially constructed internal monologues that Dörmann employed. At the same time, that the imagined Oedipal child should be longing for "dear, lovely Mummy" confirmed that Freud was very far indeed from a theory that could comfortably interpret the cases of Juliane Hummel and Marie Kutschera.

Not only was the Oedipus complex framed in terms of children hating their parents, rather than vice versa, but the notion of the child's sexual jealousy made it theoretically unnecessary to seek out the cause of that hatred in any hateful action of the hated parent. The child, the hostile force, generated the hostility independently. Freud did not absolutely rule out the possibility of hostile currents flowing from parent to child, but he made them explicitly supplementary to the central theory, and relegated them largely to the mythological past.

> The obscure information which is brought to us by mythology and legend from the primaeval ages of human society gives an unpleasing picture of the father's despotic power and of the ruthlessness with which he made use of it. Kronos devoured his children, just as the wild boar devours the sow's litter; while Zeus emasculated his father

and made himself ruler in his place. The more unrestricted was the rule of the father in the ancient family, the more must the son, as his destined successor, have found himself in the position of an enemy, and the more impatient must he have been to become ruler himself through his father's death. Even in our middle class families, fathers are as a rule inclined to refuse their sons independence and the means necessary to secure it, and thus to foster the germ of the growth of hostility which is inherent in their relation . . . In our society today fathers are apt to cling desperately to what is left of a now sadly antiquated *potestas patris familias.*

There was even perhaps a note of sympathy for that anachronistic, desperately clinging father. But what was clearly stated was that however such a father might treat his child, cruelty could do no more than "foster" an already "inherent" hostility. At any rate, by presenting parental cruelty as a thing of primeval mythology, an attribute of Kronos and Zeus, Freud made it both reassuringly dis' tant and of dubious authenticity. Freud's approach here was not so far from that of the *Neue Freie Presse*, when the paper tried to explain the "unbelievable" Hummel case as an "atavism" in an age of civilization. This similarity of perspective, however, would seem to have allied Freud with those factors and arguments that served to neutralize and evade the most troubling issues of the child abuse cases. Freud later went some way toward revising and reversing even his mythological vision of parental cruelty. In *Totem and Ta' boo,* published in 1913, the crucial event of the anthropologically primeval family became the murder and devouring of the father by his sons.

In *The Interpretation of Dreams,* Freud's evidence for the Oedi' pus complex came from dreams themselves. It was, however, his "confirmation" that gave the complex its name.

> This discovery is confirmed by a legend that has come down to us from classical antiquity: a legend whose profound and universal power to move can only be understood if the hypothesis I have put forward in regard to the psychology of children has an equally universal validity. What I have in mind is the legend of King Oedipus and Sophocles' drama which bears his name.

This recourse to legend and drama showed Freud in his cultural context, a part of fin-de-siècle Vienna. With Oedipus and Sopho' cles he achieved an historic intellectual breakthrough, but the incli' nations of his genius were not so far from the gimmicks of the *Neue Freie Presse* when it juxtaposed Hedwig Keplinger and Sarah Bernhardt's Tosca, Anna Hummel and Hauptmann's Hannele, Marie Kutschera and the stepmother of Snow White.

For Freud, however, the introduction of Oedipus was neither a cultural embellishment nor an intellectual gimmick. It was the confirmation that conferred "universal validity."

> If *Oedipus Rex* moves a modern audience no less than it did the contemporary Greek one, the explanation . . . is to be looked for in the particular nature of the material . . . There must be something which makes a voice within us ready to recognize the compelling force of destiny in Oedipus . . . His destiny moves us only because it might have been ours—because the oracle laid the same curse upon us before our birth as upon him. It is the fate of all of us, perhaps, to direct our first sexual impulse towards our mother, and our first hatred and our first murderous wish against our father. Our dreams convince us that this is so. King Oedipus, who slew his father Laius and married his mother Jocasta, merely shows us the fulfillment of our own childhood wishes.

From Sophocles' Oedipus, Freud proceeded to Shakespeare's Hamlet, arguing that Hamlet's proverbial irresolution came from unconsciously identifying with the hated Claudius—the man who had killed Hamlet's father and married his mother. Hamlet thus harbored secret wishes—as all of us do, according to Freud—whereas only Oedipus went so far as to commit the fateful acts. Under this interpretation, Oedipus murdered his father because he wanted to marry his mother: It perfectly illustrated Freud's conception of the child's "inherent" hostility, for which the parent bore no responsibility. Only recently have critics pointed out that Freud edited the Oedipus legend, deemphasizing the fact that Laius abandoned his infant child in the mountains to die, omitting the fact that Laius pierced and bound the child's ankles. The name Oedipus means "swollen foot," and it would be plausible to interpret the legend as the story of an abused child who eventually took vengeance on his father.

Freud did not see it that way in *The Interpretation of Dreams,* and his silence about the mutilated ankles of Oedipus in that book, published in November 1899, paralleled his silence about the mutilated fingers of Anna Kutschera during that same month. Furthermore, though he remarked upon the power of the Oedipus drama over modern audiences, he did not seem to notice the way Viennese audiences responded to the drama of the Hummel and Kutschera trials. Freud was much readier to recognize that children could wish to murder their parents, than that parents could wish to murder their children. Freud overlooked the ankles of Oedipus and the fingers of Anna Kutschera, but not because he had never considered the possibility that parents could behave monstrously toward their children. He had already considered that possibility—and rejected it—when his intellectual development in the nineties had led him to the controversial "seduction theory."

## "A CHILD OF HIS TIMES"

From the beginning of the decade, Freud's central clinical and intellectual interest was in patients suffering from hysteria—a complex of physiological ailments without any apparent physiological cause. On October 15, 1895, Freud wrote to Fliess that he had discovered "the great clinical secret": traumatic sexual abuse experienced as a child. In 1896 he revealed this great secret to his Viennese colleagues, presenting and then publishing a paper, "The Aetiology of Hysteria." Freud did not hesitate to hail his own discovery as nothing less than "the source of the Nile," and his description of the sexual abuse of children by adults was, in fact, everything that one expects from Freud: brilliantly intuited and articulated, and far ahead of its time.

> All the peculiar circumstances in which the ill-matched pair carry on their love relation: the adult—who can not escape his share in the mutual dependence inherent in a sexual relation, and yet is endowed with complete authority and the right of punishment, and can exchange the one role for the other in unbridled gratification of his moods; the child—helpless victim of this capriciousness.

That was the key: the child as "helpless victim," a conception that Freud had put behind him by the time he elaborated the Oedipus complex in 1899, by the time he came to read about the Hummel and Kutschera trials.

Sexual abuse, of course, was not quite the same thing as the battering abuse revealed at those trials, but Freud clearly appreciated the relatedness of these forms. He did not fail to note that the sexually abusive adult also wielded "complete authority and the right of punishment." Both kinds of abuse were monstrous violations perpetrated upon helpless victims. One cannot read a passage like this one from "The Aetiology of Hysteria," without suspecting that Freud was the one man in Vienna who could have done justice to the terrible and twisted relationship between Marie Kutschera and her stepchildren. Surely Freud could have gone far beyond the prosecutor's denunciation of her hypocrisy and *Tartüfferie,* far beyond Dörmann's poetic images of sadistic gratification.

When Dörmann wrote about the Kutschera case, he began his piece as a fairy tale—just as the *Neue Freie Presse* had introduced the case with Snow White and Cinderella. When Freud developed his new ideas about hysteria in a letter to Fliess of New Year's Day 1896, he ironically titled his observations, "A Christmas Fairy Tale." When the eminent German sexual psychopathologist, Richard von Krafft-Ebing, heard Freud's paper in April, he remarked dubiously, "It sounds like a scientific fairy tale."

Freud's paper of 1896 did inspire shock and disbelief, but in one respect it was not as shocking as it might have been. It is often supposed that Freud's seduction theory simply took for granted that the adult seducer was the child's parent. In fact, however, this was by no means an explicit feature of the fairy tale in "The Aetiology of Hysteria." There Freud grouped the seducers into three categories: adult strangers, adult attendants, and other children. The second category of adult attendants was elaborated thus: "a maid, nurse, governess, teacher, unhappily only too often a near relation." This reference to "a near relation" was the only implication of parental involvement, and so, considering the wide range of other categories and possibilities, one must conclude that in 1896 the fairy tale did not necessarily include a monstrous parent.

Freud presented "The Aetiology of Hysteria" on April 21, 1896, mentioning the unhappy possibility of an abusive "near relation." On October 23, Freud's father died. On December 6, he wrote to Fliess specifically about the possibility of "seduction by the father." Freud was at that time engaged in his pioneering "self-analysis," from which psychoanalysis would be born, and on February 11, 1897, he suggested—"unfortunately"—that his own father might be responsible for the hysteria of his son, Freud's brother. On September 21, 1897, he had again for Fliess another "great secret that has been dawning on me in the last few months": Freud no longer believed in his seduction theory, or in his patients' accounts of seduction. The supposed traumas of sexual abuse were no more than childhood fantasies. Freud's reasons for this turn-around emphasized "the surprise that in all cases, the *father,* not excluding my own, had to be accused of being perverse . . . whereas surely such widespread perversions against children are not very probable." The discovery that the adult seducer was actually a parent came as a "surprise" in 1897. Far from being an essential part of the original seduction theory of 1895–1896, it was, on the contrary, the reason for ultimately rejecting that theory as "not very probable."

Along with this "great secret" of September 21, Freud confided to Fliess that, despite the embarrassing circumstance of discovering himself in error, "I have more the feeling of a victory than a defeat." And indeed, the following month, in a letter of October 15, 1897,

Freud announced his intellectual victory. That his patients were not really sexually abused, that they were only relating fantasies, pointed to unsuspected sexual longings and rivalries in childhood—"in my own case too." And so: "we can understand the gripping power of Oedipus Rex," for "everyone in the audience was once a budding Oedipus in fantasy, and each recoils in horror from the dream fulfillment here transplanted into reality." Already in October 1897 this was the same Freud who in 1899 would analyze "Dreams of the Death of Persons of Whom the Dreamer Is Fond." The child who in 1896 was a "helpless victim" of adult monstrosity, was already being transformed into a creature of murderous wishes.

The Freud who had nothing to say about the Hummel and Kutschera cases in November 1899 was, in his view of parents and children, no longer the Freud of 1896. The author of "The Aetiology of Hysteria" might have made an ideal interpreter of those cases; this was no longer true of the author of "Dreams of the Death of Persons of Whom the Dreamer Is Fond." In 1899 Freud was publicly proposing a revolutionary conception of hostility between parents and children, but it was not quite intellectually compatible with the revelations of the child abuse sensation. Freud in 1899 presented the parent as the innocent object of the child's murderous and sexual fantasies; he had explicitly considered and rejected the idea of the child as the parent's helpless victim. For Karl Kraus, the child abuse sensation of 1899 occurred at the beginning of his intellectual development, the year that *Die Fackel* was founded; he could afford to tinker with the issues, let them go, and still find his way clearly to "Morality and Criminality" in 1902. For Freud, however, the child abuse sensation came at the end of a crucial period of intellectual development, just as his recently achieved insights were finally being published as a book. And that sensation was potentially threatening to those insights, for it pointed backwards to the hypothesis that Freud had already renounced, pointed to the child as a "helpless victim." Freud's obliviousness to the child abuse cases followed upon his earlier rejection of the seduction theory, two related aspects of the same perspective on parent-child relations. And the reasons for remaining silent about child abuse corresponded to the reasons for renouncing the "Christmas Fairy Tale."

In recent years the intellectual controversy over Freud's rejection of the seduction theory has raged through and beyond the circles of psychoanalysis. The central figure in this controversy has been Jeffrey Moussaieff Masson, a young professor of Sanskrit, who then trained as a psychoanalyst. He made such a favorable impression on

Anna Freud, then in the last years of her life, that she gave him access to her father's papers, and permission to prepare an unexpur-gated edition of the Freud-Fliess correspondence. Masson, in exam-ining the papers and letters, came to the conclusion that something had gone very wrong in Freud's intellectual development in the 1890s, and published a book in 1984, *The Assault on Truth: Freud's Suppression of the Seduction Theory*. Masson accused Freud of intel-lectual cowardice and dishonesty in dismissing his patients' traumas as mere fantasies, and argued that this constituted a false conclusion which poisoned the whole future development of psychoanalysis. "For it is unforgivable that those entrusted with the lives of people who come to them in emotional pain, should use their blind reliance on Freud's fearful abandonment of the seduction theory to continue the abuse their patients once suffered as children." With such sweeping denunciations as this one, Masson could hardly help call-ing forth furious controversy.

In the meantime, the same issues that Masson raised were being explored by other scholars in Europe and America, in a variety of fascinating and original ways. The German sociologist Marianne Krüll, in *Freud and His Father* (1979), conducted an excavation of Freud's family background, and considered its possible significance for Freud's transition from the seduction theory to the Oedipus complex. As suggested by Freud's letters, he did indeed have his own father in mind, when writing of "the surprise that in all cases the *father*, not excluding my own, had to be accused of being per-verse." In contrast to Krüll's family approach, the American histo-rian William McGrath has brought out the Austrian political con-text of Freud's intellectual development in the nineties, in *Freud's Discovery of Psychoanalysis: The Politics of Hysteria* (1986). Most relevant of all to the problem of psychoanalysis and child abuse was the work of the Swiss psychoanalyst Alice Miller, *Thou Shalt Not Be Aware: Society's Betrayal of the Child* (1981). Miller stressed that "even a genius is a child of his times," and that Freud could not escape altogether from prevailing cultural attitudes, when it came to recognizing that parents could behave abusively toward their children. By the time of the child abuse sensation of 1899, however, it would perhaps be fairer to say that Freud's vision was limited, both by his original genius and, paradoxically, by his cultural con-formity. While the latter could make him reluctant to recognize child abuse, the former had already committed him to a no less momentous, but essentially opposite, recognition—the Oedipus complex. His insight could be dazzling and daring, but at the same time he could be subject to certain cultural blinkers.

If the power of prevailing cultural attitudes played a role in the rejection of the seduction theory, then the child abuse sensation of 1899 fills a crucial gap in our understanding by offering a rare and comprehensive illustration of those attitudes. For here was the Viennese public at large responding to the same cultural dilemma—the monstrous parent, the victimized child—that Freud had faced only a few years before. Indeed one can sense the cultural affinity between Freud and his newspaper, the *Neue Freie Presse*; he looked back to Kronos and Zeus for examples of parental cruelty, just as the paper explained child abuse as an atavism. Similarly, the prosecutor's insistence that child abuse was "simply unbelievable" corresponded to Freud's conclusion that parental seduction was "not very probable." Fifteen years later, when Freud was already memorializing "The History of the Psychoanalytic Movement," he still explained that the seduction theory succumbed to its own "improbability." Since Freud himself did not feel drawn to put the mark of his genius upon these child abuse cases, by writing about them, our historical challenge must be to imagine him as simply one anonymous figure of the cultured, liberal, bourgeois Viennese public, a reader of the *Neue Freie Presse*.

Perhaps Freud was indeed "a child of his times," but in this instance it might be more accurate to see him as "a parent of his times." Really, he was both child and parent, though one could argue that with the death of his father in 1896, Freud's identity as a father in his own right now outweighed his identity as his parents' child. In 1899 he was the father of six children, including the four-year-old Anna Freud, the same name and age as Anna Hummel. Freud himself was one of seven brothers and sisters, the same number of children as the Kutschera family. These coincidences—for all that they tempt one to a "Freudian" interpretation of Freud—ultimately only emphasize the fact that all the individual members of that anonymous Viennese public must have judged the child abuse cases by implicit reference to their own complex of family relations. As Masaryk wrote about the murder at Polna that same year, "It is only the sign of a healthy moral sense that people, shrinking back from the crime with dread, should think of their own families in relation to it." Freud, of course, could not have been a part of the "parquet of mothers" at the Hummel trial, but he could have been one of the fathers of the jury who figured in Kraus's analysis of the case.

As a father Freud stood somewhat apart from the other cultural figures of fin-de-siècle Vienna. Indeed Freud was almost of a different generation, and in the Viennese cultural world the relations between generations were exceptionally meaningful; in Schorske's view, "the new culture makers in the city of Freud thus repeatedly defined themselves in terms of a kind of collective oedipal revolt." In 1899 Felix Dörmann was twenty-nine years old, just on the verge of his first marriage, which took place the following year. Hofmannsthal was twenty-five years old in 1899, and his marriage followed in 1901, his first child in 1902. Karl Kraus, the same age as Hofmannsthal, was emphatically not a family man; he never married, never had children, and once commented, "A woman occasionally is quite a serviceable substitute for masturbation, though it takes an abundance of imagination." These were the city's cultural prodigies, while Freud, destined to be its greatest name, was all of forty-three in 1899, married already for thirteen years, the father of six children, his family complete. As a nineteenth-century father, Freud could only read about the child abuse cases with the greatest unease, while as a twentieth-century genius, he could not respond to them. For however variously Dörmann and Kraus may have interpreted that "obscure and sombre poem" to match their own intellectual preoccupations, no one could have gazed into the Hummel and Kutschera cases and found "confirmation" of the universal principle that children naturally desire the death of their parents.

"We cannot reproach Freud for not knowing what we know today," writes Alice Miller about psychoanalysis and child abuse. And it is true that, if one chooses to regard "The Battered-Child Syndrome" of 1962 strictly as a new scientific sociological discovery, then one can no more reproach Freud for missing it than for failing to appreciate the double helix structure of DNA. Masson, less restrained about reproaching Freud, investigated and discovered that Freud possessed in his library three French books that touched on the abuse of children. Freud's exposure, however, went far beyond those three French books, for now we know that in Vienna, in 1899, the newspapers were filled with columns and columns about child abuse. In effect, Freud and the Viennese were given a quite comprehensive preview of the battered-child syndrome in the Hummel and Kutschera cases. That was two years after Freud rejected the seduction theory, but still before he committed himself to a public retraction.

The emergence of child abuse had to be a matter of both scientific discovery and cultural recognition, and the cases of 1899 could be both seen and not seen, at the same time, by the blinkered nineteenth-century public. They could be sensationally reported, obsessively followed, and then completely forgotten. For Freud, the power of the conventional family ideal combined paradoxically with the power of his own unconventional intellectual course, so that he could read about child abuse, but pass it over in silence. Consideration of the child abuse sensation of 1899, however, makes it impossible to suppose that Freud remained utterly naive about what parents might or might not do to their children.

## "A CHILD IS BEING BEATEN"

The child abuse sensation of 1899 received no comment from Freud, and neither did it seem to have any discernible influence on his ongoing theoretical development. In the following year, he undertook the now classic analysis of Dora. The letter to Fliess of October 14, 1900, suggested that Freud found in Dora a case ideally suited to confirm his theoretical approach: "a new patient, an eighteen-year-old girl, a case that has smoothly opened to the existing collection of picklocks." Freud noticed that Dora hated her mother, but wasted no time exploring that hatred, for the crucial dynamic of the case, for Freud, was Dora's oedipal sexual fixation on her father, on her father's lover Frau K., on her father's lover's husband Herr K., and finally, by transference, on Freud himself. Dora's hatred of her mother was treated as an incidental jealous by-product. The revelations of the child abuse sensation of the previous year had not provoked Freud to consider what a mother might have done to make her daughter hate her.

Actually, the Hummel case contained at least one specific clue that might have been relevant to the case of Dora. One of the things that made a great impression on the courtroom was that Juliane Hummel abused her five-year-old daughter for incontinence, even forcing the child's excrement into its mouth. Karl Kraus, who had very little to say about the details of abuse in the case, nevertheless could conjure up the vivid image of "the hand that was already raised to strike against a soiled child." Now, anyone who knows anything about Dora knows that she is the most famous bed wetter in European intellectual history, and among Freud's scant observations on Dora's mother, he noted a "mania for cleanliness" related to Dora's incontinence.

It would now be highly problematic to go back and explore the avenues that Freud neglected, to find out whether Dora's hatred of her mother had some foundation beyond oedipal jealousy. Exactly that, however, has been done for another famous Freud case, that of Dr. Schreber—and with alarming results. In 1911, ten years after analyzing Dora, Freud published an analysis of the autobiography of a mental patient, the German jurist and politician Daniel Paul Schreber. Schreber believed that he was suffering terrible physical tortures at the hands of "soul-murderers," and that God himself not only manipulated his excrement, but also sought to transform him into a woman in order to abuse him sexually. For Freud it was strictly a matter of paranoid delusion, and "we find ourselves once again upon the familiar ground of the father-complex." So familiar was the ground that Freud never thought of what research uncov-ered fifty years later: that Schreber's father, a well-known nine-teenth-century German doctor, dedicated to proper child rearing and physical education, had devised for the training of his own child a systematic regime whose rigors amounted to child abuse. The secret of child abuse was safe from Freud, for it could not open to his particular picklocks.

The routinely harsh corporal punishment of children was not a particular interest of Freud's, but the handful of incidental observa-tions that he made on the subject showed how easy it was to see right through the issue of abuse. The Oedipus complex, in assuming the sexual desires of the child, led Freud naturally to the idea of "infantile sexuality" in *Three Contributions to the Theory of Sex,* published in 1905. There Freud touched on the matter of the beat-ing of children.

> An erogenous source of the passive impulse for cruelty (masochism) is found in the painful irritation of the gluteal region, which is familiar to all educators since the confessions of J. J. Rousseau. This has justly caused them to demand that physical punishment, which usually con-cerns this part of the body, should be withheld from all children in whom the libido might be forced into collateral roads by the later demands of cultural education.

The rather stiff psychoanalytic phrasing did not prevent Freud's message from coming across: children should not be spanked, lest they learn to enjoy it too much. Freud could hardly suspect adults of being actively cruel as long as he perceived children as being moved by "the passive impulse for cruelty."

That this was indeed Freud's view of the corporal punishment of children was confirmed in an even more explicit passage from the famous case of the "wolf man," published in 1918 as "The History of an Infantile Neurosis." The center of the case was the child's dream of seeing white wolves sitting motionless on the branches of the walnut tree outside his window. And behind this dream Freud found the child's recollection of "the primal scene," a memory of watching his parents having sex. Along the way, Freud considered the wolf man's interesting "fantasies" about boys being beaten on their penises, and about "the heir to the throne being shut up in a narrow room and beaten." (The wolf man was Russian, and the same year that the case study was published in 1918, the doomed hemophiliac czarevitch suffered worse than beating at the hands of the Bolsheviks at Ekaterinburg.) To Freud it was clear that these were the wolf man's masochistic fantasies of being beaten himself, and Freud had no trouble tracing these back to childhood and the wolf man's father.

> By bringing his naughtiness forward he was trying to force punish-ments and beatings out of his father, and in that way to obtain from him the masochistic sexual satisfaction that he desired. His screaming fits were therefore simply attempts at seduction.

This then was the Freudian dynamic: children tried to "force" their parents to beat them, to "seduce" them into beating them, while parents were urged to "withhold" the sexually desired beatings. As for the wolf man's father in particular, Freud feared that he might have aggravated the boy's wolf obsession by perpetrating something that Freud called "affectionate abuse":

> My patient's father had the characteristic, shown by so many people in relation to their children, of indulging in "affectionate abuse"; and it is possible that during the patient's earlier years his father (though he grew severe later on) may more than once, as he caressed the little boy or played with him, have threatened in fun to "gobble him up."

The contrast between the father's "affectionate abuse" and the child's seductive sexual longing for beatings showed how very far Freud was from conceiving of child abuse as we know it.

Freud's incidental remarks on the beating of children culminated in a paper devoted especially to that subject, " 'A Child Is Being Beaten': A Contribution to the Study of the Origin of Sexual Per-versions," published in 1919. The subtitle immediately showed that Freud's concern about such beatings had not changed since the essay on infantile sexuality in 1905, that he still had in mind the spankings that Jean Jacques Rousseau confessed to having relished in the eighteenth century. The message of the subtitle was immedi-ately reinforced in the opening lines, for Freud explained that he would not be dealing with real beatings, but strictly with fantasies.

> It is surprising how often people who seek analytic treatment for hysteria or an obsessional neurosis confess to having indulged in the phantasy: "a child is being beaten." Very probably there are still more frequent instances of it among the far greater number of people who have not been obliged to come to analysis by manifest illness.

It is really striking how strangely these formulations parallel and anticipate the discovery of child abuse fifty years later—except that

Freud claimed to have discovered not an unsuspected syndrome of battered children, but rather a surprising secret world of wide-spread fantasies about battered children. It is as if once again—as with the reconsidered seduction theory—psychoanalysis could recognize as psychological fantasy that which could not yet be recognized as sociological reality.

Freud was still marked by fin-de-siècle Vienna in 1919, though the last Habsburg emperor had abdicated the year before; the great doctor wrote about these beating fantasies with an aesthetic and literary sensibility rivaling that which Felix Dörmann had employed to write about child murder and child abuse twenty years earlier. Freud observed that his patients were familiar with such works of children's literature as Uncle Tom's Cabin, and so "the child began to compete with these works of fiction by producing his own phantasies and by constructing a wealth of situations and institutions, in which children were beaten, or were punished and disciplined in some other way, because of their naughtiness and bad behaviour." Freud noted that the beating fantasies began as "simple and monotonous" stories, but then evolved to "the most complicated alterations and elaborations." Indeed the fantasy of one of his patients "rose to the level of a work of art."

That these beating fantasies could compete with works of "fiction," could even become works of "art," suggested that for Freud there was no meaningful connection to any cruel reality.

> The question was bound to arise of what relation there might be between the importance of the beating-phantasies and the part that real corporal punishment might have played in the child's bringing up at home. It was impossible, on account of the one-sidedness of the material, to confirm the first suspicion that the relation was an inverse one. The individuals from whom the data for these analyses were derived were very seldom beaten in their childhood, or were at all events not brought up by the rod.

Freud's "first suspicion" was that the fantasies were no more than fantasies, and this fit with the whole development of his ideas about parents and children. Yet the beating fantasies undeniably originated before the children were old enough to read Uncle Tom's Cabin, even before they could have learned about corporal punishment in school. That is, the cases seemed to go back to the very early years of family life. Freud, however, could discover no particular event of traumatic fixation. "The present state of our knowledge would allow us to make our way so far and no further towards the comprehension of beating-phantasies," wrote Freud modestly.

"In the mind of the analytic physician, it is true, there remains an uneasy suspicion that this is not a final solution to the problem." Freud's reluctance to force the mystery of the traumatic origin of the beating fantasies was perhaps a little out of character, consider-ing that just the year before, in the wolf man case, he had managed to uncover behind the dream of the wolves a memory of the primal scene witnessed by the wolf cub at the age of one and a half. As for his profession of intellectual uneasiness about the "final solution," if this reflected any suspicion of an undiscovered cruel reality, that did not stop Freud from resolving the problem along very different lines.

Beginning with the fantasy line—"a child is being beaten"—Freud proceeded to present a dazzling, ingenious structural analysis of the permutations and variations of the identities of the anony-mous child and the anonymous beater. The child, he discovered, could sometimes be identified as the person fantasizing, while the beater, at first simply an anonymous adult, eventually "becomes recognizable clearly and unambiguously" as the father. This path of recognition—from an adult in general to a parent in particular—recapitulated Freud's experience of the seduction theory in the 1890s, and now again, just as then, the identification of a parent only demonstrated to Freud the fantasy nature of his subject. The rejection of the seduction theory led Freud to the Oedipus complex, and now the beating fantasies led him back to the Oedipus complex again. He could go "so far and no further," for the traumatic origin of the fantasy remained beyond the reach of psychoanalysis. One could only conclude that, first, children sadistically imagined their younger siblings being beaten—a matter of inherent sexual jealousy over possession of the parents. Then, second, when those same children guiltily repressed their inherently incestuous longings for their parents, they punished themselves with the masochistic fan-tasy of being beaten. In short, the beating fantasies finally led back to the Oedipus complex, which Freud now found to be more impor-tant than ever.

> It would naturally be important to know whether the origin of infan-
> tile perversions from the Oedipus complex can be asserted as a general
> principle. While this can not be decided without further investiga-
> tion, it does not seem impossible.

As with the seduction theory in the 1890s, any hint of parents mistreating their children brought Freud irresistibly back to the Oedipus complex. And the Oedipus complex, as before, resolved everything in a theory that absolved the parents of all responsibility. Thus Freud's "first suspicion" that the beating fantasies had nothing to do with real beatings was triumphantly vindicated. He knew that the question was "bound to arise," and the Oedipus complex answered it crushingly. Another question that never did arise—and we do not know if it occurred to Freud—is whether those who were fantasizing about beaten children were perhaps beating their own children.

When one has considered Freud's handling in 1919 of the fantasy "a child is being beaten," one is certainly less surprised that he should have failed to comment on the child abuse sensation in 1899. One cannot help wondering, however, whether that fantasy, which Freud found to be so notably prevalent among his Viennese patients in 1919, could in fact be traced back in part to their awareness of the child abuse sensation twenty years before. After all, the week after the Kutschera trial in 1899, two of Freud's patients suddenly began to have viciously vengeful dreams about their dead parents' "excretory difficulties." It is certainly not too much to suppose that the unprecedented and grotesquely horrific themes and details of the Hummel and Kutschera cases should have left some sort of psychological mark on the minds of those who read the newspapers. And if in 1919 Freud found the anonymous fantasy "a child is being beaten" to be surprisingly frequent, then it seems well worth noting that twenty years before there were two children whose beaten bodies were briefly the totems of obsessional public sensation. "In death she speaks to us," said the prosecutor about Anna Kutschera. "Before our inner eye the child has raised herself up, and with a mutilated hand indicating the stigmata of her wounds, her blood accusation cries out to heaven. And she will be heard." Publicly, the case was forgotten and child abuse along with it; privately, however, the memory of the case could not have been utterly and absolutely suppressed. It would be ironically fitting if Freud, who did not respond to that mutilated body in 1899, should have unwittingly registered traces of the psychological fallout twenty years later.

There is another such moment in the Freud corpus, another observation at which one cannot help wondering—this time fifteen years later still, in 1933. In that year Freud published his *New Introductory Lectures on Psychoanalysis,* including the now virtually infamous essay on "Femininity." There the dubious notion of "penis envy" was given much play, and Freud considered how a woman might move on from "the discovery that she is castrated" to attain "normal femininity." At one point, however, there was a sort of odd digression from the topic of a girl's ambivalent "libidinous relations" to her mother.

> The attractiveness of these investigations lies in the surprising detailed findings which they bring us. Thus, for instance, we discover the fear of being murdered or poisoned, which may later form the core of a paranoiac illness, already present in this pre-Oedipus period, in relation to the mother. Or another case: you will recall an interesting episode in the history of analytic research which caused me many distressing hours. In the period in which the main interest was directed to discovering infantile sexual traumas, almost all my women patients told me that they had been seduced by their fathers. I was driven to recognize in the end that these reports were untrue, and so came to understand that hysterical symptoms are derived from phantasies and not from real occurrences. It was only later that I was able to recognize in this phantasy of being seduced by the father the expression of the typical Oedipus complex in women.

In 1933 Freud could confidently retell the story of renouncing the seduction theory in 1897; during the intervening three decades he had ascended from the position of a little known, but dubiously regarded medical eccentric, to become one of the most important cultural figures in the history of Western civilization. What was it that made the venerable sage of the 1930s think back to the abandoned seduction theory of the 1890s? It was a "surprising" detail that "we discover" when we look into how daughters feel about mothers: "we discover the fear of being murdered or poisoned." That Freud regarded these as fantasies was clear enough from the way he jumped to the seduction theory with its seduction fantasies. For Freud that was the end of the matter, but one cannot help being struck by the particular fantasy of these daughters. For some of Freud's adult patients in 1933, who told him of fears that their mothers wanted to murder them as children, were children in 1899. And in that year everyone in Vienna was reading about Hedwig Keplinger who murdered her daughter, and Juliane Hummel who murdered her daughter, and Marie Kutschera who murdered her daughter. Was this another instance of psychological fallout, registering ironically with Freud, the man who seemed not to have noticed the original explosion? By 1933 fin-de-siècle Vienna was long ago; its struggling young geniuses had achieved great things. Adolf Hitler no longer studied the social question, miserable in the streets of Vienna—in 1933 he became chancellor of Germany in Berlin. The child abuse sensation of 1899 was long forgotten, but

perhaps certain vague associations continued to haunt certain impressionable Viennese daughters.

Alice Miller has observed that Freud, in abandoning the seduction theory, "could only prolong society's sleep, which had already
lasted for thousands of years, and prevent people from becoming
aware." Freud became so famous and his writings so influential,
that one cannot help imagining that, had he held to the seduction
theory—or at least not abandoned it so absolutely—he certainly
could have made the world aware of the sexual abuse of children.
The child abuse sensation of 1899 forces upon us an equally painful
might-have-been of intellectual history. For had Freud taken note of
the Hummel and Kutschera cases, had he written about them, had
he explored the problem of child abuse, then the issue could not
have been so easily forgotten. Had Freud written about child abuse,
it would have attained some degree of international recognition
along with him, disturbed society's sleep, anticipated "The Battered-Child Syndrome" by half a century—instead of sinking into
oblivion. Felix Dörmann could not save the Kutschera case from
oblivion; indeed he was barely a significant enough cultural figure
to escape that fate himself. Karl Kraus could not preserve the memory of the child abuse trials, for child abuse in 1899 was only a
convenient vehicle for his more urgent satirical concerns. The Appeal in the *Neue Freie Presse* for the building of a "monument" to
memorialize child abuse was fantastical, but Freud could have created a meaningful intellectual monument. Only Freud could have
saved the child abuse cases from oblivion by writing about them.
And Freud remained silent.

## "ALLOW ME TO HOPE"

When all the charges against Rudolf Kutschera were withdrawn,
there was applause in the courtroom. When the prosecutor then
summed up by affirming the innocence of childhood, calling upon
Anna's mutilated corpse, and demanding that the court show no
mercy, he was received with "intoxicated applause." The ultimate
moment, however, when Marie Kutschera was condemned to
death, seemed to exercise a more solemn effect upon the spectators.
It was vividly recounted in the press.

> The condemned woman at first remained apathetic. Because of her
> deafness she must have failed to understand the verdict. So the judge
> called her to him. With a firm step she went up the stairs and bent
> over to hear the verdict, her gaze fixed upon the judge across the
> table. Sharp and penetrating, he said to her: "You are guilty of murder

and have therefore been condemned to death." She jerked herself up, and then staggered a little. "Lead this woman out!" called the judge to the soldier. He stepped toward her, but Marie Kutschera had already gained control of herself, and now left the hall with a firm step and a fixed gaze, without any expression distorting her harsh countenance. The public who remained to the end—a half hour before midnight— held itself silent.

When Joseph and Juliane Hummel were condemned to death two weeks before, there had been cries of bravo, "an acclamation the like of which we cannot remember ever before at a condemnation to death." That the public at the Kutschera verdict "held itself silent" was sufficiently noteworthy to be remarked upon in the press. If there was no applause this time, however, it was certainly not because anyone failed to appreciate the dramatic qualities of the moment. The reporter's account betrayed in every line a theatrical appreciation, and this was unquestionably a highlight among those "exciting and important scenes" of a "highly dramatic nature."

Marie Kutschera held center stage, and her performance was described with the same sensibility for theatrical nuance that a Viennese reviewer would have exercised upon a performance by Sarah Bernhardt. And the performance in the courtroom sent a message to the spectators: her self-control, her firm step and fixed gaze, her perfectly expressionless countenance, all demonstrated that Marie Kutschera left the courtroom more certain than ever that she was the martyr. The reporter, who allowed her the greatest dignity in his description of the scene, seemed almost ready to accept her implicitly enacted martyrdom. The public remained silent—perhaps because any applause, after such a performance, could only be for her. She had made herself the heroine of that final moment, and, indeed, the next day the newspapers reported that ultimate "curiosity," the anonymous telegram in which Viennese women expressed their sympathy and their faith in her innocence.

That Marie Kutschera was beckoned up to the bench, to face the judge alone and hear his verdict, offered a dramatic configuration of symbolic significance. For the resolution of the case required that she bear full and sole responsibility for the horrors that had been revealed. She was not only to bear the guilt of her husband, the post official, the children's father—but also the guilt of all Vienna, "all of us," whom the prosecution felt compelled to absolve from responsibility. If all this was to be put upon her, then the judge and the courtroom had a stake in trying to penetrate her "deafness"— here surely spiritual as well as physiological—and to make her accept that guilt. Whether her response to the verdict—staggering, then regaining control—was what everyone was looking for, we cannot tell. Her silent performance is not hard to interpret, but the silence of the courtroom remains opaque—another semiotic silence, like Freud's, which can never be definitively interpreted. Was it the silence of satisfaction—that the child abuse issue had at last been resolved and disposed of? Or was it an uneasy silence, containing the terrible suspicion that the sentencing of Marie Kutschera was only a convenient terminus to a single case, an excuse to bring down the curtain and turn away from the horrors? One way or another, the silence of the courtroom in those final moments of the trial appropriately foreshadowed the great and lasting silence that was about to descend, "society's sleep." The cases were to be forgotten, and the problem of child abuse along with them. "Christian Moosbrugger, the murderer of a prostitute," wrote Musil, "was forgotten a few days after the reports of his trial ceased to appear in the newspapers, and public excitability was diverted to other matters."

The prosecutor of the Kutschera case, in his summation, took comfort from the fact that, since child abuse had created an "unheard of sensation," benevolent societies were now being founded, and the press had taken up the issue. Thus he reassured the court that from now on the problem would be under control. The *Arbeiter-Zeitung* placed less faith in "the bourgeois press which now after the Hummel trial gushes with columns of sentimentality for its readers, publishes appeals, and even seizes the initiative for the foundation of a Children's Rescue Society." The socialist paper had tried to draw public attention to the post official Rudolf Kutschera back in December 1898, right after Anna's death—and at that time the bourgeois press had not been interested.

> We stood alone, and although we raised our voice loud and clear, it was too weak to call forth a general movement, a movement that would have prevented the death of Anna Hummel.

For Anna Hummel did not die until March 1899, three months after Anna Kutschera. In making the capriciousness of the bourgeois press responsible for the death of Anna Hummel, the *Arbeiter-Zeitung* in fact paid tribute to its class rival; only the *Neue Freie Presse* could have made out of the child abuse cases the cultural sensation that they became. Only the bourgeois press could bring child abuse to the attention of those who defined Vienna's cultural sensibilities, and by the same token only the bourgeois press had the power to let the issue drop. The *Arbeiter-Zeitung*, though it pedantically insisted on viewing child abuse as fundamentally a matter of police reform, was nevertheless able, perhaps out of consciousness of its own relative impotence, to arrive at a unique prophetic insight. On the very first day of the Kutschera trial, the *Arbeiter-Zeitung* predicted that the sensation would be a "straw fire," which would quickly "burn out," leaving "defenseless children once again to their bestial parents."

The prosecutor, Kleeborn, also addressed himself in his wildly applauded summation to the uncertain future of the child abuse issue. He personally, in the course of two weeks, obtained convictions and death sentences against Juliane Hummel, Joseph Hummel, and Marie Kutschera. He naturally felt that he had done his part against child abuse, and he was confident that the issue could now be left in the hands of the press and the benevolent societies. His words revealed more than he could have suspected; his was the perspective of a very directly concerned citizen.

> For the second time within a short while I stand before the jurors with the terrible accusation that a mother has mistreated her child to death in a murderous way. Allow me to hope that this is not the symptom of an unheard of brutalization that has suddenly caught hold, but rather that it is only a mysterious accident that has produced this quick following one on top of another. Decades passed before such a deed was perpetrated, and I hope that decades may again flow by before such a deed again comes before the courts for judgment.

His declaration strikes us, one hundred years later, as both moving and chilling. His words are moving, because this was the man who, in order to do his job, had involved himself more than anyone else in Vienna with the grisly details of the two cases—so how can one blame him for hoping what he hoped? He frankly hoped that there would be no more such cases. At the same time, his words are chilling, because that hope, which he did not cherish alone, signaled the end of the child abuse sensation and the burying of the issue for decades and decades—just as he hoped. He was perhaps right in thinking it an accident that these two cases emerged together at just the same time, but they were also symptoms of "unheard of brutalization" which remained submerged, for centuries before and for decades to come. Even after all the details of the cases had been heard, the cases themselves remained "unheard of." What he refused to recognize was the difference between the "perpetration" of the deed and the prosecution of the case, and so he could allow himself to hope that the Hummel and Kutschera parents were the only ones in Vienna who abused their children. His hopes were self-fulfilling, for it was just such hopes that constituted the power of the sentimental family ideal, and forced child abuse to remain sub-merged, unrecognized.

"In the last resort," remarked Ulrich about the Moosbrugger case, "all these cases are like a loose end of thread hanging out, and if one pulls at it, the whole tightly knit fabric of society begins to come undone." The Hummel and Kutschera cases were dangling threads in precisely this sense, and though the Viennese of 1899 could perhaps tug at them gently, even wind them around their fingers, it was unthinkable to pull hard and then follow those threads wherever they might lead. Vienna could not afford to un-ravel itself. For the historian, on the other hand, working a century later, those same dangling threads offer an extraordinary opportu-nity. By pulling carefully but persistently, one can unravel analyti-cally the whole social and cultural fabric of fin-de-siècle Vienna. Those threads take us from the home to the courtroom to the theater to the opera to the parliament, from ritual murder to politi-cal violence to literary decadence to psychoanalysis, and into the most tightly woven complexes of how the Viennese of 1899 viewed themselves and their world. We can pull and unravel now with historical fascination, but Vienna, after the trials, could only try to tuck away the threads and allow itself to hope.

# CONCLUSION

## The Case of Rosa Marianek:
## Murder and Fantasy
## at Christmas

꿍ᶴᶴᶴꟼ

*Freud's children in the woods near Berchtesgaden*
*(Reproduced by courtesy of Mark Paterson and Associates*
*for Sigmund Freud Copyrights)*

## "CHRISTIAN VIENNA WITH ITS
## GOLDEN HEART"

MARIE Kutschera was condemned to death just before midnight on Thursday, November 30. Felix Dörmann published his version of the case three days later in the Sunday
edition of the *Neue Freie Presse*. That weekend there were a number of reports in the press of child abuse cases that the police were
looking into. A glovemaker was reported by neighbors for abusing
her eight-year-old son. A tailor was anonymously denounced for
starving his child. A laundress was questioned about the suspicious
injuries of her two-year-old boy. A couple was anonymously reported for abusing their children by giving them brandy to make
them sleep. A nine-month-old baby was found suffocated by pil-
lows. It was during this first week of December, following the
Kutschera trial, that the sensation seemed to reign throughout the
city. No longer so irresistibly focused on one courtroom drama,
aroused sentiment could discover reflections of the Hummel and
Kutschera cases all over the city. Public consciousness of child
abuse had perhaps never been so high, and at this moment neither
the police nor the press could fail to respond to that consciousness.

This was the moment when the sensation seemed on the point of
becoming real sociological awareness, but this development was
highly problematic. On the one hand, the anonymous denunciation
of neighbors gave public consciousness something of the air of a
witch hunt. With reported mistreatments ranging from infant suf-
focation to brandy sedatives, the charge of child abuse already
seemed to have become a rather nasty outlet for general neighbor-
hood tensions. And on the other hand, the diffusion of attention
from one courtroom to many households, although marking an advance in sociological consciousness, also involved the risk of losing
sight of the issue altogether. Diffusion, after all, was very close to
disintegration, and the issue was, in fact, destined to disappear. For
even when the Hummel and Kutschera cases were most emphatically before the public eye, the cultural values that conditioned

225

perception and interpretation were already acting to evade, trivial-
ize, transform, and deny the facts of child abuse. Little wonder,
then, that the sensation could not survive the cases that created it.

Public awareness, even at its height, was far from soberly sociological, and this showed all too clearly in a letter to the editors of
the *Neue Freie Presse* on December 8, responding to the "Appeal to
All Feeling People" of November 26. The writer enclosed all the
money she had saved to celebrate Christmas, in order to help build
the proposed monumental asylum; she also expressed the hope that
everyone in Vienna would do the same. "It would be an atonement," the letter declared, "equal to the guilt of Vienna toward the
two little martyrs—though not great enough to obliterate the
shame that such cases were possible in Christian Vienna with its
golden heart." Thus the letter ended, almost on a refrain from
Viennese operetta—Johann Strauss, Franz Lehar—and it was
signed, simply, "a Viennese woman." Actually her message, for all
its religious intonations, was not so far from that of Karl Kraus's
blindfolded Victorian Themis: "One wouldn't have thought it possible!"

The same issue of the newspaper that announced the Christmas
donation also reported the trial of that other Viennese woman, who
had been arrested in November for abusing her seven-year-old retarded daughter. The woman was Barbara Gutsch, the wife of a
weaver's assistant, and she had been reported to the police by
someone who had been following the Hummel trial. This was not a
murder case, however, and so, one week after Marie Kutschera was
condemned to death, Barbara Gutsch was sentenced to five days of
imprisonment. At the end of December there was another abuse
trial at the other end of the social spectrum. The wholesaler's wife
was tried for "overstepping the right of discipline" with her twelve-
year-old stepson, the runaway Gustav Hohn—that is, for beating
him with a hammer and pushing his head through a window. Julie
Hohn was sentenced to imprisonment for fourteen days. Without
the complication of murder, the punitive stakes were not very high,
and public interest in the December trials of the weaver's wife and
the wholesaler's wife, judging from the press, never approached the
level of sensation that the Hummel and Kutschera cases had
achieved in November.

In fact, rather more attention was given to the December story of
Francisca Kaitl, who was stopped at the very last moment from
jumping off one of the Danube bridges with four of her children
bound to her with a cord. She was the abandoned wife of a brutal

alcoholic, a printer's apprentice; she had been unhappily blessed with eight births, including a pair of twins and a set of triplets—of which five children survived. They lived in poverty, and finally starved for two days before the mother resolved to jump from the bridge with all but the oldest boy. The passerby who stopped her from jumping had to wrestle her off the bridge, and persist against her screams and the screams of the children. The *Neue Freie Presse* thought it important to emphasize that in the case of Francisca Kaitl, "not hostility against her children led this woman to her deed, but rather the inability to look on any longer at the sufferings of those poor creatures and to bear her own." The impulse here was, unmistakably, to dissociate this poor mother on the bridge from the cases of abuse that had been aired in November.

Francisca Kaitl was never prosecuted for her murderous intentions, because a psychiatric examination found her too miserable to be held accountable for her actions. This the *Neue Freie Presse* found curiously reassuring: "Francisca Kaitl will now be able to celebrate the Christmas holiday with relief, because the brand of the murderess has been taken from her." There was, of course, something highly ludicrous about this vision of the poor woman's Christmas holiday, and probably the "relief" attributed to her was far more the relief of the press and the public that this case, at least, would not force upon Vienna the contemplation of yet another murderous parent. Just as the anonymous devotee of "Christian Vienna" invoked Christmas as the occasion for sentimental atonement, so also the Jewish editors of the *Neue Freie Presse* seemed to feel in the Christmas season an urgent concern to bring "relief" to the public on this nasty issue.

This same impulse was all the more unmistakable in the real courtroom sensation of December, the case of Rosa Marianek. It dramatically overshadowed those lesser December child abuse cases, which could anyway never live up to the fascination of the Hummel and Kutschera affairs. The case of Rosa Marianek was not one of child abuse. The issues, however, were close enough to absorb the energies and tensions generated in November, and, at the same time, sufficiently different to be able to displace those energies and neutralize those tensions. The case looked back beyond Marie Kutschera and Juliane Hummel, back to the murder and suicide of Hedwig Keplinger in October, and thus the year and the century came to an end on a less unbearably disturbing note. Indeed, by capping the child abuse sensation, the case of Rosa Marianek helped to conjure it away and allow it to be forgotten.

## "IT'S BETTER FOR THEM TO DIE"

The anonymous designation of "a Viennese woman"—she who donated her Christmas savings—signified more than a mere rubric of anonymity. Her municipal pride and shame, her complete identification with the city of Vienna, distinguished her from those other women who had filled columns and columns of the Viennese press since the middle of October. Hedwig Keplinger, Juliane Hummel, and Marie Kutschera all came to Vienna from the provinces. Not one of them was "a Viennese woman," native born, and the Viennese press did not fail to bring out this distinction as each woman, in turn, came before the Viennese public. That they were all from the provinces should not have been a very surprising coincidence, since, in the nineties, two out of three inhabitants of the city were born in the provinces—including Freud, Mahler, and Kraus. And yet, the emphasis on origins in the press had the reassuring effect of making these local horrors into the alien acts of outside intruders. The signature of the "Viennese woman," who so deplored child abuse in "Christian Vienna with its golden heart," seemed to make the same point. The case of Rosa Marianek fit the pattern perfectly, for she too was born and raised in the provinces, in Nimburg (Nymburk) in Bohemia, and Brünn (Brno) in Moravia. She came from the Czech provinces that had haunted Vienna since the Badeni language laws of two years before, and again after the Polna murder. Like Hedwig Keplinger, like Juliane Hummel, like Marie Kutschera, Rosa Marianek came to Vienna, and there achieved renown as the accused murderess of her own child.

She was the daughter of a railway employee, a locomotive cleaner; there were ten children in the family, and they all lived in one room. She left home at the age of thirteen to try to earn a living as a domestic servant, and at eighteen she was already in Vienna, pregnant and unmarried, the girl friend of a butcher's assistant. She tried to drown herself then, but failed. The baby, on the other hand, died six weeks after its birth. Two years later, in 1893, she was pregnant again, by the same butcher's assistant, and this time the child survived, a boy named Johann ("Hansel"). The parents divided the cost of foster care, since Rosa Marianek could hardly raise the child herself and remain in domestic service. Her share of the fee came to half her salary. In 1897 she was pregnant for the third time, and gave birth to a girl, Elsa, whose foster care required almost all of what remained of her small salary. Elsa's paternity was uncertain, since by that time Rosa Marianek was employed in the house of a professor's wife who rented rooms to students; that respectable lady may not have realized that her servant girl from the provinces was sleeping with both of the teenage student boarders, ages sixteen and seventeen, the sons of prosperous businessmen. When in 1898 Rosa Marianek found herself pregnant yet again at the age of twenty-five, she picked up her children from their foster homes—five-year-old Johann and one-year-old Elsa—and they all disappeared.

A few days later, she sent a letter to friends in Vienna, explaining her sudden disappearance.

> You cannot imagine what I have suffered with regard to my children. Only the dear Lord knows it. I beg you, forgive me, and tell no one that I shall yet find peace in death. My head burns like fire. I cannot go on suffering like this. No one must know about my death. You take all my clothes. I thank you many times for everything. I would beg you to pray for me, but you wouldn't do it. I held each child by one hand, and took them into the Danube. You can't imagine what I suffered to bring me to do that. But the children have no father, and I don't want people to reproach them about that when they are older. Therefore it's better for them to die.

This letter was submitted to the Viennese police, who had little trouble locating Rosa Marianek at her sister's home in Moravia. The two children were not there, and she admitted to having murdered them.

Up to this point the story was a terrible one, but the legal issues were neither complex nor problematic. However, no sooner had Rosa Marianek confessed to killing her children and was arrested to await trial, than there arose two startling developments. First, it turned out that a baby had recently been found whimpering and abandoned in a field outside the city, and this baby was now identified as the one-year-old Elsa, who, by her mother's confession, ought to have been at the bottom of the Danube. Second, two boys, ages thirteen and fifteen, reported that they had seen little Johann with his mother, who was talking to some soldiers by the city barracks—two days after she claimed to have drowned the child in the river. Thus, her straightforward confession of murder was rendered highly suspect, and the case became an exceptionally interesting one. For Elsa was undeniably alive and well, and Johann could not have died on the day his mother said she murdered him. Between the supposed murder of May 1898 and the sensational trial of December 1899, the police searched throughout the Habsburg empire—"to the last stations in Hungary"—but failed to find the boy, dead or alive. In the meantime, under arrest, Rosa Marianek gave birth to yet another child, still insisting she had drowned Johann, but conceding that she had left Elsa to die in the field where she was found. In short, it was a case in which the twists and turns of a mother's terrible intentions toward her children were so fascinating and bizarre, that it became a worthy successor to the cases of Hedwig Keplinger, Juliane Hummel, and Marie Kutschera—the last great parental sensation of 1899.

And so on December 13, the first day of her two-day trial, Rosa Marianek pleaded guilty to the murder of Johann and the attempted murder of Elsa. The prosecution was ready to demand the death penalty on the strength of her confession and guilty plea. The defense, however, found itself in the unusual position of having to undermine the testimony of the defendant, having to show that her confession was a lie, arguing that she could only be shown to have abandoned her children, nothing more. The trial immediately posed the difficult issue of how to weigh a confession against contradictory evidence, for why should a criminal confess to crimes she did not commit? This problem of her confession, the overwhelming question of whether she was lying and why, made some sort of psychological evaluation of the defendant more judicially urgent than it had been in the cases of the previous months. The lawyer for the defense raised issues far more complex than he could probably appreciate, let alone pursue, when he challenged the defendant on the witness stand: "Marianek, tell the truth for once! You have a small understanding and a great fantasy." For if the confession was not simply a lie but rather a fantasy, then that fantasy was the death of her children, nothing less. It was, in fact, very much related to the shocking dreams that Freud was analyzing in "Dreams of the Death of Persons of Whom the Dreamer Is Fond." For it was a crucial point in the presentation of the whole case that Rosa Marianek, whether she really murdered her children or not, was at any rate fond of them.

In the near-tragedy of Francisca Kaitl on the Danube bridge, the motive for murder, according to the press, was definitely "not hostility against her children." Likewise, in the far more extensive coverage and analysis of the Rosa Marianek story, there was an unmistakable and insistent determination to find a way back to before the child abuse sensation of November, back to the sociological *ancien régime,* as epitomized in the case of Hedwig Keplinger in October. For back in October a mother could murder her child, and public horror could still be easily assuaged by reassuring aestheticism and sentimentality. But the decent and naive Victorian public that found Hedwig Keplinger so sympathetic had to surrender its sentimental innocence in November, for the Hummel and Kutschera cases offered a revolutionary new appreciation of parents and children. No wonder that in December there was a nostalgia for the days when a mother might murder her children without manifesting "hostility" against them. In Felix Dörmann's October vision, Hedwig Keplinger shot her daughter out of love: "It is enough that I have had such a life, but not you, my poor little worm." In December, Francisca Kaitl was depicted as ready to jump with her children because of her "inability to look on any longer at the sufferings of those poor creatures." These were journalistic interpretations, but Rosa Marianek, in her letter, expressed herself in her own words about her selfless reason for doing away with her fatherless children: "It's better for them to die."

In October Felix Dörmann put the finishing touches on the Hedwig Keplinger sensation with his story entitled "A Servant Girl's Fate." Now in December the Arbeiter-Zeitung discussed the trial of Rosa Marianek under the heading "The Tragedy of a Servant Girl." In fact, the opening phrases of the article could have been lifted from Dörmann's piece on Hedwig Keplinger.

> The case of Rosa Marianek, which stands before the jury since yesterday, is fundamentally the typical fate of many poor girls who come from the country to Vienna to support themselves as domestic servants.

Once again it was to be the sad story of the servant girl's fate, a victim of "the swamp atmosphere of the big city." The impulse to link Rosa Marianek to Hedwig Keplinger, and to identify them both with a sympathetic social stereotype, did however come up against certain highly problematic points of analogy. For Rosa Marianek, unlike Hedwig Keplinger, did not follow through on her alleged determination to kill herself along with her children. That incontrovertible circumstance would have ruled out any possibility of public sympathy, were it not for a second flaw in the comparison. Though Rosa Marianek certainly had not killed herself, there remained the tantalizing possibility that she had not actually killed her children either. Elsa was certainly alive, and Johann had been seen. Thus the case was, potentially, even more reassuring to the public than the memory of Hedwig Keplinger, and Rosa Marianek—should she be found innocent—would serve as the perfect antidote to the horrible revelations of the Hummel and Kutschera trials.

"I ask you now," said the judge to Rosa Marianek on the witness stand, "do you hold to it, that you threw the boy into the water and saw him disappear in the waves?" He virtually invited her to recon-sider her confession, but she refused to budge from the story. Either from compulsive honesty or obstinate delusion, she forced upon the judge and the court and the public yet another case of child murder, in spite of the rather persuasive evidence against it. Her confession seemed to pose a gratuitous challenge to both testimony and senti-ment. So the judge pressed her on the possibility that the child was still alive, and he pressed her even more emphatically on the fact that she herself was unquestionably among the living.

> JUDGE: Why didn't you jump in after the child, to die with him? It was no longer possible for you to retreat. You had abandoned Elsa and thrown Hansel into the water!
> ROSA MARIANEK: (crying and wringing her hands) I was horrified and disgusted with myself, and I had no more courage.

As in the case of Hedwig Keplinger, suicide would have absolved the mother, and at the same time absolved the law and the public from having to judge the crime. The judge, discussing the all-impor-tant scene by the Danube, told Rosa Marianek to her face: "That was the point at which you should have jumped in." There was all the difference in the world between a sensational private suicide by the Danube and a sensational surrendering to public justice and execution. Rosa Marianek insisted on making the murder of her children a public issue just at the time when child murder, after the cases of November, could not but provoke much too disturbing thoughts about parents and children. It was not just Rosa Ma-rianek, but all the troublesome issues raised by her case, that Vi-enna would have preferred to consign to the bottom of the Danube.

## "AS IF MAGNETICALLY DRAWN"

Rosa Marianek—whether or not she murdered her children—did not torture and abuse them, and so it was possible to hold to the belief that she loved them. This issue had come up again and again in the cases of 1899, posing the most troubling dilemmas for Victo-rian family values. Hedwig Keplinger, after murder and suicide had closed the case, was interpreted as an all too loving mother. Juliane Hummel, on the other hand, who at first claimed to have been fond of her child, was pressed and pressed until she finally retracted. Marie Kutschera, only a stepmother at any rate, was received with blank incomprehension when she exclaimed that the dead child was "my darling." In the case of Rosa Marianek this central issue was settled neither by literary apotheosis nor by direct interrogation. Instead the courtroom became the stage for what everyone present recognized as a "scene," an extraordinary scene in which Rosa Marianek was brought face to face with little Elsa, the child she abandoned almost a year and a half before. Thus the jury and the spectators would have the opportunity to observe for themselves the sentiments of a mother who claimed to have sought the death of her children. Naturally, the reporters allowed the public at large to participate in this unique dramatic experience.

Rosa Marianek was delicate and pale. She dressed in black for the trial and tried to cover her face with a handkerchief. Now, when Elsa, already three years old, was brought into the courtroom with her foster mother, Rosa Marianek broke into such violent sobbing that she had to be led out. That was a scene in itself, but it was not enough. One of the jurors proposed that the defendant be brought back in to identify the child formally as her own before the court. This time Rosa Marianek approached her daughter "as if magnetically drawn," according to the *Neue Freie Presse*. Then, according to the *Arbeiter-Zeitung*, she "broke into loud crying again, and hurled herself upon her child," embracing and kissing her. "Among the public," reported the *Neue Freie Presse,* "there reigned deep silence and then spirited agitation." And then finally the scene was brought to an end when the judge pronounced the word, "Enough."

But enough of what? Why was it so important to set up this scene—even after Rosa Marianek had once been removed from the courtroom on account of her emotional reaction—and what had been demonstrated to the agitated public when the judge finally determined that it had gone on long enough? It was certainly much more than enough to satisfy the pretext of identification. For the sobs and kisses and embraces of the accused woman proclaimed to the public that even Rosa Marianek, who had originally confessed to the murder of this child as well as the other, was still subject to the maternal sentiments enshrined by the Victorian world. Indeed those sentiments proved themselves all the more triumphant, in spite of the case history, for Rosa Marianek appeared "as if magnetically drawn," subject to an emotional law with all the force of scientific irresistibility. The nasty and unassimilable memories of Juliane Hummel and her daughter, of Marie Kutschera and her stepdaughter, could be buried beneath the embraces and kisses that Rosa Marianek offered to her daughter. The staged encounter between mother and child was a vivid dramatic demonstration that this case was not like those of the previous month. This was all the more clear from the comment of the judge, after he had pronounced the interval of embraces to be enough. He then declared, "I take this scene in complete seriousness." The point of the scene was to observe the woman's emotional response; the judge allowed it to continue until he was convinced that her sentiments were serious and genuine.

This almost cruelly relentless interest in exposing the sentiments of the defendant marked a distinct change of emphasis from the child abuse trials of November. Neither the court nor the press had been at all eager to develop a psychological appreciation of the Hummel or Kutschera parents; it was unpleasant enough to have to establish what they had done, without having to go deeply into why they had done it. The case of Rosa Marianek, however, seemed to invite more serious consideration of the accused murderess. This was not only because she seemed so much more sympathetic, but also because in her case the contradiction of the evidence and the confession meant that she herself had to be explained and understood before she could be judged. So it was that, in contrast to the Hummel and Kutschera trials, the trial of Rosa Marianek prominently featured the testimony of a court psychiatrist—Dr. Joseph Hinterstoisser, a specialist in forensic psychiatry. His role in court showed that this time, at last, psychological issues could not be altogether ignored, but the reception of his testimony also suggested that, even in this case, those issues could not be taken quite seriously. Finally, the substance of his psychological commentary showed what conventional psychiatry had to offer in Freud's Vienna.

Dr. Hinterstoisser (whose name carries a certain comic sense of Dr. Stab-in-the-Back or perhaps Dr. Kick-in-the-Pants) promised the court that psychiatry would provide the "key" to the case. Rosa Marianek was, he insisted, neither mad nor mentally ill; she was entirely responsible for her actions. And yet, he conceded, her behavior had certain "peculiarities." From this rather unimpressive opening, he went on to observe that she was not clever—but also not an idiot—that her memory was unreliable, that she was impulsive by nature, and that she didn't reflect before speaking and acting. In short, "The will is good, but the flesh is weak." It was the sort of cliché that would never have found its way into Dörmann's writing, even at its most trite, and would certainly never have come up in the analyses of the *Neue Freie Presse*. In this sense, the level of insight of conventional psychiatry seemed to show itself distinctly inferior to the standards of contemporary literature and journalism.

Worse still, one could barely discern the applicability of the cliché: Did the "weak flesh" refer to the defendant's sexual promiscuity or the murder of her child?

As Hinterstoisser proceeded to examine more specifically the tangled problem of the confession, the quality of his insights remained unimpressive. He noted a "lack of love of truth" in Rosa Marianek, and also that her lies were of a "fantastic" nature. She herself, he thought, might have a "double character," which made it possible for her to love her children and yet contemplate their murder. Her emotional instability made her so changeable as to be "chameleonlike." In summary: "We doctors call this an hysterical character." The triviality of his observations did not, of course, prevent Hinterstoisser from assuming the professional self-importance of "we doctors," as he lectured to the laymen of the court. His clinical verdict, the one-word psychiatric diagnosis that summed up the various banalities from "weak flesh" to "double character," was hysteria. For Hinterstoisser it was the grand pronouncement; hysteria, that classic nineteenth-century syndrome of inexplicable symptoms, enabled him to put a clinical label on the "peculiarities" of Rosa Marianek, without actually analyzing or explaining them. Hysteria was the signature illness of Freud's Vienna, and it was hysteria that became the vehicle for Freud's pioneering discoveries, for the creation of psychoanalysis. Freud was one of the first to appreciate that hysteria was not simply a rubric for inexplicable symptoms and peculiarities, one of the first to insist that it was a mental illness with a psychiatric logic of its own. If the insights of Hinterstoisser were less sophisticated than those of Felix Dörmann and the *Neue Freie Presse,* they might as well have been centuries behind those of Sigmund Freud. In fact, Freud was only twelve years younger than Hinterstoisser; both had studied medicine at the University of Vienna, before specializing in psychiatry. In 1899 Hinterstoisser was by far the more eminent psychiatrist of the two.

In 1895 Sigmund Freud and Josef Breuer had published their *Studies on Hysteria.* It was Freud's emphasis on the sexual etiology of hysteria that led him to the seduction theory in 1896, and again it was his hysterical patients who caused him to question that theory in 1897, to emphasize fantasy rather than seduction, thus pointing him toward the Oedipus complex. And yet Rosa Marianek, in 1899, despite her publicly pronounced hysteria, despite her sensationally publicized sexual involvements, despite her murderous intentions (or murderous fantasies), elicited not a word of comment from Freud, not a mention in the Fliess correspondence. On December 14, the second day of the trial, Freud wrote to Fliess about his discontent in Vienna, and his satisfaction at the news that in Berlin there were people reading *The Interpretation of Dreams*. On December 21, a week later, he wrote to send Christmas greetings, to lament again that no one in Vienna was reviewing his book, and to report on a patient who discovered in analysis the memory of a "primal scene" from earliest childhood. Freud wrote, "It is as if Schliemann had once more excavated Troy, which had hitherto been deemed a fable." The patient was rewarded with a gift: a picture of Oedipus and the sphinx. Once again at the end of Freud's excavations he discovered the figure of Oedipus, murderer of his father. Other fables lurked behind the story of Rosa Marianek, as in the Hummel and Kutschera cases, but Freud's attentions remained focused upon the walls of Troy. Rosa Marianek received only the uninsightful attentions of Dr. Hinterstoisser.

Freud, on December 21, was gloomily convinced that his ideas were far too advanced to be seriously received in Vienna: "We are, after all, terribly far ahead of our time." He was right, of course, and yet, Hinterstoisser, whose psychological conceptions were anything but advanced, was also refused a serious reception at the trial of Rosa Marianek. The prosecutor several times interrupted the psychiatric testimony, objecting that it was irrelevant, and, curiously, the defense agreed. With both defense and prosecution agreeing that the psychiatric testimony was irrelevant, the judge decided to cut short the long-winded doctor. He had been prepared to go on at much greater length, and reporters noticed his "evident irritation" at being so abruptly dismissed from the witness stand. Hinterstoisser appeared almost as a comic figure, with his trite and pompous pronouncements, and certainly there was comedy in the scene of his being bustled off the stand when he had so much more to say. Several months later, in the spring of 1900, Karl Kraus brought Hinterstoisser into the pages of *Die Fackel*, viciously mocking the doctor's nonsensical psychiatric testimony in one case after another. At the trial of Rosa Marianek, the two lawyers were perhaps sufficiently cultured Viennese men to recognize the shallowness of Hinterstoisser's contributions. And yet, the improbable solidarity of judgment between defense and prosecution had other, less funny implications. For the unanimous agreement to silence the psychiatric testimony suggested a certain eager relief that psychology had nothing substantial to offer on the subject of parents murdering their children. The psychiatric issues which had remained unexamined in the Hummel and Kutschera cases could now continue to be ignored in the case of Rosa Marianek. The banality of conventional psychiatry in Freud's Vienna, combined with the same public resistance that Freud himself encountered, guaranteed that the parents who murdered their children in 1899, though they might be condemned, would not be explained.

When it came time to sum up the case for the jury, both lawyers knew that the issues were strictly sentimental. "I know that the accused excites your pity," said the prosecutor, aware that he was losing the sentimental struggle. The most he could do to resist, however, was irrelevantly to denounce Rosa Marianek for her sexual immorality. But standards of sexual propriety, for all their Victorian proverbiality, were perhaps cherished less intensely than family values and "faith in the mother." Certainly the unwed Hedwig Keplinger was able to emerge as the sympathetic heroine of her own tragedy, and Rosa Marianek fared almost as well. The defense attorney, Viktor Rosenfeld, in his summation, was not afraid to take on directly the charges of immorality. "A servant girl," he declared, "is like a lemon which is squeezed out and then thrown away." The applause in the courtroom for that observation demonstrated the powerlessness of prudery against sentiment. Only then did Rosenfeld conclude with his rhetorical masterpiece. He reminded the jurors and spectators that the supposedly murdered boy had been seen alive, that he had not been proven to be dead. Then he called upon his audience to think ahead to Christmas. He asked them all to imagine themselves sitting around their Christmas trees, then to imagine little Johann at the Christmas tree of some sympathetic woman somewhere who had taken him in, and then to have to recall that they had condemned Rosa Marianek to death. This flourish was received with more applause and with cries of bravo. The jury returned after an hour with the verdict: by ten votes against two they rejected the murder charge, and, illogically, by nine votes against three they accepted the charge of attempted murder. The judge sentenced Rosa Marianek to seven years' imprisonment, the mildest possible sentence. Once again the spirit of Christmas had been invoked against the specter of parents murdering children, and the case of Rosa Marianek was closed with a grand affirmation of sentimental "faith in the mother."

## DOUBLE ZERO, 1900

If it was Christmas that offered emotional refuge and escape from the horrors of child abuse and child murder, that enabled the Viennese of 1899 to recover their faith in the sentimental family ideal, it was New Year's that made it possible to draw a line and put the sensations decisively behind. This force was all the more decisive for the fact that it was no ordinary New Year's, but the turn of the century. And yet, not everyone agreed that the new century was about to begin. As late as December 10, only days before the trial of Rosa Marianek, the *Neue Freie Presse,* arbiter of culture, insisted that the correct chronological new century would not begin until January 1, 1901, still one year away. In England, it was reported, there were greeting cards for "A Happy New Century!"—apparently because the English were illogically susceptible to the double zero of 1900. Such superior pedantry on the part of the Viennese paper rested on the most dubious foundations, since back in November the *Neue Freie Presse* had reported the sell-out printing of the "Postcards from the End of the World." Clearly, the Viennese also believed in the magic of the double zero, believed that the new century was about to begin on January 1, 1900.

On December 16, two days after the sentimental sentencing of Rosa Marianek, the *Neue Freie Presse* reported again on the dispute over whether or not the new century was about to begin. Still the editors insisted that 1900 belonged to the nineteenth century, that the decision must be made according to logic and chronology, not under the sway of sentiment and emotion (*das Gefühl*). "A calendar," the paper proclaimed, "is not a lyric poem." The appeal against emotion and poetry had a hollow ring coming from the paper that only two weeks before had entrusted the issue of child abuse to the pen of a lyric poet. The cause of logic and chronology was doomed, and on December 31, New Year's Eve, even the *Neue Freie Presse* ungraciously conceded the question. The whole dispute was "childish," but perhaps after all there was something in the double zero, something that marked the end of an "historical epoch." In short, they surrendered to sentiment—as so often before—and allowed that even the calendar might be a lyric poem. But the explanation given for this change of heart was very revealing: "Exhausted and disillusioned by the nineteenth, the people turn their gaze longingly to the twentieth century."

There was certainly reason enough for Austrian liberalism to feel "exhausted and disillusioned" in 1899. Its years of political power were long past, and Austria was tortured with new political and social problems that liberalism could neither fathom nor resolve. Perhaps the *Neue Freie Presse* hoped that in starting a new century it would be possible to bury in the past the viciously divisive Austrian nationalities struggle and the insane virulence of Austrian anti-Semitism. If so, then liberalism was destined to be disillusioned again, for those forces would rage all the more violently and destructively in the twentieth century. But after the Hummel and

Kutschera trials, in November 1899, there was also the haunting issue of child abuse—likewise unfathomable and irresolvable—to be left behind in the nineteenth century. Those cases would be forgotten in the twentieth century, consigned to historical oblivion. That "longing gaze" toward the twentieth century was very much in the same spirit as the prosecutor's summation in the Kutschera case: "I hope that decades may again flow by before such a deed again comes before the courts for judgment."

"The new century," wrote Freud to Fliess on January 8, "the most interesting thing about which for us may be that it contains the dates of our deaths, has brought me nothing but a stupid review in the *Zeit* by Burckhard, the former director of the Burgtheater." If a lyric poet could interpret child abuse in Vienna, then, of course, a theater director could review psychoanalysis. The new century, however, contained much more for Freud than his own death; it was to bring him an astounding worldwide intellectual influence which he could hardly have dreamed of as he suffered over the stupid reviews of 1899 and 1900. And although at the turn of the century he may have been already focused on that "most interesting thing," his death, he would in fact live for decades to appreciate his amazing success. The twentieth century did, of course, hold the dates of the deaths of all those who participated in fin-de-siècle Vienna. The Emperor Franz Joseph died in 1916, and in 1918 the Habsburg empire ceased to exist at the end of World War I. In 1920 Moritz Benedikt died, leaving the *Neue Freie Presse* in the hands of his son. Felix Dörmann died in Vienna in 1928, and Hofmannsthal the following year in 1929—only days after his son committed suicide. Schnitzler died in 1931, and Karl Kraus in 1936 after being hit by a bicyclist. In 1938 the Austrian republic, the rump of the old empire, was unified with Nazi Germany in the Anschluss, and thus became part of a new empire. That same year Sigmund Freud at last left Vienna, the city he hated, and took refuge from the Nazis in London; he died of cancer the following year at the age of eighty-three, a few weeks after the outbreak of World War II. Nineteen thirty-eight was also the last year of the *Neue Freie Presse*; Hitler still remembered the newspaper with distaste from his early years in Vienna, and he would not allow it to continue publication in the Third Reich. In 1942 Stefan Zweig, like Freud a Jewish Viennese refugee from Nazi Austria, committed suicide together with his wife in Brazil. Adolf Hitler, the boy from the Austrian provinces who studied society and politics in the streets of turn-of-the-century Vienna, committed suicide in the bunker together with Eva Braun in Berlin in 1945. Anna Freud, who in

1899 was the same age as the murdered child Anna Hummel, lived until 1982; she was the guardian of her father's intellectual heritage, and herself an important psychoanalyst who took a special interest in child psychology.

The Hummel and Kutschera cases were indeed buried and forgotten in the twentieth century; the problem of child abuse, however, was not dead—but merely repressed. The first steps toward general consciousness came with improvements in X-ray technology after World War II; radiology studies revealed mysterious recurring patterns of bone fractures in children. The external mutilations of the children's bodies, described in court in 1899, could now be internally photographed. These studies appeared in specialized radiology journals under rather unsensational titles: "Multiple Fractures in Long Bones of Infants Suffering from Chronic Subdural Hematoma" (1946), "Roentgen Manifestations of Unrecognized Skeletal Trauma in Infants" (1953), "Some Traumatic Lesions in Growing Bones Other than Fractures and Dislocations" (1957). In 1962 five doctors—pediatricians, a psychiatrist, a radiologist—published the breakthrough article, "The Battered-Child Syndrome," in the *Journal of the American Medical Association*.

> The battered-child syndrome is a term used by us to characterize a clinical condition in young children who have received serious physical abuse, generally from a parent or foster parent . . . It is a significant cause of childhood disability and death. Unfortunately, it is frequently not recognized . . .

In 1899 the Viennese prosecutor had urged his audience to believe that the Hummel and Kutschera cases were freakish monstrosities, anything but sociologically symptomatic. "Allow me to hope," he declaimed, ever hopeful, "that this is not the symptom of an unheard of brutalization that has suddenly caught hold, but rather that it is only a mysterious accident." The child abuse sensation of 1899 was thus presented to the public as a "mysterious accident," the better to be able to forget about it altogether. Those cases, however, were not accidents. They were the tip of the iceberg. They were, in all their details, perfectly consistent parts of the syndrome that would finally be exposed in 1962.

"There are some things that are simply unbelievable," said the prosecutor in 1899. That conviction was at the heart of the refusal to face the implications of the Hummel and Kutschera cases: they were simply unbelievable in the light of the conventional conception of family relations. The physicians of 1962 knew that they would face the same refusal to believe, even among their medical colleagues.

> There is reluctance on the part of many physicians to accept the radiologic signs as indications of repetitive trauma and possible abuse. This reluctance stems from the emotional unwillingness of the physician to consider abuse as the cause of the child's difficulty . . . Physicians have great difficulty both in believing that parents could have attacked their children and in undertaking the essential questioning of parents on this subject. Many physicians find it hard to believe that such an attack could have occurred and they attempt to obliterate such suspicions from their minds, even in the face of obvious circumstantial evidence. The reason for this is not clearly understood.

In Vienna, after the child abuse sensation of 1899, public suspicions were indeed obliterated and the "unbelievable" cases forgotten. The revelations of "The Battered-Child Syndrome," however, surmounted contemporary disbelief, and became the starting point for a tremendous medical, psychological, and sociological exploration of child abuse. This was an heroic achievement in the history of society's self-consciousness, but the social consequences have been sadly limited. For even if we can today accept the existence of child abuse as a syndrome, even if we can then diagnose and confront it in individual cases, we remain almost helpless in the face of the tragedy. Either we leave the child with its abusive parents and place our faith in counseling and family support, or we separate the child from its parents and place our faith in foster care.

The apprehensions of the authors of "The Battered-Child Syndrome," their professions of fear that they would not be believed by their colleagues, were powerfully reminiscent of Freud's appeals to his readers in *The Interpretation of Dreams*. When he proposed the idea that children wish for the deaths of their parents, he anticipated within the text itself that his readers would refuse to believe: "They will deny the possibility of their *ever* having had such a thought with just as much energy as they insist that they harbor no such wishes now." He almost pleaded with them to give him a hearing.

> Before this idea is rejected as monstrous, it is as well in this case, too, to consider the real relations obtaining—this time between parents and children. We must distinguish between what the cultural standards of filial piety demand of this relation and what everyday observation shows it in fact to be. More than one occasion for hostility lies concealed in the relations between parents and children.

But the Oedipus complex, despite Freud's apprehensions in 1899, did indeed make its mark on our culture; this too was an heroic achievement in the history of society's self-consciousness. Since 1899, since Freud's formulation of the Oedipus complex, the ambivalence of children toward their parents has become a fundamental principle of twentieth-century psychology, has been generally accepted as far truer to life than the ideal of filial piety. It is respectfully recognized that the Oedipus complex is one of the great contributions of fin-de-siècle Vienna to twentieth-century culture. In fact, fin-de-siècle Vienna discovered not only the Oedipus complex, but also its reciprocal syndrome: the horrors of child abuse. At the very same time that Freud revealed that children dream of the deaths of their parents, anyone who read the newspapers knew that parents both tortured and murdered their children. But the latter was an even more painful discovery, more monstrous, more unbelievable. So child abuse was brought to light in Freud's Vienna for just a month, an "unprecedented" phenomenon; it played a part in the rich and tangled complications of Viennese culture and society, and then was buried again.

# Notes

## Introduction

3: **"Postcards from the End of the World"**—*Neue Freie Presse,* 13 November 1899. All translations into English from the Viennese press are by the author.

## Chapter 1. *The Story of Hedwig Keplinger*

10: **"Murder and Suicide"**—*Neue Freie Presse,* 14 October 1899.

11: **"The number of portraits"**—Robert Musil, *The Man Without Qualities,* trans. Eithne Wilkins and Ernst Kaiser (1930; New York: Capricorn Books, 1965), p. 93. For a biography of the Emperor see Joseph Redlich, *Emperor Francis Joseph of Austria* (New York: The Macmillan Company, 1929).

11: **"so bound up with the person of Franz Joseph"**—Adolf Hitler, *Mein Kampf,* trans. Ralph Manheim (1925; Boston: Houghton Mifflin, 1971), p. 159.

11: **"absolute seclusion"**—Hermann Broch, *Hugo von Hofmannsthal and His Time: The European Imagination 1860–1920,* trans. Michael P. Steinberg (1955; Chicago: University of Chicago Press, 1984), p. 73.

12: **"I went before two o'clock to the painter"**—letter of 23 October 1899. *The Incredible Friendship: The Letters of Emperor Franz Joseph to Frau Katharina Schratt,* Jean de Bourgoing (editor), trans. Evabeth Miller Kienast and Robert Rie (Albany: State University of New York, 1966), p. 310. For a biography of the Empress see Egon Corti, *Elisabeth, Empress of Austria* (New Haven: Yale University Press, 1936).

13: **"From the very earliest days of my youth"**—Stefan Zweig, *The World of Yesterday* (1943; Lincoln: University of Nebraska Press, 1964), p. 216. For the story of Mayerling see Frederic Morton, *A Nervous Splendor: Vienna 1888/1889,* (1979; Boston: Little, Brown; New York: Penguin Books, 1980).

13: **"Let us hope"**—letter of 27 October 1899, *Letters of the Emperor Franz Joseph to Frau Katharina Schratt,* p. 311.

13: **"The Emperor or Empress (or the King and Queen)"**—Sigmund Freud, *The Interpretation of Dreams,* trans. James Strachey (1899–1900, first German edition; 1953, English *Standard Edition:* New York: Avon Books, 1965), p. 389. This particular observation was added by Freud to the original text in the 1909 second edition.

14: **"A Big-City Novel"**—*Neue Freie Presse,* 14 October 1899, evening edition.

15: **"The engineer explained to the girl"**—*Neue Freie Presse,* 14 October 1899, evening edition.

16: **"I dread Vienna"**—letter of 11 September 1899, *The Complete Letters of Sigmund Freud to Wilhelm Fliess 1887–1904,* Jeffrey Moussaieff Masson, editor and translator (Cambridge, Mass.: Harvard University Press, 1985), p. 371. See also Ernest Jones, *The Life and Work of Sigmund Freud,* Volume I (New York: Basic Books, 1953).

16: **"The meaning of such dreams"**—Freud. *The Interpretation of Dreams,* p. 282.

16: **"Before this idea is rejected"**—Freud, *The Interpretation of Dreams,* p. 289.

17: **"Dear Wilhelm"**—letter of 17 October 1899, *Letters of Sigmund Freud to Wilhelm Fliess,* p. 380.

20: **"There is hardly a city in Europe"**—Zweig, p. 12.

20: **"an escape, a refuge"**—Carl Schorske, *Fin-de-siècle Vienna: Politics and Culture,* (1980, Knopf; New York: Vintage Books, 1981), p. 8. "Politics and the Psyche" was first published in the *American Historical Review* in July 1961. On Viennese aestheticism see also William Johnston, *The Austrian Mind* (Berkeley: University of California Press, 1972). On the relation between art and politics in Vienna see also William McGrath, *Dionysian Art and Populist Politics in Austria* (New Haven: Yale University Press, 1974).

20: **"Whenever I get deeply absorbed"**—letter of 14 May 1922, Ernst L. Freud (editor), *The Letters of Sigmund Freud,* trans. Tania and James Stern (1960; New York: Basic Books, 1975), p. 339.

21: **If I look back today"**—Zweig, p. 55.

21: **"At present my son Martin"**—letter of 4 October 1899, *Letters of Sigmund Freud to Wilhelm Fliess,* p. 377.

21: **"Somewhere inside me"**—letter of 21 September 1899, *Letters of Sigmund Freud to Wilhelm Fliess,* p. 373.

21: **Hedwig Keplinger: A Servant Girl's Fate**—Felix Dörmann, *Neue Freie Presse,* 15 October 1899, pp. 7–8. Translation by L. W.

25: **"In the end, not as a Jew"**—Broch, p. 105.

25: **"It was the pride and ambition of the Jewish people"**—Zweig, pp. 21–22.

26: **"I am Loris"**—in Gotthart Wunberg (editor), *Die Wiener Moderne* (Stuttgart: Philipp Reclam, 1981), pp. 38–39.

26: **"O Silberlila"**—from the poem "Sensationen" in Felix Dörmann, *Sensationen* (1892; Vienna: Verlag Leopold Weiss, 1897), p. 25. Translation by L. W. On Dörmann see the entry in *Neue Deutsche Biographie*, IV (Berlin: Duncker & Humboldt, 1957), p. 33. See also the entry for "Biedermann, Felix" (Dörmann was a pen name) in *Oesterreichisches Biographisches Lexicon*, I (Graz & Köln: Verlag Hermann Böhlaus, 1957), p. 82. See also Jens Malte Fischer, *Fin de Siècle: Kommentar zu einer Epoche* (Munich: Winkler Verlag, 1978), pp. 114–124. On Young Vienna see Jens Rieckmann, *Aufbruch in die Moderne; die Anfänge des Jungen Wien* (Frankfurt: Athenäum Verlag, 1985).

26: **"Trostlos weinende Sehnsucht"**—from the poem "Gebet" in Dörmann, *Sensationen*, p. 43. Translation by L. W.

27: **"[Hofmannsthal] is thoroughly new"**—in Wunberg, p. 40. Translation by L. W.

27: **"[Dörmann] does not speak from life"**—in Fischer, p. 123. Translation by L. W.

27: **"After a few minutes"**—in Zweig, p. 48.

28: **"A volume of poetry"**—in Fischer, p. 115. Translation by L. W.

28: **"Dear Friend"**—letter of 1 January 1892, Hugo von Hofmannsthal and Arthur Schnitzler, *Briefwechsel* (1964; Frankfurt: Fischer, 1983), p. 14. Translation by L. W.

28: **"The demolition worker taps at the window"**—Karl Kraus, *Die Demolirte Literatur* (1897; Steinbach: Anabas-Verlag Günter Kämpf, 1972), p. 36. Translation by L. W.

33: **"Dora's reticule"**—Sigmund Freud, *Dora: An Analysis of a Case of Hysteria*, trans. James Strachey (1905; New York: Collier Books, 1963), p. 95.

33: **"As regards articles of clothing"**—Freud, *The Interpretation of Dreams*, p. 391.

34: **"Heavens, I'd no idea"**—*La Ronde* (1900), trans. Eric Bentley, in Arthur Schnitzler, *Plays and Stories*, edited by Egon Schwarz (New York: Continuum, 1982), p. 63.

35: **"In hardly any German city"**—Hitler, p. 24.

35: **"The peasant boy who goes to the big city"**—Hitler, p. 26.

36: **"With open eyes"**—Hitler, p. 27.

36: **"I too had been tossed around"**—Hitler, p. 27.

40: **"In Vienna there was really only one journal"**—Zweig, p. 99.

40: **"One and all read it"**—Henry Wickham Steed, *The Hapsburg Monarchy* (1913; New York: Howard Fertig, 1969), p. 187.

41: **"the writers of the nineties"**—Schorske, p. 6.

41: **"Its editor, Moritz Benedikt"**—Zweig, pp. 99–100.

42: **"My parents"**—Zweig, p. 109–110.

42: **"Subscriber to the *Neue Freie Presse*"**—Adam Wandruszka, *Geschichte einer Zeitung* (Vienna: Neue Wiener Presse, 1958), p. 109.

42: **"I respected the exalted tone"**—Hitler, p. 53.

42: **"And I now began"**—Hitler, p. 58.

43: **"The so-called liberal Jews"**—Hitler, p. 57.

43: **"The Boer War"**—diary entry of 16 October 1899, *The Complete Diaries of Theodor Herzl*, III, edited by Raphael Patai, translated by Harry Zohn (New York & London: The Herzl Press, 1960), p. 880.

44: **"There are two fine things"**—Harry Zohn, *Karl Kraus*, (New York: Frederick Ungar, 1971), p. 16. On Kraus see also Edward Timms, *Karl Kraus: Apocalyptic Satirist* (New Haven: Yale University Press, 1986). Kraus is also a central figure in the memoir of Elias Canetti, *The Torch in My Ear*, trans. Joachim Neugroschel (1980; New York: Farrar, Straus, & Giroux, 1982). See also Walter Benjamin, "Karl Kraus" (1931), in *Reflections*, trans. Edmund Jephcott, ed. Peter Demetz (New York: Harcourt Brace Jovanovich, 1978).

44: **"I am going to start a distinguished paper"**—diary entry of 6 December 1899, *Diaries of Theodor Herzl*, p. 894.

44: **"The *Fackel* Neurosis"**—Allan Janik and Stephen Toulmin, *Wittgenstein's Vienna*, (New York: Simon & Schuster, 1973), pp. 75–76.

45: **"I have given my best"**—diary entry of 5 December 1899, *Diaries of Theodor Herzl*, p. 892.

47: **"What then?"**—*Arbeiter-Zeitung*, 15 October 1899.

48: **"The first glance"**—Zweig, p. 14.

48: **"Her silence as the murderess"**—*Neue Freie Presse*, 16 October 1899, evening edition.

49: **"People who are receptive"**—Sigmund Freud, *Civilization and Its Discontents*, trans. James Strachey (1930; New York & London: W. W. Norton, 1961), p. 30.

## Chapter 2. The Hummel Case

*page*

56: **"Hannele"**—*Neue Freie Presse*, 12 November 1899.

56: **"a dominating theatre culture"**—Hermann Broch, *Hugo von Hofmannsthal and His Time: The European Imagination 1860–1920*, trans. Michael P. Steinberg (1955; Chicago: University of Chicago Press, 1984), pp. 61–62.

57: **"Postcards from the End of the World"**—*Neue Freie Presse*, 13 November 1899.

58: **"Mothers who murder their children"**—*Neue Freie Presse*, 14 November 1899, evening edition.

60: "That which otherwise drives murderers"—*Neue Freie Presse*, 15 November 1899.

61: "an awareness of the particular nature of childhood"—Philippe Ariès, *Centuries of Childhood: A Social History of Family Life*, trans. Robert Baldick (1960; New York: Vintage, 1962), p. 128.

62: "Unhappily the results of these investigations"—William Langer, "Foreword," in *The History of Childhood*, edited by Lloyd deMause (1974; New York: Harper & Row, 1975), pp. vii–viii.

63: "The history of childhood is a nightmare"—Lloyd deMause. "The Evolution of Childhood," in *The History of Childhood*, p. 1.

63: "the utter surbordination of the child"—Lawrence Stone, *The Family, Sex and Marriage: In England 1500–1800* (New York: Harper & Row, 1977), p. 171.

63: "more children were being beaten"—Stone, p. 163.

63: "Severe and frequent whipping"—Stone, p. 434.

63: "the harsh and remote seventeenth century"—Stone, p. 456.

64: Celestine Doudet—Mary Hartman, *Victorian Murderesses* (New York: Schocken Books, 1977), Chapter 3.

65: "It is one of the most touching sights"—Jacob Riis, *How the Other Half Lives*, (1890; New York: Hill & Wang, 1957), p. 147.

65: "the curious decline of public interest"—George Behlmer, *Child Abuse and Moral Reform in England 1870–1908* (Stanford: Stanford University Press, 1982), p. 225.

66: "Among the numerous and very diverse facts"—in Jeffrey Moussaieff Masson, *The Assault on Truth: Freud's Suppression of the Seduction Theory* (New York: Farrar, Straus and Giroux, 1984), pp. 18–19.

66: Freud's library—Masson, pp. 37–40.

68: "dazzling riches and loathsome poverty"—Adolf Hitler, *Mein Kampf*, trans. Ralph Manheim (1925; Boston: Houghton Mifflin, 1971), p. 23. On Vienna see Arthur J. May, *Vienna in the Age of Franz Josef*, (Norman: University of Oklahoma Press, 1966) and May, *The Hapsburg Monarchy 1867–1914* (Cambridge, Mass.: Harvard University Press, 1951). For precise statistics for Vienna in 1899 see *Statistische Monatschrift*, herausgegeben von der K. K. Statistischen Central-Commission (Vienna: Alfred Hölder, 1900).

68: "There dwells hatefulness and vulgarity"—Hugo von Hofmannsthal, "Der Tod des Tizian" (1892), in *Gedichte und kleine Dramen* (Frankfurt: Suhrkamp Verlag, 1966), p. 66. Translation by L. W.

69: "without education, people on a low level of civilization"—*Neue Freie Presse*, 12 November 1899.

69: "Such a deed is so abominable"—*Arbeiter-Zeitung*, 15 November 1899.

69: "Imagine, for instance, the following scene"—Hitler, pp. 31–32.

70: "the little children"—Hitler, p. 28.

72: "could only in suppressed weeping"—*Arbeiter-Zeitung,* 15 November 1899.

74: "not murdered, but butchered"—*Arbeiter-Zeitung,* 15 November 1899.

74: "There can only have been one prevailing intention"—*Arbeiter-Zeitung,* 15 November 1899.

74: "the recipe for doing away with the child"—*Neue Freie Presse,* 12 November 1899.

74: "didn't kill her, no"—*Neue Freie Presse,* 15 November 1899.

75: "Was Anna a good child?"—*Arbeiter-Zeitung,* 15 November 1899.

75: "In the time right before the death of the child"—*Arbeiter-Zeitung,* 15 November 1899.

76: "In our times"—*Arbeiter-Zeitung,* 15 November 1899.

77: "It was a parquet of mothers"—*Arbeiter-Zeitung,* 15 November 1899.

78: "Do you admit to being guilty"—*Arbeiter-Zeitung,* 15 November 1899.

78: "Do you remember how you were treated"—*Arbeiter-Zeitung,* 15 November 1899.

78: "Was that hard on you"—*Neue Freie Presse.* 14 November 1899, evening edition.

79: "She was healthy"—*Neue Freie Presse,* 14 November 1899, evening edition.

80: "the banality of evil"—Hannah Arendt, *Eichmann in Jerusalem: A Report on the Banality of Evil* (New York: Viking, 1963).

80: "I can't help it"—*Neue Freie Presse,* 15 November 1899.

80: "It strikes the modern reader as unfunny"—Robert Darnton, *The Great Cat Massacre* (New York: Basic Books, 1984), pp. 77–78.

81: "the good old days"—Robert Musil, *The Man Without Qualities,* trans. Eithne Wilkins and Ernst Kaiser (1930; New York: Capricorn Books, 1965), p. 31.

81: "all the bridges"—Stefan Zweig, *The World of Yesterday* (1943; Lincoln: University of Nebraska Press, 1964), p. xix.

81: "We do not know what is giving us enjoyment"—Sigmund Freud, *Jokes and Their Relationship to the Unconscious,* trans. James Strachey (1905; New York: W. W. Norton, 1963), p. 132.

82: "Please, I never had a hostile intention"—*Neue Freie Presse,* 15 November 1899.

83: "He was given to drinking"—*Neue Freie Presse,* 14 November 1899, evening edition.

83: "Doesn't that suggest a hatred of the child"—*Neue Freie Presse,* 15 November 1899.

85: "By making our enemy small"—Freud, *Jokes,* p. 103.

85: "The species of humour"—Freud, *Jokes*, pp. 231–232.

87: "In the public and among the jurors"—*Neue Freie Presse*, 15 November 1899.

88: "You were drunk"—*Neue Freie Presse*, 15 November 1899.

89: "a good deal of the comic effect"—Freud, *Jokes*, pp. 190–196.

91: "Her wild cruelty"—*Arbeiter-Zeitung*, 15 November 1899.

91: "It remains mysterious"—*Neue Freie Presse*, 15 November 1899.

91: "A complete explanation"—*Neue Freie Presse*, 15 November 1899.

92: "So, poor Paulinchen"—letter of 9 November 1899. *The Complete Letters of Sigmund Freud to Wilhelm Fliess, 1887–1904*, Jeffrey Moussaieff Masson, editor and translator (Cambridge, Mass.: Harvard University Press, 1985), pp. 384–385.

93: "On Sunday, the 12th"—letter of 19 November 1899, *Letters of Sigmund Freud to Wilhelm Fliess*, p. 386.

94: "It is a thankless task"—letter of 19 November 1899, *Letters of Sigmund Freud to Wilhelm Fliess*, p. 387.

94: "The book has had one single review"—letter of 21 December 1899, *Letters of Sigmund Freud to Wilhelm Fliess*, p. 392.

96: "However much one may wonder"—*Arbeiter-Zeitung*, 15 November 1899.

97: "Vienna will hear us"—*Neue Freie Presse*, 26 November 1899.

98: "an iconographic index"—Carl Schorske, *Fin-de-siècle Vienna: Politics and Culture* (1980, Knopf; New York: Vintage Books, 1981), p. 27.

98: Steinhof Church—Kirk Varnadoe, *Vienna 1900: Art, Architecture, & Design* (New York: Museum of Modern Art, 1986), pp. 32–34.

99: "socially speaking"—Hitler, p. 23. On Austrian and Viennese social welfare see May, *Vienna*, chapter 2, and May, *The Hapsburg Monarchy*, chapter 13.

100: "At any rate the population"—*Neue Freie Presse*, 19 November 1899.

100: "Then I came to Vienna"—Hitler, pp. 52–60.

101: "they both tower far above"—Hitler, pp. 98–101. On Lueger and Schönerer, see "Politics in a New Key: An Austrian Trio" in Schorske, *Fin-de-siècle Vienna*; this was first published in the *Journal of Modern History* in December 1967. See also P. G. J. Pulzer, *The Rise of Political Anti-Semitism in Germany and Austria* (New York & London: John Wiley, 1964), chapters 17 and 18.

102: "the greatest German mayor"—Hitler, p. 55.

102: "overindulged out of joy"—letter of 8 November 1895, *Letters of Sigmund Freud to Wilhelm Fliess*, p. 150.

102: Leopold Hilsner—See the article "Hilsner Case" in the *Encyclopedia Judaica*, VIII (Jerusalem: Keter Publishing, 1972); and the article

"Polna Affair" in the *Jewish Encyclopedia*, X (New York & London: Funk & Wagnalls, 1905).

103: **"legends of ritual murders"**—Zweig, p. 63.

103: **"Is there no Zola"**—in Karl Kraus, *Die Fackel*, 19, Vienna, Beginning October 1899, 24.

103: **"Since they have dared"**—in Nicholas Halasz, *Captain Dreyfus: The Story of a Mass Hysteria* (New York: Simon & Schuster, 1955), p. 130.

104: **"this superstition"**—"Vorrede," Thomas Masaryk, *Die Bedeutung des Polnaer Verbrechens für den Ritualaberglauben* (Berlin: Hermann, 1900). Translation by L. W.

105: **"upper Jews"**—diary entry of 13 October 1899, *The Complete Diaries of Theodor Herzl*, III, edited by Raphael Patai, translated by Harry Zohn (New York & London: The Herzl Press, 1960), p. 879.

105: **"tasteless"**—Karl Kraus, *Die Fackel*, 19, Vienna, Beginning October 1899, 23–26.

105: **"If the whole of German art"**—Natalie Bauer-Lechner, *Recollections of Gustav Mahler*, trans. Dika Newlin (1923; Cambridge: Cambridge University Press, 1980), p. 137.

105: **"He had no defense"**—Bauer-Lechner, pp. 137–138.

106: **"A Victim of the Anti-Semitic Agitation"**—*Neue Freie Presse*, 6 November 1899.

107: **"dignified form"**—Hitler, p. 53.

107: **"I now saw the liberal attitude"**—Hitler, pp. 58–59.

108: **"Uncompromising advocacy"**—Adam Wandruszka, *Geschichte einer Zeitung* (Vienna: Neue Wiener Presse, 1958), p. 98.

108: **"centered upon rational man"**—Schorske, p. 4.

108: **"believed in what was modern"**—R. R. Palmer and Joel Colton, *History of the Modern World* (1950; New York: Knopf, 1965), p. 432.

108: **"fanatically devoted"**—Henry Wickham Steed, *The Hapsburg Monarchy* (1913; New York: Howard Fertig, 1969), p. 188. On Benedikt see Wandruszka, chapters 4 and 5.

109: **"The Fable of Ritual Murder"**—*Neue Freie Presse*, 17 October 1899.

109: **"Blood Fairy Tale"**—*Neue Freie Presse*, 25 November 1899.

109: **"transference and displacement"**—Freud, *The Interpretation of Dreams*, p. 343.

111: **"another less harmless purpose"**—*Neue Freie Presse*, 17 October 1899.

111: **"In contrast to Hilsner"**—Masaryk, pp. 55–62. Translation by L. W.

113: **"Do you still dare"**—*Neue Freie Presse*, 15 November 1899.

114: **"an acclamation"**—*Neue Freie Presse*, 15 November 1899.

115: **"In the moment when you cry bravo"**—Arthur Schnitzler, "Der grüne Kakadu" (1899), in *Das dramatische Werk*, 3 (Frankfurt: Fischer Taschenbuch, 1978), p. 40. Translation by L. W. On the production of *The Green Cockatoo* in 1899 see Renate Wagner and Brigitte Vacha, *Wiener Schnitzler-Aufführungen 1891–1970* (Munich: Prestel, 1971), pp. 31–33.

115: **"Reality enters into the play"**—Schnitzler, "Der grüne Kakadu," p. 33. Translation by L. W.

## Chapter 3. *The Kutschera Case*

*page*

119: **"With trembling hands"**—*Neue Freie Presse*, 17 November 1899, evening edition.

120: **"I could tell you all sorts of funny things"**—letter of 19 November 1899, *The Complete Letters of Sigmund Freud to Wilhelm Fliess, 1887–1904*, Jeffrey Moussaieff Masson, editor and translator (Cambridge, Mass.: Harvard University Press, 1985), p. 387.

120: **"an Affaire Hummel small-scale"**—*Neue Freie Presse*, 21 November 1899, evening edition.

121: **Gustav Hohn**—*Neue Freie Presse*, 22 November 1899.

121: **"the Zionist plan"**—diary entry of 22 November 1899, *The Complete Diaries of Theodor Herzl*, III, edited by Raphael Patai, translated by Harry Zohn (New York & London: The Herzl Press, 1960), p. 888.

121: **"If the jury members saw such an incident"**—*Neue Freie Presse*, 25 November 1899, evening edition.

122: **"And there was, furthermore, the remarkable circumstance"**—Robert Musil, *The Man Without Qualities*, trans. Eithne Wilkins and Ernst Kaiser (1930; New York: Capricorn Books, 1965), p. 76.

123: **"And by what qualities"**—Musil, p. 139.

124: **"gentle doves compared to the hawk"**—*Neue Freie Presse*, 28 November 1899, evening edition.

125: **"the so-called better circles"**—*Arbeiter-Zeitung*, 29 November 1899.

126: **"Little Anna"**—*Arbeiter-Zeitung*, 1 December 1899.

127: **"The complete contempt of humanity"**—*Neue Freie Presse*, 29 November 1899.

127: **"God help you"**—*Neue Freie Presse*, 1 December 1899, evening edition.

127: **"from far away"**—*Neue Freie Presse*, 28 November 1899, evening edition.

128: **"From the first glance"**—*Arbeiter-Zeitung*, 29 November 1899.

128: **"If she is guilty"**—*Neue Freie Presse*, 28 November 1899, evening edition.

128: "Her wrinkled, stiff, dismal face"—*Neue Freie Presse*, 29 November 1899.

128: "long-winded"—*Arbeiter-Zeitung*, 29 November 1899.

129: "Emil and I"—*Arbeiter-Zeitung*, 29 November 1899.

130: "Anna could not be brought to rest"—*Arbeiter-Zeitung*, 29 November 1899.

131: "And a little while later"—*Arbeiter-Zeitung*, 29 November 1899.

132: "Oh, he was fine, I was the martyr"—*Neue Freie Presse*, 29 November 1899.

132: Nothnagel and Söllner—G. S. Schwartz, "Devices to Prevent Masturbation," *Medical Aspects of Human Sexuality*, May 1973, 144.

134: "The children committed immoral acts"—*Neue Freie Presse*, 29 November 1899.

134: "an array of gross immoral acts"—*Arbeiter-Zeitung*, 29 November 1899.

134: "Yes, she was my darling"—*Neue Freie Presse*. 29 November 1899.

136: "It is completely out of the question"—*Arbeiter-Zeitung*, 29 November 1899.

137: "elegant"—*Neue Freie Presse*, 28 November 1899, evening edition.

139: "During my second marriage"—*Arbeiter-Zeitung*, 29 November 1899.

140: "At the time when you were living with the Felzmann"—*Arbeiter-Zeitung*, 29 November 1899.

144: "At that time the rumor spread about"—*Arbeiter-Zeitung*, 30 November 1899.

146: "It has been said, especially about Ludovica"—*Arbeiter-Zeitung*, 30 November 1899.

148: "How did you respond"—*Arbeiter-Zeitung*, 30 November 1899.

149: "The three-day jury trial"—*Arbeiter-Zeitung*, 29 November 1899.

150: "I, and all of us"—*Arbeiter-Zeitung*, 1 December 1899.

150: "The form"—*Arbeiter-Zeitung*, 1 December 1899.

151: "The children were playing"—*Arbeiter-Zeitung*, 1 December 1899.

152: "How did the Felzmann take care of the children?"—*Arbeiter-Zeitung*, 30 November 1899.

153: "Kakania"—Musil, chapter 8, pp. 29–35.

153: "the other K.K."—Harry Zohn, *Karl Kraus* (New York: Frederick Ungar, 1971), p. 33.

154: "terror clutched at my throat"—Stefan Zweig, *The World of Yesterday* (1943; Lincoln: University of Nebraska Press, 1964), p. 208. On Redl see Robert Asprey, *The Panther's Feast* (New York: G. P. Putnam's Sons, 1959).

155: "rich in exciting and important scenes"—*Neue Freie Presse*, 1 December 1899.

157: "I have nothing to say about that"—Arbeiter-Zeitung, 1 December 1899.

157: "I said to my husband"—Arbeiter-Zeitung, 1 December 1899.

158: "His pants"—Arbeiter-Zeitung, 1 December 1899.

158: "Did your mother beat Annerl"—Arbeiter-Zeitung, 1 December 1899.

159: "If you want, you can testify"—Arbeiter-Zeitung, 1 December 1899.

159: "Anna was forced to drink"—Arbeiter-Zeitung, 1 December 1899.

162: "Could you, on your accountability"—Arbeiter-Zeitung, 1 December 1899.

163: "It isn't clear to us"—Neue Freie Presse, 1 December 1899.

164: "intoxicated applause"—Neue Freie Presse, 1 December 1899.

164: The Kutschera Case—Felix Dörmann, Neue Freie Presse, 3 December 1899, pp. 7–8. Translation by L.W.

172: "The city was aroused at the elections"—Zweig, p. 66. On Austrian politics in the 1890s see Arthur J. May, The Hapsburg Monarchy 1867–1914 (Cambridge, Mass.: Harvard University Press, 1951), chapter 13. See also C. A. Macartney, The Habsburg Empire 1790–1918 (New York: The Macmillan Company, 1969), chapter 14; and Robert A. Kann, A History of the Habsburg Empire 1526–1918 (Berkeley: University of California Press, 1974), chapter 8; and Edward Crankshaw, The Fall of the House of Habsburg (London: Longman's, 1963), chapter 15.

172: "The masses"—Zweig, p. 59.

174: "I think that Count Badeni"—letter of 26 September 1897, The Incredible Friendship: The Letters of Emperor Franz Joseph to Frau Katharina Schratt, Jean de Bourgoing (editor), trans. Evabeth Miller Kienast and Robert Rie (Albany: State University of New York, 1966), p. 285.

174: "The invasion of brutality into politics"—Zweig. p. 65.

175: "psychological man"—Carl Schorske, Fin-de-siecle Vienna: Politics and Culture (1980, Knopf; New York: Vintage Books 1981), p. 22.

175: "Freud gave his fellow liberals"—Schorske, p. 203. "Politics and Patricide" was first published in the American Historical Review in April 1973.

175: "closely interwoven with the violent political history"—William J. McGrath, Freud's Discovery of Psychoanalysis: The Politics of Hysteria (Ithaca: Cornell University Press, 1986), p. 321.

176: "Schönerer, Lueger, and Herzl"—Schorske, pp. 119–120.

176: "Rudolf Kutschera is a state official"—Arbeiter-Zeitung, 29 November 1899.

180: "For torments"—from the verse play "Tubal and Lilith" in Dörmann, Sensationen, p. 91. Translation by L. W.

180: "I love the hectic, slender Narcissus"—from the poem "Was ich liebe," in Felix Dörmann, *Sensationen* (1892; Vienna: Verlag Leopold Weiss, 1897), p. 22. Translation by L. W. Kraus mocks Dörmann and notes this particular poem in *Die Demolirte Literatur* (1897; Steinbach: Anabas-Verlag Günter Kämpf, 1972), p. 29.

181: "flirtation with horrors"—Arthur Moeller-Bruck. *Das Junge Wien,* in *Die Moderne Literatur,* Band X (Berlin and Leipzig: Schuster and Loeffler, 1902), p. 16. Translation by L. W.

182: "I have lost completely"—Allan Janik and Stephen Toulmin, *Wittgenstein's Vienna* (New York: Simon and Schuster, 1973), p. 114.

183: "Indeed when one works"—letter of 10 November 1899, Hugo von Hofmannsthal and Edgar Karg von Bebenburg, *Briefwechsel* (Frankfurt: S. Fischer Verlag, 1966), p. 146. Translation by L. W.

183: "I'm not free Sunday"—letter of 17 November 1899. Hugo von Hofmannsthal and Arthur Schnitzler, *Briefwechsel* (1964; Frankfurt: Fischer, 1983), p. 133. Translation by L. W.

183: "I believe the only thing to do"—letter of 8 December 1899, Hofmannsthal and Bebenburg, p. 152. Translation by L. W.

183: "Mother and Daughter"—Hugo von Hofmannsthal, "Mutter and Tochter [Fragment]" (1899), *Gesammelte Werke: Dramen IV: Lustspiele* (Frankfurt: Fischer Taschenbuch Verlag, 1979), pp. 9–16.

185: "In Sophocles the murder of the guilty"—Alfred Kerr, *Neue Deutsche Rundschau,* December 1903, in Gotthart Wunberg (editor), *Hoffmannsthal im Urteil seiner Kritiker* (Frankfurt: Athenäum Verlag, 1972), p. 78. Translation by L. W.

185: "She is Agamemnon's hysterical daughter"—Maximilian Harden, *Die Zukunft,* 17 August 1904, in Wunberg, p. 84. Translation by L. W.

185: "Eating hate"—Hermann Bahr, 1905, in Wunberg, p. 137. Translation by L. W.

186: "My father's murder"—Sophocles, *Electra and Other Plays,* trans. E. F. Watling (New York: Penguin Books, 1953), p. 105.

186: "So did they let you starve"—Hofmannsthal, *Elektra* (1903), in *Gesammelte Werke: Dramen II: 1892–1905* (Frankfurt: Fischer Taschenbuch Verlag, 1979), p. 223. Translation by L. W.

186: "agitated, shaking itself"—Bahr, In Wunberg, p. 137. Translation by L. W.

187: "a world in which Herr Felix Dörmann can receive a poetry prize"—*Die Fackel,* 84, End October 1901, p. 2. Translation by L. W. For Kraus's comments and aphorisms see Harry Zohn, *Karl Kraus,* and also Karl Kraus, *Half-Truths and One-and-a-Half Truths: Selected Aphorisms,* edited and translated by Harry Zohn (Manchester and New York: Carcanet Press, 1986).

188: "new literature"—*Die Fackel,* 32, Middle February 1900, p. 31.

188: "Year out, year in"—*Die Fackel*, 28, Beginning January 1900, p. 1. Translation by L. W.

189: "Juliane Hummel and her spouse"—*Die Fackel*, 28, Beginning January 1900, p. 1. Translation by L. W.

191: "attempt to evade"—Janik & Toulmin, p. 273.

191: "slovenliness"—Janik & Toulmin, p. 30.

191: "Part class justice"—*Die Fackel*, 28, Beginning January 1900, p. 2. Translation by L. W.

194: "When the verdict fell"—*Die Fackel*, 28, Beginning January 1900, pp. 2–3. Translation by L. W.

195: "Before we started printing"—in Zohn, *Karl Kraus*, pp. 99–100.

196: "Was that a fragment of the trial"—Musil, p. 137.

197: "Two of my patients"—letter of 9 December 1899, *Letters of Sigmund Freud to Wilhelm Fliess*, p. 390.

199: "The meaning of such dreams"—Freud, *The Interpretation of Dreams*, p. 282.

200: "If anyone dreams"—Sigmund Freud, *The Interpretation of Dreams*, trans. James Strachey (1899–1900; New York: Avon Books, 1965), p. 283.

200: "How are we to explain"—Freud, *The Interpretation of Dreams*, p. 289.

201: "dear, lovely Mummy"—Freud, *The Interpretation of Dreams*, p. 292.

201: "The obscure information"—Freud, *The Interpretation of Dreams*, p. 290.

202: "This discovery is confirmed"—Freud, *The Interpretation of Dreams*, p. 294.

203: "If Oedipus Rex moves a modern audience"—Freud, *The Interpretation of Dreams*, pp. 295–296.

203: "swollen foot"—Alice Miller, *Thou Shalt Not Be Aware: Society's Betrayal of the Child*, trans. Hildegarde and Hunter Hannum (1981; New York: New American Library, 1986), pp. 135–147; and Marianne Krüll, *Freud and His Father*, trans. Arnold Pomerans (1979; New York: W. W. Norton, 1986), p. 61–63.

204: "All the peculiar circumstances"—Sigmund Freud, "The Aetiology of Hysteria" (1896), trans. Cecil Baines, in Freud, *Early Psychoanalytic Writings* (New York: Collier Books, 1963), p. 198.

205: "a maid, nurse, governess"—Freud, "The Aetiology of Hysteria," p. 191.

205: "the surprise"—letter of 21 September 1897, *Letters of Sigmund Freud to Wilhelm Fliess*, p. 264.

206: "we can understand the gripping power of Oedipus Rex"—letter of 15 October 1897, *Letters of Sigmund Freud to Wilhelm Fliess*, p. 272.

207: "For it is unforgivable"—Jeffrey Moussaieff Masson, *The Assault on Truth: Freud's Suppression of the Seduction Theory* (New York: Farrar, Straus and Giroux, 1984), p. 192.

207: "even a genius is a child of his times"—Miller, p. 186.

208: "improbability"—Sigmund Freud, *History of the Psychoanalytic Movement* (1914; New York: W. W. Norton, 1966), p. 17.

208: "It is only the sign of a healthy moral sense"—Thomas Masaryk, *Die Bedeutung des Polnaer Verbrechens für den Ritualaberglauben* (Berlin: Hermann, 1900), p. 56. Translation by L. W.

209: "the new culture makers"—Schorske, p. xxvi.

209: "We cannot reproach Freud"—Miller, p. 185.

210: "a new patient"—letter of 14 October 1900, *Letters of Sigmund Freud to Wilhelm Fliess*, p. 427.

210: "the hand that was already raised"—*Die Fackel*, 28, Beginning January 1900, p. 3. Translation by L. W.

210: "mania for cleanliness"—Sigmund Freud, *Dora: An Analysis of a Case of Hysteria* (1905; New York: Collier Books, 1963), p. 110.

211: "we find ourselves once again"—Sigmund Freud, "Psychoanalytic Notes upon an Autobiographical Account of a Case of Paranoia" (Doctor Schreber, 1911), in *Three Case Histories* (New York: Collier Books, 1963), p. 155–156. On Freud and Schreber see Morton Schatzman, *Soul Murder: Persecution in the Family* (New York: Random House, 1973).

211: "An erogenous source"—Sigmund Freud, "Infantile Sexuality," in *Three Contributions to the Theory of Sex*, trans. A. A. Brill (1905; New York: E. P. Dutton, 1962), p. 53.

212: "By bringing his naughtiness forward"—Sigmund Freud, "From the History of an Infantile Neurosis" ("The Wolf Man," 1918), in *Three Case Histories*, pp. 210–211.

212: "My patient's father"—Freud, "From the History of an Infantile Neurosis," p. 217.

212: "It is surprising how often"—Sigmund Freud, " 'A Child Is Being Beaten': A Contribution to the Study of the Origin of Sexual Perversions" (1919), trans. James and Alix Strachey, in *The Standard Edition of the Complete Psychological Works of Sigmund Freud*, Volume XVII (London: The Hogarth Press, 1955), p. 179.

213: "The question was bound to arise"—Freud, "A Child Is Being Beaten," p. 180.

213: "The present state of our knowledge"—Freud, "A Child Is Being Beaten," p. 183.

214: "It would naturally be important"—Freud, "A Child Is Being Beaten," p. 192.

216: "The attractiveness of these investigations"—Sigmund Freud,

"Femininity," in *New Introductory Lectures on Psychoanalysis*, trans. James Strachey (1933; New York: W. W. Norton, 1965), p. 106.

217: **"could only prolong society's sleep"**—Miller, p. 157.

217: **"The condemned woman"**—*Arbeiter-Zeitung*, 1 December 1899.

219: **"Christian Moosbrugger"**—Musil, p. 249.

219: **"We stood alone"**—*Arbeiter-Zeitung*, 29 November 1899.

220: **"straw fire"**—*Arbeiter-Zeitung*, 29 November 1899.

220: **"For the second time"**—*Arbeiter-Zeitung*, 1 December 1899.

221: **"In the last resort"**—Musil, p. 312.

## Conclusion. *The Case of Rosa Marianek*

226: **"a Viennese woman"**—*Neue Freie Presse*, 8 December 1899.

227: **"not hostility against her children"**—*Neue Freie Presse*, 13 December 1899.

227: **"Francisca Kaitl will now be able to celebrate"**—*Neue Freie Presse*, 13 December 1899.

229: **"You cannot imagine what I have suffered"**—*Arbeiter-Zeitung*, 15 December 1899.

231: **"The case of Rosa Marianek"**—*Arbeiter-Zeitung*, 14 December 1899.

232: **"Why didn't you jump in"**—*Arbeiter-Zeitung*, 14 December 1899.

233: **"as if magnetically drawn"**—*Neue Freie Presse*, 14 December 1899.

234: **Dr. Joseph Hinterstoisser**—On Hinterstoisser see entry in *Oester-reichisches Biographisches Lexicon*, Volume 2 (Graz and Köln: Hermann Böhlaus, 1959). For Kraus on Hinterstoisser see *Die Fackel*, 34, Beginning March 1900, 12–15; and *Die Fackel*, 39, End April 1900, 1–22; and *Die Fackel*, 48, End July 1900, pp. 18–20.

235: **"We doctors call this an hysterical character"**—*Neue Freie Presse*, 15 December 1899.

236: **"It is as if Schliemann"**—letter of 21 December 1899. *The Complete Letters of Sigmund Freud to Wilhelm Fliess, 1887–1904*, Jeffrey Moussaieff Masson, editor and translator (Cambridge, Mass.: Harvard University Press, 1985), p. 391.

237: **Christmas**—*Neue Freie Presse*, 15 December 1899.

238: **"A Happy New Century"**—*Neue Freie Presse*, 10 December 1899.

238: **"A calendar is not a lyric poem"**—*Neue Freie Presse*, 16 December 1899.

238: **"Exhausted and disillusioned"**—*Neue Freie Presse*, 31 December 1899.

258 POSTCARDS FROM THE END OF THE WORLD

239: **"The new century"**—letter of 8 January 1900, *Letters of Sigmund Freud to Wilhelm Fliess,* p. 394.

240: **"The battered-child syndrome is a term"**—C. Henry Kempe, Frederic N. Silverman, Brandt F. Steele, William Droegemueller, and Henry K. Silver, "The Battered-Child Syndrome," *Journal of the American Medical Association,* 7 July 1962, 17.

241: **"There is reluctance"**—Kempe et al., "The Battered-Child Syndrome," 18–19.

# Bibliography

*Arbeiter-Zeitung.* Vienna. October, November, & December 1899.

Arendt, Hannah. *Eichmann in Jerusalem: A Report on the Banality of Evil.* New York: Viking, 1963.

Ariès, Philippe. *Centuries of Childhood: A Social History of Family Life.* Trans. Robert Baldick. 1960; New York: Vintage, 1962.

Asprey, Robert. *The Panther's Feast.* New York: G. P. Putnam's Sons, 1959.

Bauer-Lechner, Natalie. *Recollections of Gustav Mahler.* Trans. Dika Newlin. 1923; Cambridge: Cambridge University Press, 1980.

Behlmer, George. *Child Abuse and Moral Reform in England 1870–1908.* Stanford: Stanford University Press, 1982.

Benjamin, Walter. "Karl Kraus." 1931. In *Reflections.* Trans. Edmund Jephcott. Ed. Peter Demetz. New York: Harcourt Brace Jovanovich, 1978.

"Biedermann, Felix." *Oesterreichisches Biographisches Lexicon.* I. Graz & Köln: Verlag Hermann Böhlaus, 1957.

Broch, Hermann. *Hugo von Hofmannsthal and His Time: The European Imagination 1860–1920.* Trans. Michael P. Steinberg. 1955; Chicago: University of Chicago Press, 1984.

Canetti, Elias. *The Torch in My Ear.* Trans. Joachim Neugroschel. 1980; New York: Farrar, Straus & Giroux, 1982.

Corti, Egon. *Elisabeth, Empress of Austria.* New Haven: Yale University Press, 1936.

Crankshaw, Edward. *The Fall of the House of Habsburg.* London: Longman's, 1963.

Darnton, Robert. *The Great Cat Massacre.* New York: Basic Books, 1984.

Dörmann, Felix. "Hedwig Keplinger: A Servant Girl's Fate." Trans. Larry Wolff. *Neue Freie Presse.* Vienna: 15 October 1899.

Dörmann, Felix. "The Kutschera Case." Trans. Larry Wolff. *Neue Freie Presse.* Vienna: 3 December 1899.

Dörmann, Felix. *Sensationen.* 1892; Vienna: Verlag Leopold Weiss, 1897.

"Dörmann, Felix." *Neue Deutsche Biographie.* IV. Berlin: Duncker & Humboldt, 1957.

Fischer, Jens Malte. *Fin de Siècle: Kommentar zu einer Epoche.* Munich: Winkler Verlag, 1978.

Franz Joseph, Emperor of Austria. *The Incredible Friendship: The Letters of Emperor Franz Joseph to Frau Katharina Schratt.* Ed. Jean de Bourgoing. Trans. Evabeth Miller Kienast and Robert Rie. Albany: State University of New York, 1966.

Freud, Sigmund. "The Aetiology of Hysteria." 1896. Trans. Cecil Baines. In *Early Psychoanalytic Writings.* New York: Collier Books, 1963.

Freud Sigmund. " 'A Child Is Being Beaten': A Contribution to the Study of the Origin of Sexual Perversions." 1919. Trans. James and Alix Strachey. In *The Standard Edition of the Complete Psychological Works of Sigmund Freud.* Volume XVII. London: The Hogarth Press, 1955.

Freud, Sigmund. *Civilization and Its Discontents.* Trans. James Strachey. 1930; New York & London: W. W. Norton, 1961.

Freud, Sigmund. *The Complete Letters of Sigmund Freud to Wilhelm Fliess 1887–1904.* Ed. & trans. Jeffrey Moussaieff Masson. Cambridge, Mass.: Harvard University Press, 1985.

Freud, Sigmund. *Dora: An Analysis of a Case of Hysteria.* Trans. James Strachey. 1905; New York: Collier Books, 1963.

Freud, Sigmund. "Femininity." In *New Introductory Lectures on Psychoanalysis.* Trans. James Strachey. 1933; New York: Norton, 1965.

Freud, Sigmund. "From the History of an Infantile Neurosis" (The "Wolf Man"). In *Three Case Histories.* New York: Collier Books, 1963.

Freud, Sigmund. *History of the Psychoanalytic Movement.* 1914; New York: W. W. Norton, 1966.

Freud, Sigmund. "Infantile Sexuality." In *Three Contributions to the Theory of Sex.* Trans. A. A. Brill. 1905; New York: E. P. Dutton, 1962.

Freud, Sigmund. *The Interpretation of Dreams.* Trans. James Strachey. 1899–1900; New York: Avon Books, 1965.

Freud, Sigmund. *Jokes and Their Relationship to the Unconscious.* Trans. James Strachey. 1905; New York: W. W. Norton, 1963.

Freud, Sigmund. *The Letters of Sigmund Freud.* Ed. Ernst L. Freud. Trans. Tania and James Stern. 1960; New York: Basic Books, 1975.

Freud, Sigmund. "Psychoanalytic Notes upon an Autobiographical Account of a Case of Hysteria" (Doctor Schreber). 1911. In *Three Case Histories.* New York: Collier Books, 1963.

Halasz, Nicholas. *Captain Dreyfus: The Story of a Mass Hysteria.* New York: Simon & Schuster, 1955.

Hartman, Mary. *Victorian Murderesses.* New York: Schocken Books, 1977.

Herzl, Theodor. *The Complete Diaries of Theodor Herzl.* Ed. Raphael Patai. Trans. Harry Zohn. New York & London: The Herzl Press, 1960.

"Hilsner Case." *Encyclopedia Judaica.* VIII. Jerusalem: Keter Publishing, 1972.

"Hinterstoisser." *Oesterreichisches Biographisches Lexicon.* II. Graz & Köln: Hermann Böhlaus, 1959.

Hitler, Adolf. *Mein Kampf.* Trans. Ralph Manheim. 1925; Boston: Houghton Mifflin, 1971.

von Hofmannsthal, Hugo. *Elektra.* 1903. In *Gesammelte Werke: Dramen II: 1892–1905.* Frankfurt: Fischer Taschenbuch Verlag, 1979.

von Hofmannsthal, Hugo. "Mutter und Tochter [Fragment]." 1899. In *Gesammelte Werke: Dramen IV: Lustspiele*. Frankfurt: Fischer Taschen-buch Verlag, 1979.

von Hofmannsthal, Hugo. "Der Tod des Tizian" (1892). In *Gedichte und kleine Dramen*. Frankfurt: Suhrkamp Verlag, 1966.

von Hofmannsthal, Hugo, and Edgar Karg von Bebenburg. *Briefwechsel*. Frankfurt: S. Fischer Verlag, 1966.

von Hofmannsthal, Hugo, and Arthur Schnitzler. *Briefwechsel*. 1964, Frankfurt: Fischer, 1983.

Janik, Allan, and Stephen Toulmin. *Wittgenstein's Vienna*. New York: Simon & Schuster, 1973.

Johnston, William. *The Austrian Mind*. Berkeley: University of California Press, 1972.

Jones, Ernest. *The Life and Work of Sigmund Freud*. New York: Basic Books, 1953.

Kann, Robert A. *A History of the Habsburg Empire 1526–1918*. Berkeley: University of California Press, 1974.

Kempe, C. Henry, Frederic N. Silverman, Brandt F. Steele, William Droegemueller, and Henry K. Silver. "The Battered-Child Syndrome." *Journal of the American Medical Association*. 7 July 1962.

Kraus, Karl. *Die Demolirte Literatur*. 1897; Steinbach: Anabas-Verlag Günter Kämpf, 1972.

Kraus, Karl. *Die Fackel*. Vienna. 1899–1901.

Kraus, Karl. *Half-Truths and One-and-a-Half Truths: Selected Aphorisms*. Trans. & ed. Harry Zohn. Manchester & New York: Carcanet Press, 1986.

Krüll, Marianne. *Freud and His Father*. Trans. Arnold Pomerans. 1979; New York: W. W. Norton, 1986.

Macartney, C. A. *The Habsburg Empire 1790–1918*. New York: The Mac-millan Company, 1969.

McGrath, William. *Dionysian Art and Populist Politics in Austria*. New Haven: Yale University Press, 1974.

McGrath, William. *Freud's Discovery of Psychoanalysis: The Politics of Hysteria*. Ithaca: Cornell University Press, 1986.

Masaryk, Thomas. *Die Bedeutung des Polnaer Verbrechens für den Ritual-aberglauben*. Berlin: Hermann, 1900.

Masson, Jeffrey Moussaieff. *The Assault on Truth: Freud's Suppression of the Seduction Theory*. New York: Farrar, Straus and Giroux, 1984.

deMause, Lloyd (editor). *The History of Childhood*. 1974; New York: Harper & Row, 1975.

May, Arthur J. *The Hapsburg Monarchy 1867–1914*. Cambridge, Mass.: Harvard University Press, 1951.

May, Arthur J. *Vienna in the Age of Franz Josef*. Norman: University of Oklahoma Press, 1966.

Miller, Alice. *Thou Shalt Not Be Aware: Society's Betrayal of the Child*. Trans. Hildegarde & Hunter Hannum. 1981; New York: New American Library, 1986.

Moeller-Bruck, Arthur. *Das Junge Wien*. In *Die Moderne Literatur*. Band X. Berlin & Leipzig: Schuster & Loeffler, 1902.

Morton, Frederic. *A Nervous Splendor: Vienna 1888/1889*. 1979, Little, Brown; Penguin Books, 1980.

Musil, Robert. *The Man Without Qualities*. Trans. Eithne Wilkins and Ernst Kaiser. 1930; New York: Capricorn Books, 1965.

*Neue Freie Presse*. Vienna: October, November, & December 1899.

Palmer, R. R., and Joel Colton. *History of the Modern World*. 1950; New York: Knopf, 1965.

"Polna Affair." *Jewish Encyclopedia*. X. New York & London: Funk & Wagnalls, 1905.

Pulzer, P. G. J. *The Rise of Political Anti-Semitism in Germany and Austria*. New York & London: John Wiley, 1964.

Redlich, Joseph. *Emperor Francis Joseph of Austria*. New York: The Macmillan Company, 1929.

Rieckmann, Jens. *Aufbruch in die Moderne: die Anfänge des Jungen Wien*. Frankfurt: Athenäum Verlag, 1985.

Riis, Jacob. *How the Other Half Lives*. 1890; New York: Hill & Wang, 1957.

Schatzman, Morton. *Soul Murder: Persecution in the Family*. New York: Random House, 1973.

Schnitzler, Arthur. "Der grüne Kakadu" (1899). In *Das dramatische Werk*. 3. Frankfurt: Fischer Taschenbuch, 1978.

Schnitzler, Arthur. *La Ronde*. 1900. Trans. Eric Bentley. In *Plays and Stories*. Ed. Egon Schwarz. New York: Continuum, 1982.

Schnitzler, Arthur. *Theresa: The Chronicle of a Woman's Life*. Trans. William Drake. New York: Simon & Schuster, 1928.

Schorske, Carl. *Fin-de-siècle Vienna: Politics and Culture*. 1980, Knopf; New York: Vintage Books, 1981.

Schwarz, G. S. "Devices to Prevent Masturbation." *Medical Aspects of Human Sexuality*. May 1973.

Sophocles. *Electra and Other Plays*. Trans. E. F. Watling. New York: Penguin Books, 1953.

*Statistische Monatschrift*. Herausgegeben von der K. K. Statistischen Central-Commission. Vienna: Alfred Hölder, 1900.

Steed, Henry Wickham. *The Hapsburg Monarchy*. 1913; New York: Howard Fertig, 1969.

Stone, Lawrence. *The Family, Sex, and Marriage: In England 1500–1800*. New York: Harper & Row, 1977.

Timms, Edward. *Karl Kraus: Apocalyptic Satirist*. New Haven: Yale University Press, 1986.

Varnadoe, Kirk. *Vienna 1900: Art, Architecture, & Design*. New York: Museum of Modern Art, 1986.

Wagner, Renate, and Brigitte Vacha. *Wiener Schnitzler-Aufführungen 1891–1970*. Munich: Prestel, 1971.

Wandruszka, Adam. *Geschichte einer Zeitung*. Vienna: Neue Wiener Presse, 1958.

*Wiener Zeitung.* Vienna. October, November, December 1899.

Wunberg, Gotthart (editor). *Hofmannsthal im Urteil seiner Kritiker.* Frankfurt: Athenäum Verlag, 1972.

Wunberg, Gotthart (editor). *Die Wiener Moderne.* Stuttgart: Philipp Reclam, 1981.

Zohn, Harry. *Karl Kraus.* New York: Frederick Ungar, 1971.

Zweig, Stefan. *The World of Yesterday.* 1943; Lincoln: University of Nebraska Press, 1964.

# Index

**Larry Wolff** is an assistant professor of history at Boston College. He lives in Cambridge, Massachusetts.